KU-300-337

THE INSIDER'S GUIDE TO

WESTERN

CANADA

THE INSIDER'S GUIDES

AUSTRALIA • BALI • CALIFORNIA • CHINA • EASTERN CANADA • FLORIDA • HAWAII •
HONG KONG • INDIA • INDONESIA • JAPAN • KENYA • KOREA • NEPAL • NEW ENGLAND • NEW
ZEALAND • MALAYSIA AND SINGAPORE • MEDITERRANEAN FRANCE • MEXICO • PORTUGAL •
RUSSIA • SPAIN • THAILAND • TURKEY • VIETNAM, LAOS AND CAMBODIA • WESTERN CANADA

The Insider's Guide to Western Canada
First Published 1994
Reprinted 1995

Moorland Publishing Co Ltd
Moor Farm Road, Airfield Estate, Ashbourne, DE61HD, England
by arrangement with Kümmerly + Frey AG, Berne, Switzerland

© 1994 Kümmerly + Frey AG

ISBN: 0 86190 396 X

Created, edited and produced by Allan Amsel Publishing
53 rue Beaudouin, 27700 Les Andelys, France
Telefax: (33) 32 54 54 50
Editor in Chief: Allan Amsel
Original design concept: Hon Bing-wah
Picture editor and designer: Gaia Text, Munich

Printed by Samhwa Printing Company Limited, Seoul, Korea

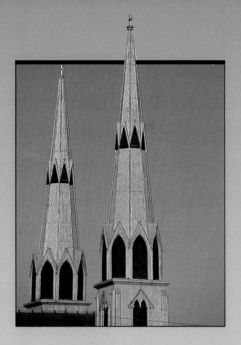

THE INSIDER'S GUIDE TO
WESTERN
CANADA

By Donald Carroll

Photographed by
Nik Wheeler and Robert Holmes

MPC

Contents

MAPS
Canada	8–9
British Columbia	36
Vancouver	39
Vancouver Island	59
Alberta	90
Saskatchawan	132
Manitoba	154
Winnipeg	157

WELCOME TO CANADA   11

THE COUNTRY AND ITS PEOPLE   19
The Historical Background   20
  The First Europeans • New
  France • British Canada • The
  Dominion of Canada • Canada
  Today
Geography and Climate   31

BRITISH COLUMBIA   35
Vancouver   38
  Background •
  General Information • What to
  See and Do • Where to Stay •
  Where to Eat • How to Get
  There
Vancouver Island   59
  Background • General
  Information
Victoria   60
  What to See and Do • Where to
  Stay • Where to Eat • How to
  Get There
The Rest of the Island   73
  What to See and Do • Where to
  Stay • Where to Eat • How to
  Get There
The Okanagan Valley   81
  General Information • What to
  See and Do • Where to Stay •
  Where to Eat • How to Get
  There
Glacier National Park   87

ALBERTA   89
Edmonton   91
  Background • General
  Information • What to See and
  Do • Where to Stay • Where to
  Eat • How to Get There
Calgary   101
  Background • General
  Information • What to See and
  Do • Where to Stay • Where to
  Eat • How to Get There
Banff and Jasper National Parks   116
  Background • General
  Information • What to See and
  Do • Where to Stay • Where to
  Eat • How to Get There

SASKATCHEWAN   131
Regina   134
  Background • General
  Information • What to See and
  Do • Where to Stay • Where to
  Eat • How to Get There
Saskatoon   142
  Background • General
  Information • What to See and
  Do • Where to Stay • Where to
  Eat • How to Get There
Elsewhere in Saskatchewan   149
  Prince Albert National Park •
  Lac la Ronge Provincial Park •
  Meadow Lake Provincial Park •
  The Western Development
  Museum at Yorkton • Cypress
  Hills Provincial Park

MANITOBA   153
Winnipeg   156
  Background • General
  Information • What to See and
  Do • Where to Stay • Where to
  Eat • How to Get There
Elsewhere in Manitoba   167
  Whiteshell Provicial Park • Lake
  Winnipeg • Riding Mountain
  National Park • Churchill •
  How to Get There

TRAVELERS' TIPS   **171**

Getting There   172
    By Air • By Rail • By Bus •
    By Car
Tourist Information   173
Embassies and Consulates   173
Travel Documents   174
Customs   174
When to Go   174
What to Take   175
Basics   177
    Time • Electricity • Weights
    and Measures
Health   178
Money   178
Crime   179
Getting Around   179
    By Air • By Rail • By Bus •
    By Car • By Ferry • By Local
    Transport • Driving
Accommodation   182
Eating out   183
Drinking   184
Tipping   185
Shopping   185
Camping   186
Hunting   188
Fishing   188

Skiing   188
Public Holidays and Festivals   189
    National Holidays • Provincial
    Holidays • Festivals
Mail   190
Telephones   191
Radio and Television   191
Newspapers and Magazines   192

RECOMMENDED READING   192

QUICK REFERENCE A–Z GUIDE TO PLACES   193
and Topics of Interest with Listed
Accommodation, Restaurants and
Useful Telephone Numbers

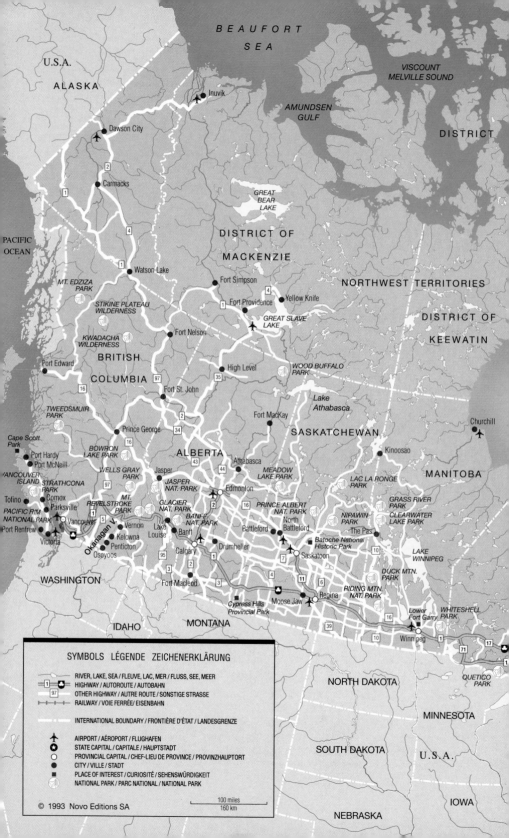

INSIDER'S GUIDE
CANADA

DENMARK

GREENLAND

BAFFIN BAY

NCASTER SOUND

RANKLIN

FOXE BASIN

HUDSON STRAIT

ATLANTIC OCEAN

HUDSON BAY

Hebron

Nain

Cartwright

NEWFOUNDLAND

POLAR BEAR PARK

WINISK WILD RIVER PARK

JAMES BAY

QUÉBEC

Happy Valley-Goose Bay

Smallwood Reservoir

LABRADOR

Churchill Falls

Labrador City

Wabush

Lourdes-de-Blanc-Sablon

L'Anse aux Meadows

Long Range Mtn.

Springdale

Trinity

Bonavista

GROS MORNE NAT. PARK

Deer Lake

Gander

St. John

Grand Falls

Clarenville

Whitbourne

CAP SPEA

Corner Brook

Marystown

AVALON PEN.

GULF OF ST. LAWRENCE

Grand Bank

Port aux Basques

ONTARIO

PARC DE LA GASPÉSIE

Sainte-Anne-des-Monts

Cap Chat

Gaspé

Gaspé Peninsula

Matane

Chéticamp

Ingonosh

Louisbourg

138

NEW BRUNSWICK

11

PR. EDWARD ISL.

105

MISSINAIBI LAKE PARK

11

PUKASKWA PARK

117

Québec

20

Grand Falls

Fredericton

Charlottetown

NOVA SCOTIA

SUPERIOR PARK

der Bay

E SUPERIOR

40

112

Grand Pré

Saint John

Windsor

Halifax

Chester

Lunenberg

Sudbury

MAINE

Annapolis Royal

Digby

Yarmouth

Shelburne

17

69

ALGONQUIN PARK

10

Montréal

Cornwall

Sault Ste. Marie

LAKE HURON

7

401

Ottawa

VERMONT

ATLANTIC OCEAN

Kingston

LAKE ONTARIO

NEW HAMPSHIRE

Waterloo

Kitchener

Stratford

Toronto

St. Catharines

Niagara Falls

London

401

Niagara Falls

NEW YORK

MICHIGAN

Windsor

LAKE ERIE

LAKE MICHIGAN

PENNSYLVANIA

Welcome
to Canada

TRUE OR FALSE? Canada is an unexciting country with no authentic voice or national identity of its own.

Answer: true.

True, that is, if you consider it exciting to walk along rubbish-strewn streets in constant danger of being mugged, or if you measure a voice's authenticity in decibels, or if you think periodic convulsions of flag-clutching jingoism are symptoms of a healthy national identity. By all of these criteria Canada will be found wanting, but if you like the idea of a gigantic country that

trated in a narrow band along the long border with the U.S.

From a strictly demographic point of view, the two most striking things about this population are that it is overwhelmingly urban — over 75 percent of Canadians live in the cities — and surprisingly heterogeneous. Unlike their American counterparts, who have been historically quick to jettison their cultural baggage in the rush to become assimilated, immigrants to Canada have tended to cherish and safeguard their distinctive traditions, preserving the old in

can be enjoyed without a gigantic wallet, a New World nation that has taken care not to squander its Old World inheritance, a place where the dazzle of the landscape is matched by the kaleidoscopic mix of peoples who inhabit it, then you will like Canada. A lot.

And there is a lot of it to like. Covering almost 10 million sq km (3.9 million sq miles), it is the second largest country in the world, after Russia. Unlike Russia, however, or its next-door neighbor to the south, Canada has only 26 million inhabitants — fewer than California. And while the land is divided up into 10 provinces and two immense territories extending well into the Arctic Circle, the vast majority of the population is concen-

order to civilize the new. Thus it is not uncommon to see signs in Finnish by Lake Superior or to hear Ukrainian spoken on the Manitoban prairies. Likewise, members of various other nationalities and ethnic groups in Canada have discovered that you can create cheery enclaves without creating dreary ghettos.

It's a pity that President Kennedy appropriated the phrase "a nation of immigrants" to describe the United States, because it actually applies more accurately to Canada (as indeed does another presidential coinage, of more recent vintage, Mr. Bush's "kinder, gentler nation"). Whereas the U.S. may have been founded by immigrants, and substantially populated by them for a century or more, Canada is still being shaped by immigration. At the turn of the century the country had a population of barely five million; since then two tidal waves of immigrants — the first before World War I and the second following World War II — have washed up on Canada's shores, helping to boost the population to its present level and helping to determine what kind of nation will enter the 21st century.

Unhappily, it appears at the time of writing that it will be a nation whose greatest triumph — the achievement of a multicultural, bilingual state — will be unraveling as the frictions between the two predominant cultures, the British and French, prompt Quebec to tear itself away from the Confederation. But of this more later. Happily, Canada's other great achievement, which is to have shared a continent with America without becoming totally Americanized, looks like it will continue to be a distinguishing feature of the Canadian way of life.

But it won't come easy. It never has. For one thing, most Canadians live close to the U.S. border, which at 6,379 km (3,964 miles) is the longest unguarded national boundary in the world. This means, among other things, that most Canadians are within reach of American radio and television stations. This has been a major concern of Canadian intellectuals for the better part of this century. It first surfaced as a worry in the twenties, when Canada was absorbed into the American radio system at a time when the U.S. was beginning to flex its imperial muscles. Then, after the end of World War II, when America was at the zenith of its power and influence, there came the new threat of cultural annexation by television.

So seriously was this threat viewed that no fewer than three royal commissions were set up between 1949 and 1961 to address "the problem of American culture in Canada", and specifically to seek ways of organizing "resistance to the absorption of Canada into the general cultural pattern of the United States." There was little the commissioners could do, however, apart from encouraging the Canadian Broadcasting Corporation in its policy of featuring homegrown material. And even this rearguard action, faithfully pursued by the CBC since its creation in 1936, has never received whole-hearted government support. And

OPPOSITE: The town that always stays up to welcome its guests; Niagara Falls fives tourists a sign or two. ABOVE: The town that stays up all summer; Inuvik, in the Northwest Territories, is backlit by the midnight sun.

ica's National Hockey League. And having been (quite rightly) converted to the glories of baseball, Canadians see their top baseball teams competing in the American major leagues. Not even their individual sporting heroes seem able to resist the Americans: within the past few years, Wayne Gretzky, "The Great One", ice hockey's all-time superstar, abandoned Edmonton for Los Angeles, and Ben Johnson, Canada's greatest-ever sprinter, was stripped of his Olym-

today that support is decidedly half-hearted: during the time I spent in Canada 11 CBC television stations had to close down because of cuts in government funding. Radio Canada International — the Canadian equivalent of the BBC World Service — is facing almost certain extinction because of lack of government support. Meanwhile, the most recent surveys show that 80 percent of total television viewing in the big metropolitan areas near the border is of American programs; even in Edmonton, which receives only Canadian stations, the figure is 66 percent.

Nor is the cross-border invasion limited to the airwaves. American films occupy most of the cinema screens, while American magazines dominate the newsagents' shelves. And of the 40 books on the national bestseller lists when I was there — fiction and non-fiction, hardcover and paperback — only six were by Canadian authors, and only three of those were published by Canadian firms!

Even Canadian sport has not escaped American colonization. All of the top teams in the one sport about which Canadians are passionate — ice hockey — play in Amer-

pic gold medal after failing a drugs test, and then had to watch while the medal was awarded to his arch-rival, the American Carl Lewis. Perhaps the only sport in which Canadians have managed to remain somewhat aloof is American football, but that is only because they enthusiastically embraced the game, made a few minor adjustments here and there, and then renamed it Canadian football. I have watched it (with more enthusiasm, it must be said, than most Canadians) and I have to say that one needs to be a real aficionado, or perhaps a theologian, to explain how it differs from the original.

It is tempting to say — no, it is true to say, so I will say it: Canadian football is symbolic of Canadian society insofar as it presents the outsider with difficulties in distinguishing

ABOVE TO BOTTOM RIGHT: Some of the faces reflecting Canda's ethnic and cultural diversity.

it from its more familiar American counterpart. And this, not surprisingly, fills Canadians with an overwhelming sense of frustration. So much so, in fact, that when I told a prominent Canadian businessman over lunch (truthfully) that I had never met a Canadian I didn't like, he reacted with exasperation bordering on disgust. "That's precisely our problem", he said. "Nobody dislikes us, because nobody knows us. To the rest of the world we're just nicer, quieter Americans." Although I felt constrained to insist that this was not a bad thing to be, I could see his point: it must be maddening to be treated forever like the Canadian dollar is treated, as a slightly discounted version of the real thing.

Equally maddening, if not more so, is the fact that most Americans regard Canadians

as nicer, quieter versions of themselves. No wonder, then, that Canadians are forever worrying about their national identitiy being obliterated by the long shadows cast by the colossus to the south. As former Prime Mininster Pierre Trudeau, in a celebrated quip, told Americans on a visit to Washington in 1969: "Living next to you is in some ways like sleeping with an elephant. No matter how friendly and even-tempered the beast, one is affected by every twitch and grunt."

John Bierman, the distinguished English biographer and author of Dark Safari who now lives in Toronto, puts it this way: "If you could perforate along the 49th parallel, tear along the dotted line and push Canada out into the Pacific or Atlantic, I'm sure they'd be a totally different people. But the identity crisis is perpetual."

To deal with this "crisis" many Canadians have chosen to reach back, sometimes way back, into their colonial past for a suitable identity. Thus there are parts of the country where stylized versions of the British and French ways of life have been lovingly, not to say fanatically, preserved. This understandably leads outsiders to the frequent conclusion that Canadians have a neurotic preoccupation with being seen as Not-Americans. And indeed in some cases they have. But in my travels around the country I have found that for all the agonizing over their soft-focus national profile, the great majority of Canadians sensibly realize that they quite probably live in the best of all possible worlds.

After all, their country is situated in a neighborhood where there is only one neighbor — and that one is so friendly that neither of them has ever bothered to put up a fence. They have the luxury of living in

cities that are not only handsome and comfortable but come equipped with the world's largest backyard, in the form of wilderness areas of awe-inspiring beauty. Their society has the civilizing patina of history while enjoying all the benefits of modern technology. In short, as a member of the Commonwealth of Nations with a large Francophone population, Canada is in the privileged position of being able to boast of a British monarch but American telephones, French cooking but American plumbing.

In the great tradition of ignoramuses who often say prescient things by accident, Al Capone once said, "I don't even know what street Canada is on." Everyone laughed, but old Scarface had put his chubby finger on one of Canada's most pressing needs. Nor could he have known that after his death Canada would come to live on one principal street, the Trans-Canada Highway. Over 90 percent of all Canadians now live within 80 km (50 miles) of this one road. What's more, the great preponderance of major tourist attractions are within easy reach of the TCH. Nearly 8,000 km (5,000 miles) long, with a water jump at each end, the highway runs all the way from Victoria, British Columbia, at the tip of Vancouver Island, to St. John's, Newfoundland. In this book we will follow it as far as Winnipeg, Manitoba, taking detours en route in order to experience the incomparable beauty and grandeur of the great national and provincial parks which have made Western Canada one of the best-loved holiday destinations in the world.

I think I should mention — though it probably goes without saying — that one detour we will not be making is to the Yukon. This is because a trip to the Yukon is not a detour; it is a tour in itself. With an area the size of France, yet with a population the size of Paris, Texas, and situated closer to Russia than to the Trans-Canada Highway, the Yukon is so remote — physically, climatically, and culturally — from most of the rest of Canada that it demands separate and special treatment for those who will separately and specially go there. Fortunately, there are a number of specialist publications available to enlighten would-be visitors.

Now, before we begin our journey eastwards from the Pacific, a word about prices. With a few exceptions, I have deliberately avoided giving exact prices. This is because I have learned that the only thing you can absolutely depend on in this business is that the prices will have changed before the ink is dry (sometimes, surprisingly, for the better — as special offers and new types of discounts are introduced). I have therefore confined myself to price categories where hotels and restaurants are concerned. HOTELS in the **Luxury** category, for example, will charge over $150 a night for a double room; **Mid-range** hotels will charge between $75 and $150; **Inexpensive** hotels will charge less, sometimes much less. At RESTAURANTS listed as **Expensive** you can

expect to pay more than $50 per person for a meal, excluding wine; **Moderate** restaurants will charge between $25 and $50; **Inexpensive** ones will cost you less — sometimes, again, much less. When hotels or restaurants fall at either of the two extremes — very expensive or inexpensive — I have so indicated.

Another word about prices. All the prices given in this book, and the categories outlined above, are in Canadian dollars. Now, most travel writers I have read will tell you to remember that the Canadian dollar is worth about 20 percent less than the American dollar. My advice is precisely the opposite: Forget that the Canadian dollar is worth less. Don't translate; think in American dollars. This is because all the prices quoted in

Canada are exclusive of the layers of taxes that are added later — sales taxes, goods and services taxes, even "taxes on taxes", as one hotelier wanly pointed out to me. So by the time your bill is added in Canadian dollars, it will come to almost exactly the original, untaxed figure in American dollars. If you keep in mind this one simple trick, you will know a real bargain when you see one.

And when you see Canada, you will rapidly begin to suspect that when it comes to shopping for countries, Canadians may have found the best bargain of all.

As the country's Chinatowns attest, Canadians have managed to create cherry enclaves without creating dreary ghettoes.

The Country and Its People

THE HISTORICAL BACKGROUND

Just when the first immigrants arrived in Canada is a matter of considerable debate among the experts — some say it could have been up to 40,000 years ago, while others insist that it was no more than 11,000 years ago — but there is no argument over who they were or where they came from. They were nomadic tribes from Asia, principally Siberia and Mongolia, who crossed into North America across a land bridge which

around 1000 AD. Arriving at the northwestern tip of Newfoundland, which they named Vinland ("land of grapevines"), they established a settlement at the site of present-day L'Anse aux Meadows. Unfortunately, the archaeological remains don't tell us how long the settlement survived or what finished it off, but it is generally assumed that a combination of the harsh winters and harsh Indians drove the settlers away before they had a chance to establish a viable colony.

The next proven landing in Canada was not for another five centuries, when in

appeared over the Bering Strait during successive Ice Ages. They and their descendants then fanned out across the continent, establishing different Amerindian societies and civilizations which in some cases became highly developed as early as the eighth millenium BC.

THE FIRST EUROPEANS

There is evidence, although inconlusive, to suggest that the first European to set foot in North America was a sixth-century Irish monk, St. Brendan, who according to legend landed briefly on the coast of Newfoundland. But the earliest verified landing was made by Vikings sailing from Greenland

1497 the Venetian John Cabot (*né* Giovanni Caboto) arrived in Newfoundland, and then Nova Scotia, to claim these new-found lands for England and Henry VII. (For all practical — i.e., fishing — purposes the nearby sea had already been claimed by the Portuguese, Basque, and Breton fishermen who in the previous century had discovered the Grand Banks fishing grounds off the coast of Newfoundland to be among the richest in the world.) The next claimant to what was already shaping up as another stage for the worldwide Anglo-French rivalry was the Breton Jacques Cartier, who in 1534 sailed into the Gulf of St. Lawrence, touching land at Prince Edward Island, which he named Ile St. Jean, and the Gaspé

Peninsula before sailing down the St. Lawrence as far as an Indian village in the shadow of an impressive hill, which he named Mont Réal. He claimed the entire area for France, referring to it by the Algonquin Indians' word for "settlement": Kannata.

NEW FRANCE

Since Cartier didn't return to France laden with the hoped-for gold and gems, French interest in Canada quickly waned, only to be revived at the start of the seventeenth century by, of all things, the demands of *haute couture*. In a word, furs. Thus in 1605 the French explorer Samuel de Champlain established the first permanent European settlement in Canada at Port Royal, Nova Scotia, on the Bay of Fundy, in hopes of trading with the Indians for their beaver pelts. Three years later Champlain founded another settlement on a plateau overlooking the St. Lawrence River at the bend where the river suddenly narrows. He named the village Quebec, and as the center of the fur trade it rapidly grew into the most important city in New France.

Following in the footsteps of the explorers and the fur traders, the Jesuits swiftly began the spiritual and intellectual colonization of the region. Their more contemplative lay counterparts, the Société de Notre Dame, moved in on Cartier's "royal mountain" and founded the settlement of Montreal in 1642. Before long it had supplanted Quebec as the center of the fur trade in New France.

The two decades spanning the middle of the seventeenth century were difficult ones for the French settlers, as they became inexorably drawn into the bitter tribal conflicts between the Hurons, their principal trading partners, and the warlike Iroquois. But the real threat to their colonial supremacy came, as always, from the British. Although the British had watched uneasily as New France expanded, their primary concerns had remained the settling and securing of their American colonies and the exploitation of the fertile fishing grounds off the Canadian coast. Canada itself was of interest only insofar as somewhere within its precincts there had to be the long-sought Northwest

Passage to the Orient. Gradually, however, it began to dawn that Canada, or New France, was part of a continent that was itself a treasure trove of riches — and Britain had the key to the back door.

In 1610 the English navigator Henry Hudson sailed into the giant bay that now bears his name. Sixty years later Hudson Bay in turn gave its name to a commercial enterprise, the Hudson's Bay Company, which was to leave an indelible mark on the history of Canada. Formed by British fur merchants to provide an alternative to

Quebec as an outlet for the fur trade, it was granted by Charles II right to all the lands drained by rivers flowing into Hudson Bay. Thus backed by a solicitous sovereign and a powerful navy, it was to become the largest fur trading company in North America, and is still today a force to be reckoned with in Canadian retailing.

Although British military activity in Canada was minimal during the War of the Spanish Succession (1701–1713), under the Treaty of Utrecht France was forced to relinquish all claims to Hudson Bay and

OPPOSITE: A bridal party of Kwakiutl Indians, photographed by Edward Curtis in 1914, arrives at the groom's village. ABOVE: Another early way of arriving at villages.

The Country and Its People

Newfoundland, and to give up Acadia, which the British promptly renamed Nova Scotia ("New Scotland"). There was a period of relative peace and tranquility for the next 40 years, broken only in 1744 by the British seizure of the French fortress of Louisbourg on Cape Breton Island. It was handed back four years later under the Peace of Aix-la-Chapelle.

The Seven Years' War, known in America as the French and Indian War, was to be the decisive turning point in Canadian history. The war began well for the French and their

Indian allies, as the British forces in battle after battle showed themselves to be tactically unprepared for what amounted to quasi-guerrilla warfare. But the tide began to turn in 1758 with the arrival of British land and naval reinforcements. A successful siege of the fortress at Louisbourg led to its recapture, giving the British control of the entrance to the Gulf of St. Lawrence, while at the Lake Ontario end of the St. Lawrence River the British took the vital Fort Frontenac. Then, in the summer of 1759, an assault force under the command of 32-year-old General James Wolfe, the youngest general in the British army, sailed from the Atlantic down the St. Lawrence to Quebec. All summer long Wolfe's artillery pounded the city, reducing it to rubble but without budging the French forces under the Marquis de Montcalm in their citadel atop the steep cliffs above the town. Then, on the night of September 12, Wolfe tried a daring maneuver. He led a force of 5,000 infantrymen in boats to a point behind the city, where they silently scaled the cliffs and assembled on

the Plains of Abraham. The next morning, the startled French forces, flushed out of their fortified redoubt, were slaughtered. Quebec had fallen. Both Wolfe and Montcalm were killed. The battle had lasted 15 minutes.

Although it was one of the shortest battles on record, its consequences ultimately reverberated around the world. The fall of Quebec effectively marked the fall of New France, and when the French handed over all of Canada under the terms of the Treaty of Paris in 1763, the British were left as undisputed masters of the entire North American continent. Some historians argue, however, that it was a Pyrrhic victory in that the British were also left over-confident and over-stretched, not to mention out-of-pocket, while the many American colonists who fought on the British side, including one George Washington, had gained wartime experience as well as insights into British military strategy that would prove invaluable a few years later when the Americans launched their War of Independence.

BRITISH CANADA

The conquest of Canada brought another problem for Britain: what to do about the predominantly French population in the new territory over which they now ruled. In the end, they did the decent thing — and paid dearly for it. By passing the Quebec Act of 1774, the British gave the French Canadians the right to continue using their own language, the secure ownership of their property, the primacy of French civil law, and the freedom to practice the Roman Catholic religion (including the Church's right to collect tithes). This did not go down at all well with the overwhelmingly Protestant population in the 13 American colonies, who were already incensed over what they considered unjust taxes imposed by Britain to help pay for the war against France. And when the boundaries of the province of Quebec were extended to protect the French Canadian fur traders operating in the Ohio and Mississippi River valleys, the American colonists decided that they had had enough.

The colonial rebellion became the American Revolution late in 1775 with attacks on Montreal and Quebec City which, had they been successful, would almost certainly have heralded a fairly swift victory for the Americans. In fact, the attack on Montreal was successful, but so brutish was the behavior of the "liberators" that most French Canadians decided they would prefer not to be thus liberated and went on to fight fiercely alongside the British, thus denying the Americans an early knockout.

By the time the war ended in 1783, Canadians had a new neighbor, the United States of America, and also a lot of new Canadians, for about 50,000 Americans who remained loyal to the British Crown had fled northwards. Most of them settled in Nova Scotia and what is now New Brunswick, although about 7,000 made their way to present-day Ontario. More still arrived at the end of the war claiming to be Loyalists, but their devotion to George III might possibly have been influenced by the offer of free land to Loyalist immigrants. In any case, as a result of the American Revolution, Canada received a large transfusion of English-speaking immigrants, many of whom were well-educated and had occupied positions of responsibility and influence under the old colonial regime. Thus did the balance of power in Canada begin to shift away from the French Canadians.

In the years following the war Canada became transformed both politically and territorially. In 1791 the province of Quebec was divided into Upper Canada (mainly English-speaking, now Ontario) and Lower Canada (mainly French-speaking, now Quebec), each with its own lieutenant governor and parliament. Meanwhile, the vast and hitherto neglected lands to the west were gradually being opened up in the wake of the pioneering explorations of Alexander Mackenzie, who in 1793 became the first white man to cross Canada all the way to the Pacific coast, and Simon Fraser and David Thompson, who were the first to map the great mountains and rivers from the Rockies to the Pacific.

The War of 1812 was the last neighborhood brawl before the United States and Canada settled down to live together more or less happily ever after. The war had a number of causes: border disputes, British interference with American shipping, fierce rivalry in the lucrative fur trade, American claims that the British were behind Indian raids on American border settlements, British claims that Americans were trying to export republicanism to Canada, and so forth. Whatever the justice of any of these claims, they added up to war. Although both sides got in some telling blows — the Americans captured Toronto (or York, as it then was) and burnt it to the ground, whereupon the British retaliated by capturing Washington and burning the White House — neither side really seemed to have much appetite for the fight. The Americans wanted to get on

with nation-building and the British wanted to get on with countering the Napoleonic threat at home, while the Canadians wanted to be left in peace. So in 1814 they got together and declared the war over.

Not surprisingly, considering the enormous size of the two countries, the border issue was not immediately resolved. The first major step was taken in 1818 when they agreed on the 49th parallel as their mutual border from the Great Lakes to the Rockies, but it was not until 1842, after much haggling and a little skirmishing, that the Canadian border with the New England states was established. The last link, the border with the Oregon Territory west of the Rockies, was established along the 49th parallel in 1846.

As increased immigration swelled the population, French Canadians became convinced that the British were deliberately trying to dilute their power by swamping them with English-speaking newcomers.

ABOVE: The opening ceremony at Expo 86 in Vancouver, British Columbia. OPPOSITE: The view from Fort Anne in Annapolis Royal, Nova Scotia.

As a result, in 1837 French Canadians under the leadership of Louis-Joseph Papineau demanded automony for Lower Canada (Quebec) so that they could establish an independent republic. When the British refused, a violent rebellion broke out which was not finally defeated until 1838. It was the first time that the call for an independent Quebec had been heard. It would not be the last.

Nor were the French Canadians the only ones growing impatient with British rule around this time. In Upper Canada (Ontario) a rough and ready coalition of economic have-nots led by newspaper editor William Lyon Mackenzie rose up against the oligarchic Tory establishment and demanded that the government be remodeled along American lines. When these demands, predictably, were not met, Mackenzie too resorted to armed rebellion with even less success than Papineau, whom he soon joined in exile in the U.S.

Although both insurrections had been easily put down, they succeeded in lighting an anti-colonialist fuse that would prove unquenchable.

Nevertheless, Canada at mid-century was a picture of expansion and growth. New waves of immigrants boosted the population of the Maritime Provinces, which were beginning to prosper as a result of their flourishing lumber, fishing, and shipbuilding industries. The population explosion also led to the creation of settlements further westward, in addition to providing the labor needed to build the canals, roads, and railways that made the westward expansion possible. In less than 20 years, over 3,000 km or 2,000 miles of railroad tracks were laid. All that was needed for Canada to become a truly coast-to coast country was for some sort of tug to be exerted from the other side of the Rockies. That tug, when it came, turned out to be a powerful yank: in 1858 gold was discovered in the Fraser River Valley.

The Gold Rush that followed was so frenetic, and so dominated by Americans rushing northwards to stake their claims, that Britain quickly proclaimed a new Crown colony, British Columbia, to control the stampede into the territory.

British colonies now straddled the continent from the Atlantic to the Pacific.

THE DOMINION OF CANADA

With the old Anglo-French strains still causing problems, and with the turmoil to the south caused by the American Civil War, not to mention the ordinary growing pains brought on by rapid population growth and territorial expansion, it was widely felt that the colonies should come together and forge a stronger union among themselves. So in 1864 delegates from the various colonies convened in Charlottetown, Prince Edward Island, to begin laying the groundwork for a new confederation. Three years later, the British North America Act of 1867 created

The entrance to Ottawa's Confederation Building.

the Dominion of Canada, in which the colonies of Nova Scotia, New Brunswick, Ontario, and Quebec became provinces in a confederated union with self-rule under a parliamentary system of government. Manitoba joined the Confederation in 1870, British Columbia in 1871, and Prince Edward Island in 1873. Alberta and Saskatchewan joined in 1905; Newfoundland, typically, held out until 1949, when it finally became Canada's tenth province.

As important as this political union was to Canada's development, it was more symbolic than real so long as there was no corresponding physical link between the provinces. In fact, three of the provinces — Nova Scotia, Prince Edward Island, and British Columbia — only agreed to join the

Confederation on condition that a transcontinental railway was built to tie the new nation together. Work on this mammoth project began in 1881 and, incredibly, was completed in only four years. In 1885, at Rogers Pass in the Selkirk Mountains, the last spike was driven: the Canadian Pacific Railway was in business.

As was to be expected, however, this mighty triumph of engineering was not achieved without casualties. The coming of the Iron Horse meant the virtual disappearance of the buffalo, the driving of Indians from their ancestral homelands, and the deaths of hundreds of (mostly Chinese) laborers on the railroad itself. It also precipitated a bloody uprising in 1885 on the part of the Matis, who were the descendants of

French trappers and Indian women, aided and abetted by several tribes of Plains Indians, all of whom felt threatened by the armies of new settlers swarming over their land. Already driven out of Manitoba as far west as the southern banks of the Saskatchewan River, the Matis and their Indian allies, under the leadership of Louis Riel, overwhelmed the Mounted Police post at Duck Lake, attacked the town of Battleford, and captured and burned Fort Pitt. But their successes were short-lived. Before long they were subdued by the superior firepower of

Prairie Provinces became one of the great grain-producing areas of the world. And, for icing on the national cake, in 1896 gold was discovered in the Klondike, setting off the biggest gold rush in history as 100,000 fortune-seekers poured into the Yukon. These were heady times.

Thus Canada entered the twentieth century in a buoyant mood. It was also blessed during the years 1896–1911 with one of its greatest prime ministers, Sir Wilfrid Laurier, a French Canadian and Roman Catholic who set himself the Herculean task of end-

the Canadian forces, and Riel was hanged. His execution became another source of resentment among French Canadians, who felt that he would not have been treated so harshly had he not been a Roman Catholic of French ancestry.

With the country now linked literally and politically from sea to sea, the final years of the nineteenth century saw Canada blossom dramatically as a nation. As thousands upon thousands of new immigrants arrived, new lands were settled and cultivated, hydroelectric projects were initiated, new manufacturing industries were started up alongside the already-thriving industries of lumbering, fishing, mining, pulp and paper. Above all, agriculture boomed as the

ing the antagonism and suspicion between Canada's Anglo and French communities. But World War I came along and deepened the rift: French Canadians violently objected to military conscription, which was introduced in 1917 after the Canadian volunteer forces fighting alongside the British in the trenches had suffered such appalling losses that there were no volunteers left to fight. The French Canadian point of view — that the war had nothing to do with them, and therefore they shouldn't be drafted to fight in it — left much residual bitterness on both sides after the war was over.

A happier legacy of the war was an economy enriched by a vastly increased manufacturing capacity, streamlined industrial development, expanded mining activity, and burgeoning exports of wheat. Along with Canada's post-war prosperity came growing independence from Britain, acknowledged by the British at the Imperial Conference of 1926 when Canada was granted the right to conduct its own international affairs without reference to London, and sealed by the Statute of Westminster in 1931 which made Canada an independent nation.

Then came the Depression, which was even worse in Canada than in the U. S. Suddenly the Promised Land was a ravaged land, as drought erased the wheat fields and unemployment stalked the cities. The misery of the "Dirty Thirties", as the Canadians called the decade, lasted until September 1939 when Hitler marched to the rescue by marching into Poland. Canada, following Britain's lead, immediately declared war on Germany, whereupon the economy coughed, spluttered, then roared back to life.

Also revived, sadly, was the bitter Anglo-French debate over military conscription, which once again split the country. And, again, Canada suffered battlefield losses out of all proportion to its population. On the other side of the ledger, the Canadian economy prospered out of all proportion to its pre-war capacity as almost 10 percent of the population were engaged in war-related industries. Thanks to the war, Canada became one of the world's major industrial nations as well as an important military power, a co-founder of the United Nations, and a member of NATO.

Peace was as good to Canada as the war had been. A huge oil field was discovered near Edmonton, Alberta, in 1947; giant uranium deposits were discovered in Ontario and Saskatchewan; its extraordinary mineral riches made Canada the world's leading producer of nickel, zinc, lead, copper, gold, and silver; its inexhaustible water resources made possible countless hydroelectric projects, including the world's biggest; its forests made it the world's foremost exporter of newsprint, while its oceans made it the world's foremost exporter of fish. And as if that weren't enough, Canada was fortunate in having the world's best customer for raw materials right on its doorstep.

Another milestone in Canada's rise among the world's top industrial nations was the opening in 1959 of the St. Lawrence Seaway, a joint U.S.–Canadian project that made possible shipping from the Great Lakes to the Atlantic. Three years later the Trans-Canada Highway was completed, a concrete link spanning all 10 provinces.

In 1967 Canada celebrated its hundredth birthday by throwing itself a big party in the form of a World's Fair — Expo '67 — in Montreal. And Canadians had much to celebrate: a vigorous and rapidly expanding

economy, one of the highest standards of living in the world, advanced social welfare programs providing health care and other benefits for all citizens, virtually unlimited natural resources, and a history of international conduct such that Canada had managed to join the front rank of the world's nations without making any enemies. What better reasons for having a party?

CANADA TODAY

Alas, there was a ghost at the birthday party. The old specter of separatism which had haunted the Confederation during the entire century of its existence was suddenly summoned up in a speech by visiting President de Gaulle. Speaking to a large throng outside the Montreal City Hall, he declared, *"Vive le Québec libre!"* Considering that he was present in Canada as a guest of a nation

OPPOSITE: Similar headgear, but worlds apart: faces from the Northwest Territories (left) and the southern prairies. ABOVE: The Prince and Princess of Wales at the opening of Vancouver's Expo 86.

celebrating its "unity through diversity", this was mischief-making on an epic scale.

With their clamorings having thus been endorsed by the President of France, Quebec's separatists found new heart for the struggle to wrench the province away from the rest of the nation. The Parti Québecois was formed under the militant leadership of René Lévesque, and won 23 percent of the vote in the 1970 provinical elections. That same year the separatist movement turned nasty around its fringes, as the so-called *Front de Liberation du Québec* (FLQ) resorted

became a brushfire and Lévesque's Parti Québecois were swept into power in the provincial elections. Immediately Lévesque embarked on a campaign to emphasize Quebec's separation. In particular, strict language laws were passed to ensure that French, and only French, would be the official language of Quebec. Not only that, but a Commission de la Langue Française was created to operate as a kind of language police in stamping out every last trace of English in the province — even down to the humble apostrophe, if caught being used in

to outright terrorism, kidnapping the British Trade Commissioner and murdering the Canadian Labour Minister, Pierre Laporte. Prime Minister Pierre Trudeau responded by invoking the War Measures Act and sending 10,000 troops into the province. The crackdown succeeded; the FLQ was crushed and Laporte's killers were caught. Three years later the Parti Québecois won only six seats in the 110-seat provincial parliament.

Despite this electoral setback, and the Trudeau government's concessions to the Quebecois, including the Official Languages Act by which French became Canada's second official language, the flames of separatism refused to die out. Then in 1976, to widespread astonishment, the flames

a non-French way (e.g., to create a possessive noun).

Alarmed by the Anglophobia underlying this outbreak of cultural chauvinism, English-speaking people and businesses fled the province in droves — much to the delight of the Quebecois extremists but much to the detriment of Quebec's economy. Then, in 1980, the pendulum swung back the other way again; in a referendum on separation, Quebecois rejected the proposal by a large majority. And at the next election Lévesque's separatists were voted out of office. In 1987 the Conservative government of Brian Mulroney made a significant gesture towards the Quebecois when the prime minister signed a document recognizing them as a "distinct society". The following year, in what seemed like a reciprocal gesture of appreciation, Quebec gave Mulroney's Conservatives a large part of their majority in the national elections. It seemed, at last, that the flames of separatism had finally been extinguished.

Not so. As before, the desire for separation among the Quebecois simply smoldered unnoticed, waiting to be re-ignited into the burning issue it had so often been in the past. And, sure enough, it blazed back into prominence at the start of the nineties.

ment recommended that a new referendum on sovereignty for the province be held in 1992 and, if approved by the voters, that Quebec should become an independent sovereign state one year from the date of the referendum. Although the voters rejected the idea in 1992, the betting is that next time the proposition is put to them they *will* vote to let Quebec go its own way.

The reason is that *next* time — for the first time — the other Canadians are not going to beg them to stay. All across Canada I heard the same message: every time the people in

This time, however, nobody was able to say precisely what set it alight. The best explanation I heard came from Don Johnson, a columnist for the Toronto *Globe and Mail*. "We are merely advised that Quebeckers feel humiliated, the status quo is unacceptable and unhappiness prevails", he said with a helpless shrug. He then went on to compare it to the breakdown of a marriage — "where neither party can point to a specific cause, but there is a general feeling that a divorce would be preferable."

At any rate, whatever the cause of the latest "unhappiness", it looks increasingly likely that this 125-year-old marriage is headed for eventual divorce. In March 1991 a commission set up by the Quebec parlia-

Quebec throw a tantrum we give them what they want, and they're always demanding special treatment; if they want to go, let them go. That is obviously a crude paraphrase of a more complicated sentiment, but it is nonetheless a sentiment that I encountered everywhere I went in Canada. And my experience is borne out by a recent opinion poll showing that over 75 percent of English-speaking Canadians would be happy to bid *adieu* to Quebec. This means, among other things, that any federal government would be severely limited in the inducements it could offer the Quebecois to reconsider, which

The maple leaf or the fleur-de-lis? Will it be the national or the provincial flag that flies over Quebec in future?

in turn would hurt feelings that are already bruised. No, Canada's prospects of surviving in its present shape do not look good.

I suppose it is impertinent for a non-Canadian to offer an opinion in the matter, but I will anyway. I find it terribly, terribly sad to contemplate the idea of a great nation dismembering itself, especially when it had seemed so close to finding the right formula for becoming — multiculturally, bilingually — a near-perfect example to the rest of the world of how to build a terrific country. One can only hope that good sense and good will ultimately will prevail.

GEOGRAPHY AND CLIMATE

William Lyon Mackenzie King, Canada's longest-serving prime minister, observed at the beginning of his third term of office in 1936: "If some countries have too much history, we have too much geography."

It's hard to argue with that. Spread over almost 10 million sq km, Canada stretches more than 5,500 km (3,400 miles) from Cape Spear, Newfoundland, in the east to the Alaskan border in the west, and 4,600 km (2,900 miles) from Lake Erie's Pelee Island in the south to Cape Columbia on Ellesmere Island in the north (which is only 800 km or 500 miles from the North Pole). Yes, *much* geography.

Within this vastness, predictably, one finds stunning topographical extremes. Almost half the country, for example, is forested — one single forest zone of conifers extends for 6,000 km (3,730 miles) in a wide sweep from Newfoundland to the far north — while similarly enormous tracts of land are empty, treeless prairies. There are millions of acres of flood plains and marshy lowlands, and there are the majestic Rocky Mountains. (Canada's highest mountain, at 5,951 m or 19,525 ft, Mt. Logan, is not in the Rockies but in the St. Elias Mountains of the southwestern Yukon.)

And then there is the water. Canada is awash in lakes and rivers; they account for over seven percent of the country's total

The spectacular Mackenzie Mountains divide the Yukon from the Northwest Territories.

area. There are 400,000 of them in Ontario alone. Three of the 20 longest rivers in the world are to be found in Canada. In all, the country has a staggering 25 percent of the world's fresh water resources.

Geologically, Canada can be divided into five distinct regions, not counting the archipelago of islands inside the Arctic Circle. The **Appalachian** region is that hilly, wooded part of the country bounded on the west by the St. Lawrence River and on the east by the Atlantic, and includes the Maritime Provinces, Newfoundland, and the Gaspé Peninsula. It belongs to an ancient mountain system, now eroded to modest elevations, that reaches as far south as Alabama.

The **St. Lawrence Lowlands** comprise that swath of land from the mouth of the St. Lawrence River to the Great Lakes. This fertile flood plain is home to most of Canada's people, industry, and commerce.

The **Prairies** spread across the provinces of Manitoba, Saskatchewan, and Alberta, and on up into the Northwest Territories. The rich soil in the southern reaches, where the prairies join the Great Plains of the U.S., yields great golden seas of wheat which gradually dry up in Alberta, giving way to huge cattle ranches.

The **Western Cordillera** is bounded on the east by the Rocky Mountains and on the west by the Coast Mountains. In between is the spectacular diversity of British Columbia, a province of soaring mountain peaks, alpine lakes and meadows, large boreal forests, intricate networks of rivers, deep blue lakes and long green valleys.

The fifth region, the **Canadian Shield**, encompasses everything else: the immense, horseshoe-shaped land mass that surrounds Hudson Bay, and stretches from the coast of Labrador down to the St. Lawrence Lowlands, over to the Prairies, and up to the Arctic. Covering some 4.7 million sq km (1.8 million sq miles), about half the entire area of Canada, this rough-hewn, rock-strewn, lake-pitted wilderness is one of the oldest sections of the earth's crust.

Dotted throughout all of these regions are enclaves of particular note: Canada's 34 national parks. With a total area of over 140,000 sq km (54,000 sq miles), the national parks system is designed to protect

wildlife of all kinds — wild flowers as well as wild animals — from the predations of man.

The flora and fauna that decorate and populate the Canadian landscape naturally vary from region to region. There are, however, some animals that can be found just about everywhere: squirrels and chipmunks, rabbits and hares, porcupines and skunks. Equally widespread throughout the country's forests and woodlands are deer, moose, black bears, beavers, wild geese, and ducks. The richest fishing grounds in Canada — possibly in the world — are to be found in the Gulf of St. Lawrence and the waters of the continental shelf off Newfoundland: cod, herring, mackerel, tuna, oysters, clams, lobsters, and scallops are only the best-known of the 800 species of edible marine life with which the area teems.

In the St. Lawrence Lowlands the coniferous forests of spruce, firs, and pines that sweep from Labrador to the Rockies begin to be infiltrated by aspen, birch, oak, elm, beech, hemlock, and ash. In southern Quebec the sugar maples appear, and in southwestern Ontario the walnut and tulip trees, the hickories and dogwoods. As for its animal life, the region is better known for its bipeds than its quadrupeds.

In the prairies, one animal in particular is conspicuous by its absence: the plains buffalo. The few who have survived are now in the national parks, while their place has been taken by great herds of cattle. Denizens of the semi-arid grasslands of the southern prairies include kangaroo rats, hares, pronghorn antelopes, and the ranchers' nemesis, coyotes.

In the mountain ranges of the Western Cordillera one can find, if one tries hard enough, brown bears, elk, mountain goats, bighorn sheep, and the bosses of the upper slopes, grizzly bears. In the lakes and rivers there is some of the best trout and salmon fishing to be found anywhere in the world.

In the great expanse of forests across northern Canada are the largest concentrations of fur-bearing animals: mink, ermine, marten, muskrat, beaver, river otter, weasel, lynx, bobcat, wolves, and wolverines. Further north, in the tundra, are the arctic foxes, lemmings, musk ox, and caribou, as well as snow geese and trumpeter swans. Still further north, where the frigid waters are full of whales, seals, and walrus, the mighty polar bear patrols the ice packs of the Arctic.

Because words like "frigid" and "polar" and "ice" and "Arctic" — and even the subtly prejudicial "north" — are all words that we readily associate with Canada, most foreigners think that Canada's climate can probably be summed up in one word: cold. This is a mistake. True, Canada occupies the northern — and therefore colder — part of the continent, but this ignores the fact that Pelee Island, Ontario is on the same latitude

tion in Canada falls as snow, compared to a worldwide average of five percent. And the only national capital colder than Ottawa is Ulaan Bataar, the capital of Mongolia; Winnipeg is the coldest city in the world with a poulation of more than half a million; and residents of Montreal shovel more snow every year than residents of any other city.

But there is a bright side to all this. It's just that: brightness. Canada may be refrigerated half the time, but it is sunlit most of the time. Which means that it is beautiful all the time, brilliantly white in winter, infinitely

as Rome. True, the dominant images of western Canada are the snow-capped peaks of the Rockies, but this obscures the fact that those same Rockies form a protective wall that guarantees Vancouver milder winters than, say, Dallas. True, the eastern coast takes a beating from the Atlantic, but parts of it are also caressed by the Gulf Stream, creating swimming beaches equal to any in the Mediterranean.

Having said that, one has to admit that for much of the year Canada is a theme park called Winter. Harold Town, one of Canada's leading artists, once said: "We are a nation of thermometers monitoring cold fronts…. We jig to the crunch of snow." Indeed, over a third of the annual precipita-

and variously green the rest of year. What's more, its meteorological diversity mirrors its geographical diversity, so that the visitor has the luxury of choosing not only the scenery and activities that most appeal, but also the precise climate in which to enjoy both.

In the following chapters, and in the WHEN TO GO section of TRAVELERS' TIPS, I will give information about the sort of weather you can expect to find in different places at different times. For now, though, let me just assure you that in Canada there is truly a time and place for everything.

The Canadian prairies in bloom.

British Columbia

B.C., as it is commonly known, is the country's third largest and most westerly province, and perhaps its most beautiful. It stretches from the Rockies to the Pacific, and from the 49th to the 60th parallel. It is thus bordered by the U.S. states of Washington, Idaho, and Montana at its southern edge, the Yukon and Northwest Territories to the north, Alaska at its northwest corner, and Alberta to the east beyond the Rockies. The rugged, snowcapped Coast Mountains rise above the deeply indented Pacific coastline, and beyond them the landscape is rippled by mountain ranges running northwest to southeast that give way to valleys and wide, rolling prairies carpeted with ancient forests and dotted with lakes.

B.C.'s climate is as varied as its landscape. The coast, warmed by the Pacific current and shadowed by the high Coast Mountains, has mild, wet winters and cool summers. The more exposed interior is generally drier, with more extreme temperatures, while northeastern winters are the coldest of all and have the heaviest snowfall.

The province covers an enormous area — 947,800 sq km (366,255 sq miles) — big enough to hold a handful of European countries. There are only three million inhabitants in the entire province, the majority of whom live in the southwestern corner, and almost half the entire population can be found in Greater Vancouver. This leaves an awful lot of space. There are literally hundreds of parks covering millions of acres of wilderness, making ideal habitats for all kinds of wildlife and a heaven for outdoor enthusiasts. With so many people huddled in its bottom corner, and with the great barrier created by the Rockies, it is not surprising that B.C. seems separated from the rest of the country. It has often been observed that its lifestyle and easy-going attitudes owe more to California than to Canada.

The Indian tribes who once inhabited the West Coast enjoyed prosperity and had a highly developed culture, expressed in art forms that are still much in evidence. Stunning examples of wood carving are carefully preserved, most strikingly in the form of totem poles, and the craft is still practiced.

Europeans were slow to arrive here because of the enormous physical barriers presented by the terrain. It was 1774 when tentative Spanish exploration began, and 1778 when Captain James Cook landed on Vancouver Island, where he traded with Indians for furs, later sold to the Chinese at a large profit. News of this began to speed things up, and the inevitable skirmishes ended with the Spanish conceding control to the British. So in 1792 Captain George Vancouver was despatched by the British to map the coast. In the meantime intrepid fur traders were exploring overland routes to the Pacific and establishing trading posts.

The Hudson's Bay Company established its headquarters on Vancouver Island. In 1849 the island was colonized by the Crown and Victoria was declared its capital. The discovery of gold along the banks of the Fraser River brought a rush of prospectors, and to secure its hold on their territories the British Government made the mainland (then known as New Caledonia) a British colony and renamed it British Columbia in 1858. In the 1860's the construction of the Cariboo Road opened up the area, lumber mills and canneries began to spring up, and in 1866 the colonies of Vancouver Island and British Columbia joined together. When the United States acquired Alaska, a further attack of nerves prompted B.C. to consider joining the Confederation as a security measure against American invasion, but it was with caution and only upon the promise that a trans-continental railway would reach its coast that in 1871 B.C. finally joined.

A farm off Highway 1 in British Columbia.

This promise was fulfilled by 1885 and industries based on the province's natural resources were able to develop. A further boost came with the opening of the Panama Canal, which made transportation easier and therefore cheaper. Today the economy still rests largely on natural resources such as fishing, forestry, mining, energy, agriculture (particularly in the lower Fraser Valley and the irrigated Okanagan), and the tourism attracted by the area's extraordinary natural beauty. The logging industry is currently at the center of a battle between con-

servationists and the B.C. government, with the province's image of caring environmentalism being severely challenged over the rapid destruction of the rain forests and the pollution resulting from logging activities.

VANCOUVER

Magnificent in its setting, sophisticated and cosmopolitan in character, Vancouver must rate as one of the world's most livable and beautiful cities. The air is fresh, the atmosphere is vibrant and youthful, and being only a little over 100 years old, this youngster is suitably seated in the lap of nature. To the north it is shadowed by the Coast Mountains, to the west are the peaks of Vancouver Island, and wilderness surrounds the city. Water is all around: Burrard Inlet separates the city core from the residential North Shore area, while the Strait of Georgia lies to the west and the Fraser River to the south.

The miniature railway in Vancouver's magnificent Stanley Park.

Water of another kind also figures largely in the life of Vancouverites. The rain is a popular topic of conversation — which is hardly surprising, as the city averages 57 inches a year of the stuff. However, protected by the bulk of Vancouver Island and warmed by the Japan Current, Vancouver has a gentle climate and, unlike so much of Canada, has very little snowfall. May to September are the warmest months with least rainfall, although even in July and August there may be days when the mountains will be shrouded in mist. On the bonus side, the rain keeps the air fresh and the city green.

Vancouver is the third largest city in Canada as well as being B.C.'s business center, but with a metropolitan population of only 1.4 million, and being so close to nature, it can afford a small-town lifestyle. Here, where there is a noticeable tendency to stroll instead of rush, the residents positively rejoice in the delights of their park-like city. It is said that Vancouverites are considered by Eastern Canadians to be a little too hedonistic. With the endless recreational opportunities offered them by the sea, the mountains, and the parks, who can blame them? There are nine miles of beaches within the city limits, a rain forest is within walking distance of the business core, and ski slopes are only 20 minutes away. Although spoiled by nature's bounty, Vancouverites do not take their surroundings for granted, and like the Indians before them they have a healthy respect for their environment.

The sea plays a major role in the city's economy, for Vancouver has the largest port on the North American Pacific coast. It's from here that grain, timber, and minerals are exported, and especially valuable trade links with Japan have been forged. Timber, fishing, and tourism are Vancouver's major industries, but increasingly the economy is becoming more dependent on international finance. With the high rate of foreign investment here and the increasing immigration from Hong Kong, in some quarters the city has been dubbed "Hongkouver".

BACKGROUND

When in 1791 the Spanish explorer José María Narváez sailed up the Georgia Strait,

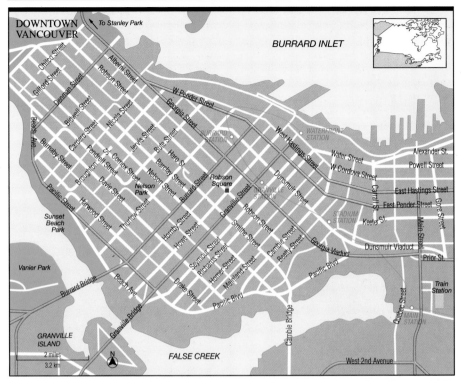

the shores on which Vancouver now stands were densely carpeted with trees and inhabited by Salish Indians who fished the waters. The following year Captain George Vancouver quite literally put the area on the map when he explored and charted Burrard Inlet on behalf of the British Navy. The next white man to explore the area was Simon Fraser who in 1808 reached the Pacific by means of an overland route. This brought him to the mouth of the river now named after him, and in his wake fur trading posts were set up.

The site then seems largely to have been ignored until the 1860's when sawmills started to appear around Burrard Inlet. Alcohol was not allowed on company land, and so when a Yorkshireman named Jack Deighton turned up with a keg of whiskey, he answered the prayers of the thirsty workers. He persuaded the men to help him build a saloon, and that was when things began to happen. The year was 1867, and the rough-and-ready community that quickly sprang up around the bar was named Gastown after its loquacious saloonkeeper, who by then had become known as "Gassy Jack". The town kept on growing and in 1869 the

provincial government officially renamed it Granville.

The next major development came in 1884 when William Van Horne, builder of the Canadian Pacific Railway (C.P.R.), decided to make Granville the site of the West Coast terminus. He also suggested that the town be renamed and so in 1886 it became incorporated as the city of Vancouver. Within months the city was destroyed by fire but with speed and determination it was rebuilt by the time the first C.P.R. passenger train chugged into town in 1887.

It was at this time that unpleasantness and disgrace shadowed Vancouver's history. Many Chinese had arrived to work on constructing the railroad, and a series of clashes between them and the white community spurred Vancouver authorities to deport them to Victoria. The incensed provincial government intervened to right this injustice and the Chinese community continued to live in the area that developed into the city's Chinatown. The racism did not end there, however, and to the city's further shame the Chinese were denied many of the rights granted to other citizens until the late 1940's.

The twentieth century saw Vancouver's rapid growth: the port grew in importance as trade with the Far East developed, the fishing and timber industries thrived, the opening of the Panama Canal in 1914 facilitated export of grain to Europe, thus increasing the port's importance, and the demands created by the Second World War served to boost the mining and timber industries. After that, urban development hurtled onwards, making Vancouver the envy of many older cities.

Where once impenetrable wilderness

free (800) 663-6000. The main North Vancouver Infocentre is at 131 East 2nd Street, ((604) 987-4488. There is an information kiosk at Lonsdale Quay by the SeaBus Terminal, another at the airport, and several more dotted within and around the city.

WHAT TO SEE AND DO

Sights

DOWNTOWN

One of the city's most distinctive landmarks is the delightful white-sailed structure of

greeted the eyes of the first explorers, shiny high-rise buildings glitter against the splendid background of the Coast Mountains. The city gently tends the little past that it has so that old buildings have been restored and native art has been carefully preserved.

GENERAL INFORMATION

For information on British Columbia as a whole, contact Tourism British Columbia, Parliament Buildings, Victoria V8V 1X4, ((604) 387-1642 or toll-free (800) 663-6000. For information on Vancouver itself, contact its main tourist office: The Travel Infocentre, 1055 Dunsmuir Street (near Burrard Street), Vancouver V7X 1L3, ((604) 683-2000 or toll-

Canada Place that boldly projects into the harbor north of Burrard Street. With its unmistakable roof of white teflon-coated "sails" that whiten in the sunlight, it has inevitably been referred to as "Vancouver's answer to the Sydney Opera House", and like the Opera House it has quickly become an emblem of the city it graces. Originally built as the Canada Pavilion for Expo 86, the complex now comprises the World Trade Centre, the Vancouver Trade and Convention Centre, a luxury hotel, the gigantic **CN IMAX Theatre**, restaurants, shops, and a major cruise ship terminal. An outdoor promenade runs around the structure and offers excellent views of the harbor and mountains of the north shore.

Also of architectural note is the nearby **Canadian Pacific Railway Station** on Cordova Street. This splendidly restored structure was built in the 1880's as the C.P.R. terminus, and now the SkyTrain elevated rail line to the eastern suburbs and the SeaBus ferry operate from here.

To fully appreciate the city's glorious setting you should take a trip up the nearby 40-story-high **Harbour Centre** at 555 West Hastings Street, ((604) 689-0421. The views from the top will take your breath away, if you have any left to take after the journey up the outside of the building in the glass "Skylift" elevator. The circular observation deck is equipped with telescopes and information plaques, and an excellent special-effects film about the city is shown. It is open daily until 10 pm.

Three blocks south of the Harbour Centre and then a couple east along Georgia Street lies **Robson Square**, which covers the area between Howe and Hornby Streets. This complex, built in 1979, contains government buildings, a seven-story law court building with a vast sloping glass roof, a media center, restaurants, terraces, waterfalls, and, during the colder months, an ice-skating rink in the open-air plaza. The old courthouse building still stands across from the modern complex, and this dignified neo-classical building has been converted to house the **Vancouver Art Gallery**. The building was designed in 1907 by B.C.'s foremost architect of the time, Frances Rattenbury, and it seems fitting that the interior of the building was redesigned by Arthur Erickson, the internationally-renowned Vancouver architect who was responsible for the square's modern complex. The gallery holds temporary exhibitions of international and Canadian art and its permanent collection includes Canadian, European, and North American paintings. One of its main attractions is the large collection of works by the famous B.C. artist Emily Carr, whose paintings capture the mystery of the rain forests and echo the native art of Canada's Pacific coast. The Art Gallery is at 750 Hornby Street, Robson Square, ((604) 682-5621, and is open daily.

You can soak up a bit of European atmosphere when you stroll along the section of

Robson Street that runs between Howe and Broughton Streets. Once a mainly German neighborhood, this stretch is known locally as **Robsonstrasse**, and here you can sample all varieties of European food in the restaurants, cafes, and delicatessens that line the street, or take a look at the high fashion on display in its trendy shops.

A few blocks east of the Harbour Centre between Richards and Columbia Streets lies the neighborhood of **Gastown**, the birthplace of Vancouver and the oldest part of the city. It was here in 1867 that the Englishman

John "Gassy Jack" Deighton built his saloon with the willing help of thirsty mill workers. The shanty town that sprung up around it grew to eventually become Vancouver, and although in 1886 a fire destroyed the town, it was quickly rebuilt using more robust materials. By the 1960's these buildings had degenerated into slums, and so it came about that during the 1970's Gastown underwent the familiar rags-to-riches story of renovation. The nineteenth-century buildings were restored, modern but matching additions were built, streets were cobbled, imitation nineteenth-century street lights

OPPOSITE: Statue in Stanley Park.
ABOVE: Downtown Vancouver.

British Columbia

popped up, and the area filled with bistros, restaurants, galleries, and shops. This recipe proved yet successful again and Gastown is now a major tourist draw both by day and by night. The center of Gastown is Maple Tree Square, where the original Globe Saloon once lay and where a statue of Gassy Jack and his barrel of whiskey now stands in memory. At the corner of Cambie and Water Streets there's a Heath Robinson sort of affair which a plaque proudly proclaims to be the first **steam-powered clock** in the world. It pipes out its very own version of the Westminster chimes on the quarter-hour and lets off steam on the hour.

Just south of Gastown between Carrall Street and Gore Avenue, centered along Pender and Main Streets, is **Chinatown**, home to Canada's largest Chinese community. The neighborhood developed in the 1880's and some of the original buildings still stand. It's a bustling area filled with the noises and smells of Hong Kong, and it brims with restaurants, bakeries, herbalists, and shops selling all kinds of Chinese goods. Behind the **Chinese Cultural Centre** on East Pender Street is the delightful **Dr Sun Yat-Sen Classical Chinese Garden** which offers peaceful sanctuary from the city. The only one of its kind outside China, it was designed in Ming Dynasty style by a team from the city of Suzhou in honor of the revolutionary Sun Yat-Sen, who visited here while planning the overthrow of China's last dynasty. It is an exquisite composition of sculptural limestone rocks, plants, trees, bridges and water, and it's a good idea to join the guided tour which explains the principles behind the design. While you're in the area, you'll have to keep your eyes peeled if you don't want to miss the **Sam Kee Building**, reputedly the world's narrowest building, which stands at the corner of Pender and Carrall Streets, a mere 1.3 m (six ft) deep.

Stanley Park is the city's pride and joy and Vancouverites regard it with great reverence. This 405-hectare (1,000-acre) urban park covers the whole of the western tip of the downtown peninsula which juts out into Burrard Inlet, and consists of some 700 acres of lush rain forest. The rest is given over to gardens, sandy beaches, and public facilities. Back in 1886 Ottawa granted

this land to Vancouver and in 1889 Canada's governor-general Lord Stanley dedicated it "to the use and enjoyment of people of all colors, creeds and customs for all time." It is laced with hiking trails and dotted with picnic sites. There are tennis courts, a running track, miniature golf courses, cricket pitches, restaurants and snack bars, an open-air theatre, and a miniature railway. At the Georgia Street entrance is the marshy lake known as the Lost Lagoon, a bird sanctuary where you'll see Canada geese, Trumpeter swans, and other wildfowl. The 10-km (six-mile) scenic seawall that encircles the park is popular with cyclists and strollers, and for the less energetic there's a **Scenic Drive** which starts from the Georgia Street entrance to the park, taking you

around the peninsula in an anti-clockwise direction.

At **Brockton Point** there are great views across Burrard Inlet of the north shore mountains, and nearby is a display of totem poles. At **Prospect Point**, the Lion's Gate Bridge forms the only link between the downtown area and the north shore, and from here you get a good view of the ships passing through First Narrows to and from the port. At the southwest tip of the park peninsula, **Ferguson Point** looks over to Third Beach and the peaks of Vancouver Island.

Also in the park, the **Vancouver Aquarium**, ((604) 682-1118, is well worth a visit. It's the largest of its kind in North America: over 8,000 aquatic specimens are on display here. Star performances are given by the acrobatic killer whales, who can be watched through glass, with strong support from the playful beluga whales and the dolphins. While you're here you can take a turn in the Amazonian jungle, re-created under cover with plant, animal, aquatic, and bird life indigenous to that area.

OUTSIDE DOWNTOWN

Over on the south side of False Creek is **Granville Island**, which is in fact a small peninsula connected to the downtown core by Granville Bridge. Once the center of Vancouver's shipbuilding industry, by the

Vancouver's Chinatown not only has the largest Chinese Community in Canada, but many of its buildings were erected by the original settlers.

1960's the area had degenerated into a particularly grim spot full of dingy factories and warehouses. Renovation began in the 1970's and it is now a lively neighborhood of businesses, craft studios, industry, theatres, galleries, restaurants, markets, and shops. A huge warehouse underneath Granville Bridge has been converted to house the popular **Public Market**, where stalls sell seafood, produce, and foods of many countries. On the west of the island you'll find the **Maritime Market** which sells just about everything needed for pleasure boating.

The island is a fun place to have lunch and enjoy some views. To get there from the center peninsula you can take the passenger ferry that runs from Sunset Beach near the Aquatic Centre or take a bus from downtown.

Close by and to the west of Burrard Bridge in **Vanier Park** stands the **Vancouver Museum**, 1100 Chestnut Street, ((604) 736-4431. The museum has a gallery devoted to West Coast Indian culture, where some stunning examples of native art and artifacts are displayed. In a gallery that charts the area's history, exhibits include a replica of a Hudson's Bay Company trading post and reconstructed period interiors. Open daily. Situated on the second floor of the museum is the **H.R.Macmillan Planetarium**, ((604) 736-3656, which has up to four astronomy shows daily, and laser shows set to rock music at night. It is closed on Mondays dur-

ing the winter months. Next to the museum is the **Gordon Southam Observatory**, ((604) 738-2855, where you gaze at the heavens with the aid of a Zeiss telescope. Ring for opening times as they are subject to weather conditions. Admission is free.

A short distance away from the museum, also in Vanier Park, the **Maritime Museum**, ((604) 736-2211, traces the history of shipping in the area and the development of the port of Vancouver. The prime exhibit is the *St. Roch*, the fully restored Royal Canadian Mounted Police ship that during the Second World War became the first vessel to navigate the Northwest Passage in both directions. Guided tours are given. Outside you can see some of the museum's restored boats in **Heritage Harbour**.

Moving west, the **University of British Columbia** is magnificently sited on the headland of Point Grey, which is tipped with forest and overlooks the Georgia Strait and English Bay. Its **Museum of Anthropology** at 6393 NW Marine Drive, ((604) 228-3825, is a concrete and glass building worthy of its dramatic setting. Designed by Vancouver architect Arthur Erickson, the building's huge glass windows embrace the splendid views of cliffs, mountains, sea, and trees, giving context to wonderful exhibits of West Coast Indian art and craft. The museum has a splendid collection of totem poles, some of which are displayed alongside other huge exhibits in the vast **Great Hall**. The museum does not limit itself to representing the Northwest Pacific area and there are works of art and artifacts from many other cultures. Some galleries are set aside for temporary exhibitions and some house the research collections where items are thoughtfully stored in glass filing drawers and clearly catalogued. Outside, totem poles and some reconstructed Haida Indian dwellings are set in the rain forest. The museum is closed on Mondays and admission is free on Tuesdays.

Should you feel so inclined, from here you can follow the marked trails that lead down to **Wreck Beach**, a well-known and popular nudist beach. Or you can enjoy nature in a much more cultivated form at the **Nitobe Memorial Garden**, 6565 NW Marine Drive, a serene Japanese garden with a

ABOVE: Shopping in Granville Island's Public Market. OPPOSITE TOP: A street entertainer on Granville Island. BOTTOM: The joys of pleasure boating attract many to Granville Island.

ceremonial tea-house. At the southwest end of the campus there's the **UBC Botanical Garden**, at 16th Avenue and SW Marine Drive, ℂ (604) 228-4208, where highlights include the **Asian Garden** and the **Physick Garden**, a sixteenth century-style garden of medicinal plants.

In the eastern corner of False Creek, the silver geodesic dome that was built for Expo 86 is now home to **Science World**, 1455 Quebec Street at Terminal Avenue, ℂ (604) 687-7832, where visitors come to grips with science and have fun through imaginative hands-on displays. If you've always wanted to be in the movies, maybe you should settle for a visit to the center's **OMNIMAX Theater**, ℂ (604) 687-OMNI. Specially-made films are shown on the world's largest domed screen with effects that give a new meaning to the words "audience participation". Sky-Train runs to the nearby Main Street Station. Open daily.

Keen gardeners and those who enjoy floral displays will love **Queen Elizabeth Park**, at 33rd Avenue and Cambie Street, ℂ (604) 872-5513. At a height of 150 m (492 ft) it is the city's highest point, where wonderful views and magnificent gardens make a delightful place to stroll. Inside its dome-shaped **Bloedel Conservatory** exotic plants grow and brightly-colored tropical birds fly free. A few blocks away there's yet another manifestation of Vancouver's love affair with nature at the **Van Dusen Botanical Gardens**, at 37th Avenue and Oak Street, ℂ (604) 266-7194. In this 22-hectare (55-acre) garden there are geographical and botanical groupings of plants, a fragrance garden, a children's topiary garden where hedges are cut into animal shapes, and a maze. Both Queen Elizabeth Park and the Van Dusen Gardens are open daily.

THE NORTH SHORE

On Vancouver's north shore the Coast Mountains rise steeply out of the sea, cut deeply by inlets and canyons. On the lower slopes are the smart residential suburbs of North and West Vancouver and beyond them peaks and parks beckon hikers in the summer, skiers in the winter, and lovers of the Great Outdoors all the year round. To get there you can cross the spectacular **Lions**

Gate Bridge** that links the northern end of Stanley Park to Western Vancouver or the Second Narrows Bridge at Burnaby in East Vancouver. Alternatively, take the SeaBus, a commuter catamaran that runs from the old C.P.R. station to Lonsdale Quay on the northern shore. From there buses will take you to the view of your choice.

Next to the SeaBus terminal is the **Lonsdale Quay Market**, a lively new waterfront development of shops and eateries centered around a busy public market selling produce. There are lovely views across Burrard Inlet of the city and it is a good spot to pause and orientate oneself before exploring the spectacular sights the north shore has to offer.

At the north end of Capilano Road, the **Skyride**, 6400 Nancy Green Way, awaits to lift you 1100 m (3,700 ft) up **Grouse Mountain**. The ride takes about eight minutes and on a clear day it's a chance to enjoy yet more panoramic views that take in Washington's Olympic Peninsula. In the winter this is one of the most popular ski resorts, being the closest to the city, but in the summer it's known as Cypress Beach because it's a great place to laze around soaking up the brilliant sunshine. There's a restaurant and snack bar up here and year-round paths and hiking trails make it a popular recreation area.

Near the foot of Grouse Mountain, the fantastically dramatic **Capilano Suspension Bridge** offers thrills, though hopefully no spills, for those with a head for heights. Set in a wild and wonderful parkland, this plank-and-cable bridge is 137 m (450 ft) long and sways 70 m (230 ft) above the Capilano River as it rushes through a deep and narrow canyon surrounded by Douglas firs and Western Red cedars. It's a commercialized place and a charge is made to cross the bridge; nevertheless it is a beautiful and awe-inspiring sight. It's at 3735 Capilano Road and if you're driving from downtown, pick up the Capilano Road from Lions Gate Bridge.

You can, however, enjoy a similar but less commercialized experience at **Lynn Canyon Park** (ℂ 604/987-5922). This thickly forested parkland has nature trails through the rain forest, an ecology center, and a suspension bridge that crosses Lynn Creek. It is like the bridge at Capilano though only half as long and it crosses the creek at a height of 80 m (240 ft). There is no admission charge. If you're traveling by car, cross at Second Narrows Bridge, take Lynn Valley Road, and then head east along Peters Road.

A little further afield, the **Mount Seymour Provincial Park** overlooks the waters of Indian Arm, offering opportunities for hikers, horse riders, mountaineers, picnickers, viewseekers, and during the winter months skiiers. Trail paths and a road climb eight kilometers (five miles) up the moun-

at 10:30 am and begins its 66-km (41-mile) journey northwest to the small logging community of Squamish along a route that runs through forests, up mountains, by waterfalls, at a leisurely 20 m.p.h. The train arrives at Squamish at approximately 12:30 pm and passengers have one and a half hours to explore — enough time to get to **Shannon Falls** for some lunch. There's an attractive option of returning to Vancouver by sea aboard the *MV Britannia*, a route which takes a little longer. The *Royal Hudson* runs from mid-May to September, and as it's a

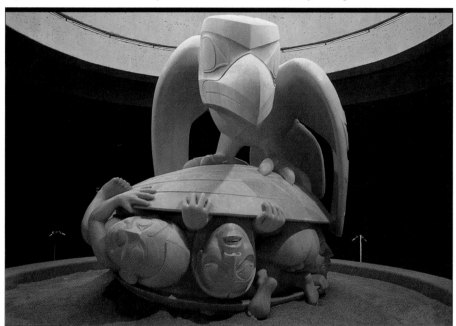

tain to a lookout where there's a cafe, an information center, more trails, and views of eastern Vancouver. From here a chairlift takes visitors to the mountaintop in July and August, while the more rugged follow the trail to the summit. To get there by car, take the Mount Seymour Parkway from Second Narrows Bridge, then turn off to the north on Mount Seymour Road.

A delightful way to see the impressive coastal scenery of **Howe Sound** is to take a trip aboard the refurbished *Royal Hudson 2860*, a stately old C.P.R. steam locomotive that pulled trains across Canada in the 1940's and 1950's. With a shrill whistle, a hiss, and the squealing of wheels, the train pulls away from North Vancouver Station

popular excursion you must book in advance. Contact B.C. Railways, 1311 W. First Street, ☏ (604) 987-5211.

North of Squamish and 120 km (75 miles) northwest of Vancouver is the fashionable **Whistler Resort**. It is primarily famous for its skiing but also offers all manner of recreational activities that include fishing, hiking, water sports, heli-hiking, and simply sightseeing. The pseudo-European Whistler Village nestles between Blackcomb and Whistler Mountains, and caters for every need, including those of conventioneers. You can get there by train from North

A stunning sculpture greets visitors to the University of British Columbia's Museum of Anthropology.

Vancouver, by bus with Maverick Coach Lines that operate from downtown Vancouver, or by car along the scenic Highway 99. For information on Whistler Resort call (604) 932-4222 or toll-free (800)685-3650 from Vancouver.

SOUTHEAST OF VANCOUVER

To the east of Vancouver lies the fertile **Fraser Valley**, an area of parklands shadowed by mountains all around, a popular weekend escape for Vancouverites. The Trans-Canada Highway follows the Fraser

Sports

The B.C. Lions, a Canadian **Football** League team, play their home games from late June to November at the enormous 60,000-seat BC Place Stadium, 777 Pacific Boulevard, ((604) 681-5466. **Baseball** fans can see the Vancouver Canadians, contenders in the Pacific Coast League, at home in the Nat Bailey Stadium, 4601 Ontario Street, ((604) 872-5232, and from October to March there's **ice hockey** at the Pacific Coliseum in Exhibition Park, ((604) 254-5141, where the Vancouver Canucks take on National Hockey League

River along its south shore, while Highway 7 runs along the north side. **Fort Langley National Historic Park**, 56 km (35 miles) from Vancouver on the south side of the river makes an interesting stop. Once a trading post for the Hudson's Bay Company, the fort dates from 1827, and it was here in the Big House that B.C. was officially proclaimed a crown colony. The fort with its wooden palisade has been restored and the buildings are open daily to the public. For information telephone (604) 888-4424.

opponents. Also at Exhibition Park there's **horse racing** from April through October, ((604) 254-1631, and **harness racing** takes place at Cloverdale Raceway, 6050 176th Street, in the suburb of Cloverdale. In March, World Cup **ski racing** takes place on the slopes of Grouse Mountain, and during July it's the site of the World Invitational **Hang Gliding** Championship.

With so many excellent opportunities within easy reach of the city center, outdoor pursuits are very much part of the lifestyle here. From late November through Easter, it's a **skiers'** paradise. Grouse Mountain offers runs that are suitable for those of all abilities. An aerial tramway takes skiers to the top, runs are lit at night, and being only

ABOVE: B.C. Place Stadium in Vancouver.
OPPOSITE: Sails charmingly interrupt Vancouver's shoreline and skyline.

13 km (eight miles) from downtown it's very popular. For information telephone (604) 984-0661. Neighboring **Mount Seymour** (**(** 604/986-2261) and **Cypress Bowl** (**(** 604/926-5612) also have good skiing and nighttime illumination during the winter months. At the world-famous Whistler Resort, Whistler Mountain has a rise of 1,530 m (5,020 ft) and Blackcomb Mountain has the greatest vertical rise in North America at 1,609 m (5,280 ft). Both are well served by high-speed lift systems and between them they have about 190 marked trails. The area

beautiful alpine and mountain trails, go to the Whistler/Blackcomb area. There are countless **hiking** trails of all kinds and lengths throughout the north shore parks, and, close to the city center, Stanley Park has some scenic trails. There are some excellent private **golf** clubs in the area, and several public courses, the best of which is the University Golf Course, 5185 University Boulevard, **(** (604) 224-7513, which is a par-71 course. Over in Whistler, there's a par-72 championship course designed by Arnold Palmer. For information telephone (604)

has some particularly beautiful cross-country skiing, and there is the possibility of **heli-skiing** for strong intermediate or advanced skiers. During the summer months there's glacier skiing on Blackcomb, and many other recreational activities. For information contact Whistler Resort Association, 4010 Whistler Way, Whistler, B.C. V0N 1B4, **(** (604) 932-4222 or toll-free (800) 685-3650 from Vancouver. For ski information on the Vancouver area you can telephone (604) 669-SNOW.

Cycling is another of Vancouver's popular pastimes, and there's no problem with bike rentals. Stanley Park has many cycling paths, and there are miles more of them through the city. For some exceptionally

932-4222. **Tennis** players will find plenty of courts throughout the city, particularly in Stanley Park and Queen Elizabeth Park.

With so much water around, there's plenty of activity both in and on it. If you fancy **sailing**, there are schools to teach you how to do it, and plenty of places where you can charter something, particularly around the Coal Harbour area and on Granville Island. **Windsurfing** tuition and equipment rentals are available at Kitsilano, Jericho, and English Bay beaches, and also over in Whistler at Alta Lake. The Fraser Canyon is a good area for **canoeing** and **whitewater rafting**, while nearer downtown there's canoeing at False Creek. The Vancouver area has some excellent **scuba diving**, particularly in Howe Sound. Divers World, at 1523 West 3rd Avenue, and The Diving Locker, 2745 West 4th Avenue, ℂ (604) 736-2681, rent out equipment and organize scuba trips.

With so many beaches within the city limits **swimmers** are also spoiled for choice. The closest to downtown are the beaches in Stanley Park, all of which are good for swimming, and at Sunset Beach there's the Aquatic Centre, 1050 Beach Avenue, ℂ (604) 689-7156, which has indoor Olympic pools, a saltwater pool and a diving tank. The UBC Aquatic Center is on the campus at University Boulevard, ℂ (604) 228-4521, and there's an outdoor saltwater pool at Kitsilano Beach.

The Vancouver area has exceptionally good freshwater and saltwater **fishing**, with a good choice of lakes, rivers, streams, bays, and a variety of fish, being particularly well-known for its salmon. You'll need a license and you should check the regulations carefully. Information is available from the Greater Vancouver Regional District Parks Department, 4330 Kingsway, Burnaby B5H 4G8, ℂ (604) 432-6350. The B.C. Department of Fisheries can be contacted at ℂ (604) 666-2268 or toll-free (800) 663-9333.

Shopping

Normal shopping hours are 9 am to 5:30 pm, with late-night shopping downtown on Thursdays and Fridays, and Sunday opening from noon to 5 pm.

Downtown at Georgia and Granville Streets, the giant **Eaton**'s department store links up to the **Pacific Centre**, Vancouver's largest underground shopping mall with about 180 stores. It adjoins the **Vancouver**

Centre, which is linked to another major department store, **The Bay**, and also joins up to the Granville SkyTrain station. Above this underground complex the pedestrianized **Granville Mall** stretches from Smithe to Hastings Streets, offering a mix of specialty shops, department stores, and a bit of everything. Over at West Hastings and Howe Streets is the upmarket **Sinclair Centre**, a mixture of shops, galleries and eateries housed in four restored heritage buildings, and close by at West Hastings and Seymour Streets there's another smart mall at the **Harbour Centre**. Over Lions Gate Bridge at Marine Drive and Taylor Way, the chic **Park Royal Shopping Centre** has some major department stores and a good range of shops and services.

ABOVE: This gallery on Granville Island features animate as well as inanimate works of art.
OPPOSITE: Beyond the lights of Vancouver are the illuminated runs of the Grouse Mountain ski resort.

Gastown has some unusual shops mixed in with the usual souvenir outlets and it's quite good for antiques. **Water Street** is the place to go for native arts and crafts. **Granville Island** is renowned for its busy **Public Market** where you can buy fresh seafood, local produce, and foods of all descriptions. It is located under the Granville Bridge, and is open daily except on Mondays during the winter months. There is also a **Maritime Market**, a collection of shops known as the **Kid's Only Market**, and lots of arts and crafts studios. Another of Vancouver's main

has a vibrant nightlife that draws visitors and residents alike, while **Granville Island** has a concentration of theatres and art centers. To check the listings you can pick up a free copy of the weekly arts and entertainments paper the Georgia Strait, buy a copy of the weekly *West Ender*, or check the listings in the daily *Vancouver Sun* or *The Province*. Tickets for most cultural events are available, subject to handling charge, through the **Vancouver Ticket Centre** (Ticketmaster) which has lots of outlets around the city. Telephone (604) 280-3311 for

markets is the **Lonsdale Quay Market** on the North Shore by the SeaBus terminal, which has food stalls on its lower floor, and boutiques, children's stores, specialty and craft shops on its upper floor.

Robson Street is the city's high fashion center, and is also known for its international food stores, food market, and unusual gift shops. When shopping for gifts, bear in mind that one of the specialties of the region is salmon: you can buy it beautifully packed from department stores and various outlets around the city.

Nightlife
True to its pleasure-seeking reputation, Vancouver is geared to entertainment. **Gastown**

information or (604) 280-4444 for credit card booking. Bear in mind that reduced-price tickets are often available close to the time of performance.

The cultural heart of Vancouver beats downtown at the **Queen Elizabeth Theatre**, 649 Cambie Street, ((604) 665-3050, the city's largest theatre, where musicals, drama, ballet, opera, and concerts of all kinds are staged. The complex incorporates the smaller **Vancouver Playhouse**, 600 Hamilton Street, ((604) 665-3050, home to the city's main theatre company of the same name, and also host to a season of dance during the winter months. A few blocks away stands the other cultural mainstay, the **Orpheum Theatre** at 884 Granville Street, ((604) 684-2787. This is a splendidly restored 1920's building that is home to the Vancouver Symphony Orchestra and is the major venue for musical events.

There's usually some free entertainment such as music, theatre, dance, films, readings or exhibitions at the **Robson Square Media Centre**, 800 Robson Street, ((604) 660-2830, either in its theatre or outdoors in the plaza. **The Arts Club Theatre**, 1585 Johnston Street, Granville Island, ((604) 687-1644, stages major theatrical productions, while smaller ones are performed in the adjoining **Arts Club Revue**. At the Arts Club Theatre's original location at 1181 Seymour Street you can see Canadian plays and experimental theatre. **The Vancouver East Cultural Centre**, 1895 Venables Street, ((604) 254-9578, holds musical and theatrical events, and in Gastown the **Firehall Arts Centre**, 280 East Cordova Street, ((604) 689-0926, offers innovative theatre.

There are **Theatresports** twice nightly on Fridays and Saturdays at the Back Alley Theatre, 715 Thurlow Street, ((604) 688-7013, when two teams of actors compete for laughs by improvising plays on themes suggested by the audience. Front seats run the risk of audience participation. More improvised comedy takes place at the **Comedy Punchlines Theatre**, 15 Water Street, ((604) 684-3015, where stand-up comics take the stage at weekends and amateurs have their chance on Monday nights.

Ballet lovers can see local troupes perform in the **Vancouver Playhouse**, 600 Hamilton Street, ((604) 665-3050, and also at the **Robson Square Plaza** where free performances are held during the summer months. The **Ballet British Columbia**, ((604) 669-5954, can be seen at the Queen Elizabeth Theatre (see above) where world-class companies visit, and there's some exciting contemporary dance at the **Anna Wyman Dance Theatre**, 1705 Marine Drive, West Vancouver, ((604) 662-8846.

The widely acclaimed **Vancouver Symphony Orchestra**, 400 East Broadway, ((604) 684-9100, plays mainly in the Orpheum Theatre, Granville Street, and has a varied program that ranges from classics to pop. The **Vancouver Chamber Choir**, 1254 West

7th Avenue, ((604) 738-6822, also performs at the Orpheum, and the **Vancouver Opera** presents four productions each season at the Queen Elizabeth Theatre.

Vancouver likes its jazz, and there's quite a mixture of venues. **The Hot Jazz Society** at 2120 Main Street, ((604) 873-4131, offers a wide variety, as does the **Landmark Jazz Bar** in the Sheraton Landmark Hotel, 1400 Robson Street, ((604) 687-9312. A good place for modern jazz is the **Alma Street Cafe**, 2505 Alma Street, ((604) 222-2244, and also at the **Glass Slipper**, 185 East 11th Avenue, ((604) 682-0706. There's a casual, intimate atmosphere at **The Classical Joint Coffee House**, 231 Carrall Street, ((604) 689-0667, and a tinge of the blues at the fashionable **Basin Street Cabaret**, 23 West Cordova Street, ((604) 688-5351. **The Railway Club**, 579 Dunsmuir Street, ((604) 681-1625, is a popular spot, as is the **Town Pump**, 66 Water Street, ((604) 683-6695, which also has live country and western music. If C&W is what you want, then you should consider a visit to the **JR Country Club**, Sandman Inn, 180 West Georgia Street, ((604) 681-2211.

Large rock concerts are often held in the **BC Place Stadium**, and you can see touring and local rock bands at the **Metro**, 1136 West Georgia Street, ((604) 687-5566, and also at **Club Soda**, 1055 Homer Street, ((604) 733-4141. **Richard's on Richards**, 1036 Richards Street, ((604) 687-6794, is a dance club which features live music nightly. The **Commodore Ballroom**, 870 Granville Street, ((604) 681-7838, is a major venue for rock and many other kinds of music.

On the disco circuit, **Sneaky Pete's**, on the fifth floor at 595 Hornby Street, ((604) 681-9561, attracts the late-twenties to thirties age group, while **Graceland** at 1250 Richards Street, ((604) 688-2648, is an altogether more off-beat and *outré* place. **Amnesia**, 99 Powell Street, ((604) 682-2211, is a very large club, with frequently changing arty decor, and a noise level that's conducive to conversation. The **Pelican Bay** in the Granville Island Hotel, 1253 Johnston Street, ((604) 683-7373, is a smart restaurant/disco with lovely views that attracts all age groups. In **Stanley Park**, Shampers at the 1733 Comox Street, ((604) 684-6262, is a popular disco in an elegant setting.

Vancouver can match the needs of the most demanding movie buff with its concentration of cinemas in Granville Mall, several multi-screen complexes, and many outlets for foreign and non-mainstream movies. The **Pacific Cinémathèque**, 1131 Howe Street, ((604) 688-3456, shows major foreign films and obscure North American ones; non-mainstream movies can also be seen at the **Hollywood Theatre**, 3123 West Broadway, ((604) 738-3211, **The Ridge Theatre**, 3131 Arbutus Street, ((604) 738-6311, and the **Vancouver East Cinema**, 2290 Commer-

nished; the facilities include a fitness spa, indoor and outdoor swimming pools, saunas, and tennis courts. There are three restaurants, including the first-rate Chartwell restaurant, and piano music plays in the delightful Garden Lounge. The hotel is centrally located and has the added convenience of being linked to the fashionable shops of the Pacific Mall.

The **Delta Place**, 645 Howe Street, Vancouver V6C 2Y9, ((604) 687-1122, toll-free (800) 268-1133, is another leading hotel which is part of the Delta chain. The 197

cial Drive, ((604) 253-5455. There's the ultimate in special effects at the **CN IMAX Theatre** at Canada Place, ((604) 682-4629, where specially-made films are shown on a gigantic curved screen.

WHERE TO STAY

Luxury

One of the city's top hotels is the **Four Seasons**, a high-rise that overlooks the Pacific Centre at 791 West Georgia Street, Vancouver V6C 2T4, ((604) 689-9333, toll-free (800) 268-6282. It embodies the excellent service, ultimate comfort and good taste which has become the trademark of this first-rate hotel chain. Rooms and suites are beautifully fur-

well-furnished rooms and suites are individually designed and have marble bathrooms with telephones, and bedside control panels. The hotel has a business center, a fine restaurant, indoor swimming pool, fitness suite, sundeck, racquetball courts, and even a library. Everywhere the needs and comforts of its guests are anticipated, and service is always close at hand.

For old-fashioned grandeur look to the **Hotel Vancouver**, 900 West Georgia Street, Vancouver V6C 2W6, ((604) 684-3131, toll-free (800) 268-9411, one of the great railway hotels which is now a Canadian Pacific Hotel with over 500 accommodations. With a

The Pan Pacific Vancouver Hotel in the Canada Place waterfront complex.

classical facade crowned with a steep green copper roof, this hotel is a Vancouver landmark, and within it the spacious public areas are furnished in grand style with chandeliers, antiques, an excess of marble, and comfortable old-fashioned sofas and armchairs. The rooms are also spacious but decorated in a much more low-key fashion, and business- and executive-class accommodation is offered. There's an indoor swimming pool, a fitness center, saunas, shops, cocktail lounges, a couple of good restaurants and a popular nightspot. The service here is impeccable and the overall picture one of comfort and elegance.

Rising above the Royal Centre mall is the city's largest hotel, the **Hyatt Regency Vancouver**, 655 Burrard Street, Vancouver V6C 2R7, ((604) 687-6543, toll-free (800) 233-1234. There are 646 accommodations, conference and banqueting facilities are available, and floors set aside for executive suites. Rooms are smartly decorated, some have balconies, and there are lots of nice touches. It has a good seafood restaurant, pleasant lounges, an outdoor swimming pool, health club, and access to racquetball and squash courts. The staff are knowledgeable and extremely helpful, and there's a bright and lively atmosphere.

Magnificently sited in the remarkable Canada Place waterfront complex is the **Pan Pacific Vancouver Hotel**, 300-999 Canada Place, Vancouver V6C 3B5, ((604) 662-8111, toll-free (800) 663-1515. This hotel really does have everything. It's a member of the Leading Hotels of the World group, and all rooms and suites are luxurious, although there is an ultra-deluxe class available. With the Trade and Convention Centre also in the complex, it comes as no surprise to find that the excellent dining facilities include a Japanese restaurant and a dim sum bar. It has a business and conference center, remarkably good health and fitness facilities, and a soaring, glass-topped lobby complete with waterfall. The Pacific Centre is literally at your feet, and the views are unsurpassed.

Le Meridien, 845 Burrard Street, Vancouver V6Z 2K6, ((604) 682-5511, toll-free (800) 543-4300, is owned by Air France and has a distinctly French accent. This is a relatively new hotel, furnished in classical French style

with marble, antiques, and great elegance. The rooms, although a little on the small side, match the public areas for style and grace, and the service is superb and personal. The hotel has 397 units and an adjoining block provides suites for long-stay guests. The excellent Restaurant Gerard is located here, and there's an attractive cafe, piano bars, a well-equipped health club, and tennis courts. Also European in style is **The Georgian Court Hotel**, 773 Beatty Street, Vancouver V6B 2M4, ((604) 682-5555, toll-free (800) 663-1155, located opposite the BC Stadium and only a block away from the Queen Elizabeth Theatre. Antiques adorn the elegant lobby, the airy rooms are beautifully furnished, well-equipped, and many offer splendid views. There is an executive floor, a health club, and the first-rate William Tell restaurant.

Across from Robson Square the **Wedgewood Hotel**, 845 Hornby Street, Vancouver V6Z 1V1, ((604) 689-7777, toll-free (800) 663-0666, is a smaller, privately-owned hotel with 94 accomodations. It has a charming, intimate atmosphere and is tastefully decorated with antiques. Executive facilities and rooms are available, and there's a restaurant, a piano bar, and fitness facilities.

In the city's west end **The Westin Bayshore**, 1601 West Georgia Street, Vancouver V6G 2V4, ((604) 682-3377, toll-free (800) 228-3000, is beautifully positioned near the edges of Stanley Park and set in its own grounds overlooking Coal Harbour. The hotel offers 519 accommodations with large windows and lovely views, a wide range of services, restaurants, and indoor and outdoor pools. The *pièce de résistance* is the private marina which brings fishing trips and cruises to the doorstep.

Mid-range

The **Hotel Georgia**, 801 West Georgia Street, Vancouver V6C 1P7, ((604) 682-5566, toll-free (800) 663-1111, is an old red-brick building near Robson Square. The place has an old-fashioned air about it, the service is friendly, and there are 314 comfortable accommodations. It has a restaurant, and there's an English-style pub in the basement. **The Barclay Hotel** at 1348 Robson Street, Vancouver V6E 1C5, ((604) 688-8850, is within walking distance of Stanley Park and offers some of the best value around. It has 85 accommodations and is attractively decorated throughout in French style. It has a French restaurant, licensed lounge, and meeting facilities.

In North Vancouver, the **Lonsdale Quay Hotel**, 123 Carrie Cates Court, N. Vancouver V6M 3K7, ((604) 986-6111, is located next to the SeaBus Terminal on the top floors of the lively Lonsdale Quay Market. It has 58 rooms and suites, all attractively decorated, and there are some good views across Burrard Inlet. It has fitness facilities, a sauna, a restaurant, and a pub, and downtown is only 12 minutes away by SeaBus. Just north of Lions Gate Bridge, you'll find the lovely **Park Royal Hotel**, 540 Clyde Avenue, W. Vancouver V7T 2J7, ((604) 926-5511, set in attractive grounds on the banks of the Capilano River, well-situated for beaches and mountains, and close to the Park Royal shopping center. The 30 accommodations are all attractive and airy, and there is a restaurant, an outdoor terrace for dining, and an English-style pub.

South of downtown, the **Granville Island Hotel and Marina**, 1253 Johnston Street, Vancouver V6H 3R9, ((604) 683-7373, toll-free (800) 663-1840, is a lively waterfront place that tends to attract a sporty crowd who take advantage of the tennis courts and the various charters that operate from the marina. The building has the warehouse-like appearance characteristic of Granville Island, rooms have window shutters, large, well-equipped bathrooms, AM/FM cassette stereos, and most have waterfront views. The building incorporates a night-club, restaurant, and a popular pub.

At the edge of Stanley Park on English Bay stands the much-loved **Sylvia Hotel**, 1154 Gilford Street, Vancouver V6G 2P6, ((604) 681-9321. This delightful ivy-covered stone building has 115 units which include housekeeping suites, some of which are located in a modern extension. The decor throughout is attractive, each room is different, and there's a restaurant and bar which both have beautiful views of the bay. Its popularity means that it is necessary to book well in advance. Prices range from moderate to inexpensive.

Inexpensive

The **Nelson Place Hotel** at 1006 Granville Street, Vancouver V6Z 1L5, ((604) 681-6341, is conveniently placed for the theatres, shops, and BC Place. There are 100 small, pleasant rooms, all with private bathrooms. The **Kingston Hotel** at 757 Richards Street, Vancouver V6B 3A6, ((604) 684-9024, is a European-style place where continental breakfast is included in the price. The rooms are small but clean; some have private bathrooms while others have hand basins. There's a sauna and laundry facilities. It is excellent value for money. The **St Regis Hotel** at 602 Dunsmuir Street, Vancouver V6B 1Y3, ((604) 681-1135, is an older place with large comfortable rooms, all with private bathrooms, and there's a bar and restaurant on the premises.

East of downtown, **The Patricia**, 403 East Hastings Street, Vancouver V6A 1P6, ((604) 255-4301, has 195 simply-furnished rooms with private bathrooms. For accommodation in the Gastown area, try the **Dominion Hotel**, 210 Abbott Street, Vancouver V6B 2K8, ((604) 681-6666. This characterful hotel is a late nineteenth-century brick building with antiques and relics of old Vancouver scattered throughout, and rooms that have been renovated.

The **YWCA** at 580 Burrard Street, Vancouver V6C 2K9, ((604) 662-8188, has accommodation for women, couples and families, and has a very good fitness center for women. A few blocks away, also in downtown, the **YMCA**, 955 Burrard Street, ((604) 681-0221, offers rooms for men, women and couples, and has fitness facilities. At the attractive location of Jericho Beach the **Vancouver International Hostel**, 1515 Discovery Street, ((604) 224-3208, has over 350 beds and good self-catering facilities. **University accommodation** is available from May to August at the Simon Fraser University 20 km (12 miles) east of downtown. For details contact SFU Housing and Conference Services, Simon Fraser University, Room 212 McTaggart-Cowan Mall, Burnaby, Vancouver V5A 1S6, ((604) 291-4201. The University of British Columbia at Point Grey 16 km (10 miles) southwest of the center also has rooms and self-contained suites; information is available from the UBC Conference Centre,

5961 Student Union Boulevard, Vancouver V6T 2C9, ((604) 228-2963.

There's a wide range of **Bed & Breakfast** accommodation in metropolitan Vancouver. Among the agencies offering a good choice are: A B & C Bed and Breakfast of Vancouver, 4390 Frances Street, Burnaby, Vancouver B5C 2R3, ((604) 986-5069; the Old English Bed and Breakfast Registry, Box 86818, North Vancouver V7L 4L4, ((604) 986-5069; the Town and Country Bed and Breakfasts in B.C., Box 46544 Station G, Vancouver V6R 4G6, ((604) 731-5942; and Canada-West Accommodations, Box 86607, North Vancouver V7L 4L2, ((604) 929-1429.

You won't find any campgrounds in the center of Vancouver, and many of the ones in the suburbs are primarily for RV's. Check with an Infocentre for details.

WHERE TO EAT

Vancouver's large number of restaurants reflect the city's rich ethnic mix in the wide variety of food they offer. You'll also find Northwestern cuisine here, the region's own brand based on plentiful supplies of seafood, game, herbs, and flowers.

Expensive

Chartwell at the Four Seasons Hotel, 791 West Georgia Street, ((604) 689-9333, is named after the English country home of Winston Churchill, and the restaurant imitates that ambience with its warm wooden paneling and a glowing fireplace. Some say it is the best restaurant in Vancouver, and its inspired continental cuisine certainly makes it a strong contender. Those who count the calories will find the menu especially pleasing. **William Tell** at the Georgian Court Hotel, 765 Beatty Street, ((604) 688-3504, is another top Vancouver restaurant where a traditional interior and tables set with the finest china and crystal provide the setting for its haute cuisine. Swiss-French specialties appear alongside the classics, and local produce is mostly used. The wine list here is particularly good and the service superb.

Located in the French-run Meridien hotel, **Gerard's**, 845 Burrard Street, ((604) 682-5511, is a beautiful dining room with an atmosphere that is both refined and relaxed.

The cuisine is French with an emphasis on seafood, and the menu is innovatively and expertly put together. Vying with Gerard's for the title of best French restaurant is **Le Gavroche** at 1616 Alberni Street, ((604) 685-3924. Set in a lovely old house in the city's west end, this restaurant has a mouth-watering menu, a democratic wine list, and excellent service. It is an ideal choice for a special occasion.

South of the downtown peninsula, **Tojo's** at 777 West Broadway, Suite 202, ((604) 872-8050, offers Japanese food in sleek, sophisti-

cated surroundings with an outdoor terrace and mountain views. You can choose to dine in a traditional tatami room, at a conventional dining table, or at the small sushi bar. The menu features all kinds of Japanese specialties as well as the chef's own innovative dishes, and freshness is the hallmark. Prices here range from expensive to moderate.

Moderate

The best place in Vancouver specializing in Northwestern cooking is probably the highly-acclaimed **Raintree**, 1630 Alberni Street, ((604) 688-5570. The imaginative use of local seafood and organically-grown produce results in some wonderful dishes, and an exceptionally good wine list together with stunning views over the water of Grouse Mountain combine to make a memorable meal. Over in West Vancouver, **Salmon House on the Hill**, 2229 Folkstone Way, ((604) 926-3212, is another good place to sample Northwestern cuisine. Perched high above Vancouver, the restaurant commands wonderful views of Stanley Park and the city across the inlet. Seafood dominates the menu here, and it really is delicious.

At a beautiful location on Granville Island's waterfront, **Bridges**, ((604) 687-4400, has a good seafood restaurant, a bistro, and

guson Point, the **Teahouse Restaurant**, ((604) 669-3281, serves fine continental fare in a delightful Victorian house overlooking the bay.

Over in Kitsilano, at **Bishop's**, 2183 West 4th Avenue, ((604) 738-2025, exciting continental food is presented with great style and served with enthusiasm. The restaurant is small and chic, and the atmosphere relaxed. Celebrated Italian chef Umberto Menghi has several restaurants in Vancouver, the most popular being **Il Giardino**, 1382 Hornby Street, ((604) 669-2422. Here Italian classics reign, with game featuring prominently

a large terrace where you can enjoy beautiful mountain views. Across the creek, **A Kettle of Fish**, 900 Pacific Street, ((604) 682-6661, serves deliciously fresh fish in a conservatory-style setting, and east of downtown, **The Cannery**, 2205 Commissioner Street, ((604) 254-9606, has an extensive seafood menu and great harbor views.

If steak is what you're after then you should go to **Hy's Mansion**, 1523 Davie Street, ((604) 689-1111. Located in the city's west end, this grand Victorian building provides a beautiful setting to enjoy one of Hy's substantial and expertly-prepared steaks. For excellent French food, few places better the bistroesque **Le Crocodile**, 818 Thurlow Street, ((604) 669-4298, and in Stanley Park at Fer-

on the menu. It's extremely popular and reservations are required for both lunch and dinner. For imaginative Italian country cooking, go to **Piccolo Mondo**, 850 Thurlow Street, ((604) 688-1633, where you'll find a seemingly endless menu and some very interesting dishes.

For some of the city's best Chinese food go to the **Kiri Mandarin Restaurant**, 1166 Alberni Street, ((604) 682-8833, where the menu is diverse, the surroundings sophisticated, and lobster and crab come fresh from the tanks. For a taste of Japan, try the **Kamei Sushi**, 811 Thurlow Street, ((604) 684-5767, which also has branches on West Broadway.

OPPOSITE and ABOVE: Produce for sale in Chinatown.

Inexpensive

To complete your visit to Vancouver you should have a meal at **Quilicum**, 1724 Davie Street, ((604) 681-7044, where the food is native West Coast Indian and dishes include specialties such as barbecued oysters, caribou, seaweed with wild rice, and barbecued goat ribs. The interior resembles that of a native longhouse and it is decorated with Indian art. Prices here range from inexpensive to moderate.

When you're in Gastown, you should call in at **The Only Fish and Oyster Cafe**,

20 East Hastings Street, ((604) 681-6546, or rather, join the queue, because although this well-known and well-loved cafe has absolutely no finesse and no alcohol, it does have the freshest seafood you'll find anywhere. Also in the area is the popular **Old Spaghetti Factory**, 53 Water Street, ((604) 684-1288, part of a Canadian chain that serves several varieties of spaghetti and a few other standard Italian dishes in surroundings decked with old curiosities, such as a 1910 trolley bus now fitted with tables.

Chinatown has a wealth of restaurants, but some of the best Cantonese food can be found at **The Pink Pearl**, 1132 East Hastings Street, ((604) 253-4316, a large restaurant where the emphasis is on seafood. There's first-rate Szechuan-Peking cuisine at the much smaller **Yang's** at 4186 Main Street, ((604) 873-2116, and you can enjoy Vietnamese food at very good prices at **Saigon**, 1300 Robson Street, ((604) 682-8020. Robsonstrasse, as it's some-

times known, is noted for its European restaurants, and one of its old favorites is **Heidelberg House** at 1164 Robson Street, ((604) 682-1661, a pleasant place in which to sample German specialties.

If Californian-Mexican food appeals, go to **Topanaga**, 2904 West 41st Avenue, ((604) 733-3713, a small cafe that serves hearty portions. For Indian food, try the **Heaven and Earth India Curry House**, 1754 West 4th Avenue, ((604) 732-5313, in the Kitsilano area, or look around the section of Main Street between 49th and 51st Avenues, where Vancouver's Indian community is centered.

HOW TO GET THERE

Vancouver International Airport handles flights from North and South America and all around the world. The airport is 18 km (11 miles) from downtown and about a 25-minute drive away. There's an Express Bus which leaves the airport at 15-minute intervals, stopping at major downtown hotels and the Greyhound Bus Terminal. The cheapest way of getting to the center is by the public bus service, which involves taking the Nº 100 bus to 70th Avenue, where you transfer to the Nº 20 bound for downtown.

VIA Rail runs a once-daily service connecting Vancouver to eastern Canada along the Trans-Canada Railway, a route that is famous for its stunning scenery. The station is at 1150 Station Street, ((604) 669-3050, toll-free (800) 665-8630. Amtrak, the American railway, does not connect directly to Vancouver but it's possible to take a bus from Seattle or to connect with VIA Rail at Winnipeg. BC Rail connects Vancouver with northern B.C. and has its station at 1311 West First Street, North Vancouver, ((604) 984-5246, toll-free (800) 665-8630.

BC Ferries run from the Tsawwassen Ferry Terminal, 30 km south of downtown Vancouver, to Swartz Bay and Nanaimo on Vancouver Island, and they also operate a ferry to Nanaimo from Horseshoe Bay, west of Vancouver. For information ring (604) 669-1211.

Greyhound buses run from the U.S. to the Vancouver Greyhound Terminal, 150 Dunsmuir Street, ((604) 662-3222. Maverick Lines, ((604) 662-8051, toll-free (800) 972-6301, run from Vancouver Island and

The First Narrows leads out from Vancouver into the Strait of Georgia.

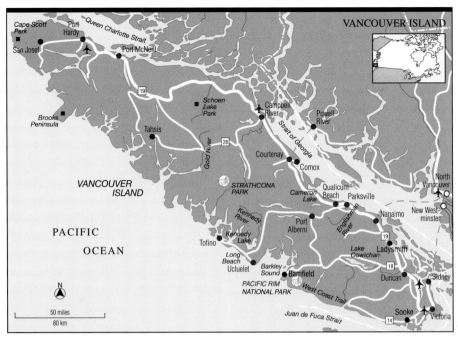

the Sunshine Coast to the Greyhound terminal, and Pacific Coach Lines, ((604) 662-8074, also connect Vancouver Island to the terminal. Motorists coming from the east will want to take the Trans-Canada Highway, while those coming from Washington in the U.S. will take Highway 5, which becomes Highway 99 at the B.C. border.

VANCOUVER ISLAND

Moored alongside the west coast of the B.C. mainland and separated from it by the Strait of Georgia, Vancouver Island stretches 450 km (280 miles) and covers an area of 32,000 sq km (12,000 sq miles). It is thus the largest island off North America's Pacific Coast, and violates the 49th parallel, much to the annoyance of some. A chain of snow-tipped mountains runs north-south through the center of the island, splitting its personality between a wild and woolly west, with an exposed Pacific coastline cut by deep inlets, and a sheltered eastern shore of a much tamer character with white sandy beaches, farmlands, gentle slopes, and seaside towns.

The island is blessed with a gentle climate throughout the year, although the rainfall varies dramatically from place to place.

The lowest rainfall and mildest temperatures are found at the southern end of the island which is sheltered by the Olympic Mountains across the Juan de Fuca Strait. It is not surprising therefore that most of the island's 500,000 population live in Victoria and the cozy seaside towns of the southeast, leaving the west side uninhabited for the most part, with a few small fishing communities dotted around.

The rain forests with their soaring Douglas firs and the lonely west coast shores seem a far cry from the neat lawns of Victoria and the snug towns of the southeast. It is this combination of ruggedly beautiful scenery, the sedate charm of Victoria, and people as gentle as the climate itself that makes Vancouver Island so appealing to vacationers. The culture is equally diverse, for the British Empire was not the only society to leave its mark. The Haida, Kwakiutl, Cowichan, and Sooke Indians who lived in fishing villages here long before the arrival of the white man have scattered the island with their totem poles, their crafts and legends, while their fishing skills seem to have found their way into the blood of the inhabitants.

Together with fishing, mining and logging are the island's main industries, and they are mostly found to the east of the mountain range. Stubbled mountainsides stand testimony to the latter and an impassioned battle rages over the island's particularly active logging program.

BACKGROUND

In 1774 Juan Perez of Spain visited Vancouver Island, and when Captain Cook landed at Nootka Island on the west coast in 1778 he did a little trade with the Indians. In 1792 Captain George Vancouver put the island on the map when he charted the waters of

Johnstone Strait. These visits had little effect on the lives of the island's native tribes and it wasn't until 1843, when the Hudson's Bay Company took control and founded a trading post on the island's southeastern tip, that things started slowly to change.

In 1849 Vancouver Island was declared a crown colony, with the Hudson's Bay Company administering it from Fort Victoria. Apart from some company farms established by the subsidiary Puget Sound Agricultural Company, little happened by way of colonization and the main concern remained fur trading.

The discovery of gold in the Fraser River during the 1850's and '60s brought prospectors to Victoria, B.C.'s only port and source

of provisions. As a result, the area developed into a typical boom town, but when the gold fields were exhausted Victoria continued as an administrative center. The island united with B.C. in 1866, and in 1871 Victoria was declared the provincial capital. It was intended to be the western terminus of the C.P.R., but this did not come to pass and the railroad stopped at Vancouver. This meant that industrialization also stopped at Vancouver and Victoria was left free to build itself a reputation as a center of genteel society. The other gift that the C.P.R. gave Victoria was the building of the beautiful Empress Hotel in 1908, boosting a tourist industry that has flourished ever since.

GENERAL INFORMATION

For information on Victoria contact the Infocentre at 812 Wharf Street, Victoria V8W 1T3, ((604) 382-2127. The office is open daily and is located on the waterfront across from the Empress Hotel.

For information on the rest of Vancouver Island you should contact the Tourism Association of Vancouver Island, Suite 302, 45 Bastion Square, Victoria V8W 1J1, ((604) 876-3088. There are also information centers in towns throughout the island, but the other major branch is in Nanaimo at 266 Bryden Street, ((604) 754-8474.

VICTORIA

Victoria has overcome its rough and ready beginnings, and has developed into a graceful city that is both conservative and relaxed. Baskets of flowers adorn the lampposts, nineteenth-century buildings have been carefully renovated, tidy lawns and flower beds are all around. Victoria has been transformed from a raucous gold rush town into a colonial fantasy of a British seaside resort.

Victoria is B.C.'s capital, and with a population of 250,000 it is the province's second largest city. It is situated around a beautiful natural harbor at the southeastern tip of the island, sheltered by the mountains of Washington State, which lies only 32 km (20 miles) away across the Juan de Fuca

Strait to the south. It boasts Canada's mildest climate with only 68 cm (27 inches) of rainfall a year and plenty of sunshine. While the rest of Canada is struggling through snow, Victoria is busy taking its official bloom count.

The love of beautiful gardens is not the only feature that Victoria has inherited from its British connections. It is a place that revels in and capitalizes upon its image as a last bastion of the British Empire. Old British traditions are fiercely preserved. Wander through one of the city's parks and the chances are that you'll see some croquet, cricket, or bowls being played. You can ride around the city on a double-decker bus, stock up on Wedgwood china, Waterford crystal and tweeds in the shops, or take refreshment in one of the many pubs or tea rooms. Just to make sure you get the picture, somewhere around the Parliament Buildings you'll hear the whine of bagpipes.

Part of the reason for this "forever England" image is that the population is largely of British extraction, and the mild weather and low rainfall continues to make Victoria an attractive retirement home for the British. The main employers here are the government and tourism, and to keep the latter industry thriving the Britishness is carefully preserved and reinforced wherever possible, sometimes in ways that are rather garish, but it still keeps the visitors coming.

WHAT TO SEE AND DO

Sights
DOWNTOWN
Downtown Victoria is compactly laid-out within a small area, so walking is the easiest and most pleasant way of exploring it. The hub of the city is the **Inner Harbour** area, where Victoria's most majestic buildings overlook the lively little harbor which is constantly busy with the comings and goings of ferries, fishing boats, and yachts.

A very large portion of the Inner Harbour is filled with the ivied grandeur of the **Empress Hotel**, a resplendent castle-like building that is the heart and very much the soul of Victoria. Designed by Francis Rattenbury and built by the C.P.R. in 1908, the Empress

became the place where Victorian polite society came to take tea. Today visitors flock here to experience an afternoon tea of cucumber sandwiches and scones with jam and clotted cream, served among silver teapots and cake stands in the desperately British ambience of the Empress lobby. Tea at the Empress is very popular and should you wish to partake you should telephone (604) 384-8111 to make a reservation. Behind the hotel stands **The Crystal Garden**, 731 Douglas Street, ((604) 381-1213, a large glass structure that was designed by Rattenbury

and built in 1925. It once held an enormous saltwater pool, and its elegant ballroom was the scene of many social events. It is now an exotic conservatory with colorful tropical birds and monkeys among the greenery, overlooked by the ever-popular tea rooms.

Across from the Empress, neatly clipped lawns and carefully arranged flowerbeds surround the stately **Parliament Buildings**, a Gothic extravaganza of towers and domes that also overlooks the lovely harbor. Completed in 1898 and designed by the ir-

OPPOSITE: A descendant of the original inhabitants of British Columbia. ABOVE: The fearsome image of the thunderbird sits atop a totem pole in Victoria's Thunderbird Park.

repressible Francis Rattenbury, these buildings remain the home of the provincial legislature. A statue of Queen Victoria dignifies the lawn to the front, statues of eminent Victorians stand either side of the elaborate arched entrance, and the central copper-covered dome is crowned with a gilt statue of Captain George Vancouver. Free guided tours of the interior in a choice of languages operate daily during the summer months and on weekdays only during the winter. The buildings remain a remarkable sight at night when they are outlined by thousands of little lights.

On the corner between the Empress and the Parliament Buildings stands the excellent **British Columbia Provincial Museum**, ℂ (604) 387-3701. The museum occupies part of a modern complex of buildings known as **Heritage Court**, to the front of which stands a 62-bell **Carillon Tower** which was a gift from the province's Dutch community. This is one of Canada's very best museums and the skill and imagination of its displays have made it one of Victoria's top attractions. It is devoted to all aspects of B.C.'s natural and cultural history from prehistoric times through to the present day. The second floor covers the province's natural history, while beautifully constructed dioramas depict aspects of the region's natural environment such as the rain forest, seashore, mountains, and ocean. The section dealing with the province's cultural history has some of the most popular and fascinating displays where sight, sound, and smell combine to give vivid and memorable impressions of life in the past. There is, for example, a detailed re-creation of an early twentieth-century street, complete with a cinema that runs old movies, a pioneer village, a sawmill, and a reconstructed section of Captain George Vancouver's ship, *The Discovery*. In the section that deals with Indian history, realistic displays allow the visitor to glimpse life in a Pacific Coast Indian village, and the museum's extensive collection of Indian art and artifacts includes a collection of totem poles. The museum is open daily and admission is free on Mondays. Telephone (604) 387-3041 for recorded information or (604) 387-3701 during office hours.

To the rear of the museum is a small grassy plot known as **Thunderbird Park** which is forested with modern totem poles carved with the image of the legendary thunderbird. At the southern edge of this park stands **Helmcken House**, a heritage building dating from the 1850's that was originally the home of Fort Victoria's surgeon. Inside you can see period furnishings and a display of the doctor's medical equipment. Admission is free.

Victoria has its share of more commercialized attractions, especially in the area

around the Parliament Buildings. One of the better ones is the **Undersea Gardens**, 490 Belleville Street, ℂ (604) 382-5717, where you descend to the bottom of the harbor to look, through glass, at the marine life and some frolicsome scuba divers. Next to it the **Royal London Wax Museum** (ℂ 604/388-4461) is worth a look. The building was designed by Rattenbury and originally built in 1924 as the C.P.R. Steamship Terminal.

For a pleasant waterfront stroll continue westwards along Belleville Street past the ferry terminals and follow the coast to **Fisherman's Wharf**, a lively spot where fishing boats come and go and houseboats are moored. If you'd like to see Victoria from the water, boat trips leave from the Inner Harbour, in front of the Empress.

The **Old Town** section of Victoria lies to the north of the Empress, along Wharf Street and the nearby streets and alleys. This is an

OPPOSITE TOP: Dignified survivors from the last century: a horse and carriage and the Parliament Buildings in Victoria. BOTTOM: The Empress Hotel. ABOVE: Victoria's Wharf Street.

area of narrow streets, squares, gaslights, cobbles, and buildings that date from the 1860's. The area has undergone extensive renovation and, as is so often the case, many of the old buildings now house chic restaurants, cafes, and shops. At **Centennial Square** you can see Victoria's original City Hall, and at nearby Bastion Square, site of the original Fort Victoria in 1843, the old criminal courthouse now houses the **Maritime Museum** ((604) 385-4222. On display here are model ships, nautical paraphernalia, and a Native American dug-out canoe

came into being in the 1850's when many Chinese arrived to work on constructing the Trans-Canada Railway. Over the years Chinatown has dwindled in size and now scarcely covers two blocks, but it is still the site of the narrowest street in Canada and has a few interesting buildings.

At the southeastern edge of downtown, behind the B.C. Provincial Museum, **Beacon Hill Park** offers a delightful retreat and a lovely spot to picnic. This hilly parkland of gardens, trees, ponds, and views stretches southwards to the Juan de Fuca Strait. At its

that sailed from Victoria to England at the beginning of the century.

Close by at 1107 Wharf Street is the **Emily Carr Museum,** ((604) 387-3080, where you can see the works of this famous B.C. artist whose landscapes and portrayals of Indian life are painted in a style that partially reflects Native American influences. The gallery is open daily, except on Mondays during the winter months. Admission is free.

Just north of Centennial Square, on the corner of Fisgard Street and Government Street, an ornate red gateway known as the **Gate of Harmonious Interest** marks the entrance to Victoria's old and colorful **Chinatown**. Once a flourishing community, it

southwestern corner a plaque marks the terminal of the Trans-Canada Highway.

OUTSIDE DOWNTOWN

About one and a half kilometer (one mile) east of downtown in the Rockland area, a nineteenth-century mansion houses the **Art Gallery of Greater Victoria**, 1040 Moss Street, ((604) 384-4104. It exhibits art from a variety of countries and periods, and has a particularly fine collection of Asian art that includes a Shinto shrine. The gallery is open daily, except on Mondays during the winter, and admission is free on Thursdays. Nearby stands the imposing **Craigdarroch Castle**, 1050 Joan Crescent, ((604) 592-4233, a turreted baronial-style mansion of palatial proportions. It was built in 1890 by Robert Dunsmuir, a wealthy Scottish coal tycoon, in order to persuade his wife to leave her home in Scotland. The interior is richly decorated with wood panelling, stained glass, and period furniture. It is open daily and admission is free.

Moving west of downtown, **Craigflower Manor** at 110 Island Highway, ((604) 387-3067, is one of Victoria's earliest buildings, dating from 1856. It was built on a farm for the Hudson's Bay Company subsidiary, Puget Sound Agricultural Company, in an early attempt to develop a settlement around the trading post. With original furnishings and household appliances, it makes for an interesting visit. Nearby stands the **Craigflower Schoolhouse**, which was built in 1855 and ended its days as a schoolhouse in 1911 to serve as a museum. Open daily.

To the west of Victoria Harbour, the **English Village** at 429 Lampson Street, ((604) 388-4353, is a collection of replicated old English buildings. The highlight is the accurately reconstructed **Anne Hathaway's Cottage** furnished with sixteenth- and seventeenth- century antiques, and the **Olde English Inn** offers accommodation and a restaurant. The village is open daily.

The best way of appreciating Victoria's eastern coast and the beautiful homes and gardens of her suburbs is to follow the 13-km-long (eight miles) scenic route known as **Marine Drive** (a bus tour also follows this route). You can start the drive at Thunderbird Park by going south along Douglas Street or by joining Dallas Road at Beacon Hill Park and then just follow the signs. There are some good views of Washington's Olympic Mountains and the coastline along the Dallas Road section of the drive. The road then continues through the lovely golf course that overlooks the sea at Gonzales Point with views of the San Juan Islands. A little further along the road, now Marine Drive, at the Oak Bay Marina you'll come to a big tourist attraction called **Sealand**, 1327 Beach Drive, ((604) 598-3373, an oceanarium where you can view marine life through the glass walls of huge tanks. There's also an octopus grotto and outside pools containing the larger mammals such as killer whales,

sea lions and harbour seals. It is open daily and there are hourly shows starring the inhabitants of the outdoor pools.

The route continues past the wealthy residences of Oak Bay, through Uplands Park, skirting around Cadboro Bay where you'll see the Royal Victoria Yacht Club, passing by the university campus, and continuing along the coastline past parks and gardens. By the time you get to Cordova Bay the road has become the Cordova Bay Road, and you come to another tourist draw called the **Fable Cottage Estate**, 5187 Cordova Bay

Road, ((604) 658-5741. Here a story-book house stands amid themed floral gardens where mechanical elves do their stuff, and there are such wonders as "the World's Largest Hanging Basket".

The route continues a little way before joining up with Highway 17. Then you can either head south to return to downtown or continue northwards to Keating Cross Road and make this the time to see the famous Butchart Gardens, which you really ought not to miss (see below).

Highland dancers OPPOSITE, and a morris dancer ABOVE, step out in Victoria.

EXCURSIONS

The outstanding **Butchart Gardens** are located 21 km (13 miles) north of downtown on Tod Inlet at 800 Bennevuto, ((604) 652-4422 . Their history makes a classic ugly-duckling-to-swan story. Jenny Butchart was the wife of a wealthy cement manufacturer who, in the process of beautifying their large estate, decided to do something about the unsightly hole left by her husband's abandoned limestone quarry. In 1904 she began the task of landscaping this eyesore by setting lawns, planting trees,

flower beds, but the Horticultural Centre can answer any questions you may have. Even in their winter greenery the gardens are worth the trip, and flowers will still be blooming in the greenhouses. The Butcharts' house has a dining room which serves lunch and afternoon tea so that you can make this the leisurely visit that the gardens deserve. To get there from downtown Victoria either take Highway 17 to the turn-off to Keating Cross Road, where you continue your journey in a westerly direction, or take the 17A direct. Open daily.

creating beautiful arrangements of flowers, and by covering the sides of the pit with ivy. The success of this sunken garden inspired the Butcharts to continue their horticultural activities, and now their gardens cover an area of some 20 hectares (50 acres). There's a magnificent rose garden which is best seen in July, a Japanese garden with lacquered bridges, summer houses, and waterfall, and a formal Italian garden with topiary hedges, a lily pond, and statuary. In the summer you can enjoy music in these delightful surroundings on the Concert Lawn and take a nighttime tour of the illuminated gardens.

These are very much pleasure gardens so you won't find botanical labels among the

To take a look at the coastal scenery northwest of Victoria, travel north out of the city on the Trans-Canada Highway, and after 16 km (10 miles) you'll hit **Malahat Drive**. The road skirts along Finlayson Arm and then climbs Malahat Ridge where you have views across Saanich Inlet of the Gulf Islands, the mainland, and the distant peak of Mount Baker in Washington State.

If you'd like to explore some of the beaches and forests of the southwest corner of Vancouver Island, then pack your picnic hamper, maybe your tent as well, and head out of Victoria picking up Highway 14 bound for **Sooke**, some 34 km (22 miles) out of town. If you don't have your own transport there are buses that run from downtown to Sooke. In this logging town you'll find a museum, an Infocentre, and supplies for the rest of your journey. North of Sooke along Highway 14 you'll probably stop and follow a forest trail to one of the lovely beaches that line the coast here. The highway ends at the small one-horse settlement of Port Renfrew, where you can observe some marine life in the tidal pools at **Botanical Beach** when the tide is low. The rugged West Coast Trail — a serious hiking undertaking — runs from here to Bamfield and forms a section of the famous Pacific Rim National Park. From here you can either retrace your steps along Highway 14 back to Victoria or you can take the logging road to Lake Cowichan where you have a choice of two roads, both of which connect with the Trans-Canada Highway at Duncan.

Northeast of Victoria in the Strait of Georgia lie the lovely and temperate **Southern Gulf Islands**. Some of the islands are inhabited by artists, retirees, and others drawn by the peace or the prospect of an alternative lifestyle. They offer the visitor quiet beaches, beautiful vistas, accommodation, fishing, diving, and a host of other outdoor opportunities. From Swartz Bay, B.C. Ferries runs at regular intervals to Salt Spring Island, and operates another service to Pender, Mayne, Galiano, and Saturna Islands.

Sports

There are plenty of places offering **boating** or **sailing** charters, with or without crew. If you'd like to learn how to do it, there are a few schools around, one of which, Horizon Yacht Centre at the Oak Bay Marina, ((604) 595-6677, is also a useful source of information for anyone considering a trip. There are plenty of opportunities for **canoeing** in the area and sports outfitters can often supply information on package trips. There's **freshwater fishing** at Elk and Beaver Lakes, which are only about a 15-minute drive north of Victoria, and there are several other lakes and streams a little further out. The waters that surround Victoria are renowned for salmon and offer some excellent **deep sea fishing**. There are many companies in town who offer charters. Fishing licenses are required and information is available from the Ministry of Environment, Fish & Wildlife

Information, Parliament Buildings, Victoria V8V 1X5.

The waters, particularly in the Georgia Strait, are excellent for **diving**, and are inhabited by a wide variety of marine life. Thetis Lake Park is a very pleasant spot for **swimming**. It is a short drive northwest of downtown and has a very popular beach as well as more secluded spots. You'll also find some beautiful beaches on the southwest coast along the stretch of Highway 14 between Sooke and Port Renfrew. There are several recreation centers in the Victoria area that have

pools. One of the best is the Crystal Pool Recreation Centre at 2275 Quadra Street, ((604) 383-2522, which has a lap pool, diving pool, whirlpool, and sauna. **Windsurfing** is quite a popular pursuit in these parts and there are plenty of places that give lessons. Some popular spots are Cadboro Bay, east of downtown near the university, and Elk Lake, which is about a 15-minute drive north of Victoria.

There are good **hiking** trails around some of the parklands northwest of Victoria, and lots more along the southwest coast between Sooke and Port Renfrew. At Port Renfrew, about 107 km (66 miles) from Victoria, there's the very testing West Coast Trail to Bamfield (see section on the Pacific Rim National Park under REST OF THE ISLAND).

Victoria and vicinity is ideal **golfing** country, with several private and public courses.

OPPOSITE: The beautiful Butchart Gardens on Tod Inlet outside Victoria. ABOVE: Rugby is another Old World activity that thrives in Victoria.

The closest public courses to downtown are the Cedar Hill Golf Course, 1400 Derby Street, ((604) 595-3103, and the Mount Douglas Golf Course at 4225 Blenkinsop Road, ((604) 477-8314. Of the many private clubs, the Victoria Golf Club, 1110 Beach Drive, Oak Bay, ((604) 598-4321, has to be one of the most beautiful courses anywhere, with wonderful sea views from Gonzales Point.

Shopping

Shop opening hours are usually 9:30 am to 5:30 pm with late night shopping on Thurs-

days and Fridays, and opening between 12 and 5 pm on Sundays.

Government Street, particularly where it runs through the Old Town, has some of the city's most interesting stores. Here are shops that have remained unchanged for the last 70 or so years and they wouldn't seem out of place in London's Jermyn Street. You can buy plaids, tartans, Waterford crystal, Wedgwood china, have yourself measured for a suit that will be made for you in England, buy your cigars at an old-fashioned tobacconist, or treat someone to delicious handmade chocolates. Also along the street are outlets for Canadian arts and crafts, and you'll see hard-wearing Cowichan sweaters on sale that are made of naturally waterproof undyed wool and decorated with traditional Indian designs. This is also the best street for fashionwear. The department store Eaton's has a branch at the **Victoria Eaton Centre**, a multi-story complex

ABOVE: The Victoria Eaton Centre.
OPPOSITE: Afternoon tea in the Empress Hotel.

located between Government and Douglas Streets at Fort Street.

There's a two-level shopping complex at **Harbour Square** between Government and Wharf Streets, and five blocks north at **Market Square** an attractive group of renovated buildings have been converted to house shops, services, and eateries. Moving a couple of blocks north to Fisgard Street, the city's **Chinatown** offers souvenirs, crafts, and some exotic groceries. Along the waterfront, the brightly painted houses of **Waddington Alley** contain some interesting boutiques and art galleries; for antiques you should visit the shops and auction rooms that cluster along the stretch of **Fort Street** between Blanshard and Cook Streets. You'll find some of the best outlets for native arts and crafts along **Douglas Street**, and there's also a branch of **The Bay** near the junction with Fisgard Street.

Nightlife

There are several free magazines which carry entertainment listings for the area. The Arts Council of Greater Victoria publishes Arts Victoria, and there's the Monday Magazine that comes out on Thursdays, as well as the monthly Night Moves.

The **Royal Theatre**, 805 Broughton Street, and the **McPherson Playhouse**, 3 Centennial Square, are both renovated older theatres that stage plays and concerts. For information on both theatres telephone (604) 386-6121. The **University Centre Auditorium**, University of Victoria, Finnerty Road, ((604) 721-8299, also stages plays and dance events, and the intimate **Belfry Theatre**, 1291 Gladstone Street, ((604) 385-6815, tends towards contemporary drama. For stand-up comedy there's **Yuk-Yuk's** at 514 Fort Street, part of a chain of comedy cabaret clubs.

The **Pacific Opera** stages productions at the McPherson Playhouse, while the **Victoria Symphony Orchestra**, ((604) 385-6515, performs mainly at the Royal Theatre but can also can be heard at the University Centre Auditorium at Finnerty Road, ((604) 721-8299.

Victoria holds its own annual **"Terrifvic"** Jazz Festival in April: you can obtain information from the **Victorian Jazz Society**, ((604) 388-4423. **The Alhambra Club** on Government Street near Parliament Buildings is quite a smart spot where you can catch some big-name performers. Downtown, **Hermann's Dixieland Inn**, 753 View Street, ((604) 388-9166, has lots of atmosphere, hearty food, and the kind of jazz you'd expect from its name. **Pagliacci's** at 1011 Broad Street, ((604) 386-1662, is a friendly Italian restaurant with live jazz of all varieties, but not a lot of space.

If you'd like to hear some rock music, check out **Harpo's** at 15 Bastion Square, ((604) 385-5333, where there's a wide variety of music and often some top names playing. Close by on the waterfront, **Merlin's Nightclub**, 1208 Wharf Street, ((604) 388-6201, has live rock music, as does **The Rail** at the Colony Motor Inn, 2852 Douglas Street, ((604) 385-2441. **The Forge** at The Strathcona Hotel, 919 Douglas Street, ((604) 383-7137, is a bigger place where the music tends towards hard rock and the crowd tends to be fairly young.

Priding itself on its Englishness, Victoria has several pubs that serve British-style beer. **Spinnaker's** at 308 Catherine Street overlooks the harbor to the west of downtown, and is a pleasant place where you can sample some very good ale brewed on the premises. **Swan's Pub** at 506 Pandora Avenue is another popular place serving its own brand of beer.

WHERE TO STAY

Luxury

It is virtually impossible to think of Victoria without the image of the chateau-like **Empress Hotel** springing instantly to mind. This ivy-clad dowager dominates the Inner Harbour and remains a bastion of Englishness and old-fashioned glamor. The hotel underwent major renovation in 1989 and has emerged triumphantly with upgraded facilities and sympathetic redecoration. It is the island's largest hotel with 481 rooms and suites, all beautifully decorated with traditional prints and fresh flowers. Popular with honeymooners are the more secluded rooms in the attic which have four-poster beds as well as window seats for enjoying the beautiful views of the harbor. The hotel also caters for handicapped guests and the security system is designed to accommodate the hearing-impaired. Business class accommodation is available and the hotel is adjacent to the Conference Centre. Formal dining is in the lovely Empress Room, while the Bengal Lounge offers an Indian buffet in Raj-style surroundings. There is a modern bistro, and the famous afternoon tea is served in the 1920's elegance of the Palm Court or the Tea Lobby. There's a swimming pool, fitness facilities, and shops. The address is 721 Government Street, Victoria V8W 1W5, ((604) 384-8111 or toll-free (800) 828-7447 in the U.S. and (800) 268-9411 in Canada.

Close to Beacon Hill Park, **The Beaconsfield Inn**, 998 Humboldt Street, Victoria V8V 2Z8, ((604) 384-4044, is a restored early twentieth-century mansion beautifully decorated with wood paneling, stained glass, and furnished with antiques. This Old World elegance extends to the 12 unique and lovely rooms, some of which have special features such as canopied beds or wood-burning fireplaces, and there are also a few celebration suites. The old-fashioned atmosphere is preserved by the absence of telephones or televisions in the rooms. The hotel has a lovely library where guests can attend a hospitality hour each afternoon, and breakfast is served in the attractive conservatory. Prices here vary between luxury and mid-range. Its sister hotel is the nearby **Abigail's Hotel**, 906 McClure Street, Victoria V8V 3E7, ((604) 388-5363, which is a heritage Tudor-style mansion in much the same mould. It has 16 accommodations with similar features to the Beaconsfield, and again the library serves as a delightful social center. Prices also vary between luxury and mid-range.

In complete contrast is the modern high-rise **Executive House Hotel**, 777 Douglas Street, Victoria V8W 2B5, ((604) 388-5111, toll-free: (800) 663-7001 in the U.S. and (800) 663-7563 in Canada. It is one block away from the Inner Harbour and has 179 large accommodations, including suites with self-catering facilities. There's a health spa, a formal restaurant and one that is more casual, a popular pub, and an oyster bar. The **Hotel Grand Pacific** at 450 Quebec Street, Victoria V8V 1W5, ((604) 386-0450 or toll-free (800) 663-7550, is another modern hotel that overlooks the Inner Harbour and has 150 rooms and suites. Rooms are attractive, well-equipped, and each has a balcony and bathroom. The hotel has an athletic center, an indoor pool, a business center with conference facilities, and a pleasant dining room.

The **Laurel Point Inn** at 680 Montreal Street, Victoria V8V 1Z8, ((604) 386-8721, toll-free (800) 663-7667, stands on a headland overlooking the Inner Harbour and is surrounded by gardens. The coolly elegant rooms all have balconies with harbor views, and there is a swimming pool, tennis court, sauna, and a bistro. Prices vary between mid-range and expensive.

If you're considering a trip to the South Gulf island of Saltspring, you should make sure of a stay at **Hastings House**, Box 1110, Ganges V0S 1E0, ((604) 537-2362 or toll-free (800) 661-9255. If you weren't considering it, it's worth the trip just for the delight of staying at this inn. It belongs to the prestigious Relais & Châteaux association and has 12 lovely accommodations well-stocked with life's little luxuries. The house resembles an old English country house set in lovely grounds with views of Ganges Harbour, and first-class gourmet food is served in the graceful dining room. The price includes breakfast and lunch. Book well in advance.

Mid-range
The **Victoria Regent Hotel**, 1234 Wharf Street, Victoria V8W 3H9, ((604) 386-2211, stands at the water's edge and has excellent harbor views. There are 48 well-appointed accommodations, mostly one- and two-bedroom suites, some with fireplaces and all with kitchens. There's a waterside restau-

rant and marina facilities. Close to Parliament Buildings, the **Château Victoria Hotel**, 740 Burdett Avenue, Victoria V8W 1B2, ((604) 382-4221, toll-free (800) 663-5891, is a high-rise building with 178 accommodations each with a balcony. The hotel offers a good range of services; rooms and suites are available, some with kitchen. Also in the downtown area you'll find the **Best Western Carlton Plaza** at 642 Johnson Street, Victoria V8W 1M6, ((604) 388-5513, housed in a heritage building and offering the usual good value and service that characterizes this hotel chain.

Close to Parliament Buildings you can enjoy some old-fashioned comfort in an intimate atmosphere at the **Holland House Inn**, 595 Michigan Street, Victoria V8V 1S7, ((604) 384-6644. This is a 1930's house, casually elegant with contemporary art adorning its public areas. There are 10 cheerful, antique-furnished rooms with balconies, some of which have four-poster beds and fireplaces. It's worth staying here for the gourmet breakfast alone. Overlooking the harbor just one block from Parliament Buildings, **The Captain's Palace**, 309 Belleville Street, Victoria V8V 1X2, ((604) 388-9191, occupies three mansions and dates from the late nineteenth century. Frescoed ceilings hung with chandeliers, walls clad with wood paneling, and maids in pinafores give you the feeling that nothing much has changed here. There are 17 accommodations furnished with antiques, all with private bath, and the attractive dining room has views of the harbor.

Some five kilometers (three miles) east of downtown there's the delightful Tudor-style **Oak Bay Beach Hotel** at 1175 Beach Drive, Victoria V8S 2N2, ((604) 598-4556. This seaside hotel has antiques in the lovely lobby and rooms which all differ in size and design. The hotel operates cruises and fishing charters from the nearby marina, and has a pub and a good dining room. The prices here vary tremendously and can be very high. For some fantasy accommodation try the **Olde England Inn**, 429 Lampson Street, Victoria V9A 5Y9, ((604) 388-4353. It is part of a group of reconstructed sixteenth-century English buildings that include a replica of Shakespeare's birthplace, Anne

Hathaway's Cottage and the like, located just a short drive west of downtown in the Esquimalt district. Genuine antiques, including some canopy beds, furnish the rooms. The bathrooms are not, thankfully, sixteenth-century replicas. Prices again vary widely from the lower end of the luxury category to the high end of inexpensive.

If you're planning an excursion to the southwest coast of the island, you might consider staying at the **Sooke Harbour House**, 1528 Whiffen Spit Road, R.R. 4, Sooke V0S 1N0, ((604) 642-3421, about 37 km (23 miles) from Victoria. Primarily an internationally-famous gourmet restaurant, this large white house perched high above a bay also has 15 guest rooms. The rooms are lovingly decorated with original artworks and antiques, each with a name that underlines the theme reflected in the decor. All rooms have fireplaces and private bathrooms, while some have four-posters, double jacuzzis, balconies, or sundecks. Rates include breakfast and lunch, and special honeymoon packages are available.

Inexpensive

Close to Parliament Buildings is the **James Bay Inn**, 270 Government Street, Victoria V8V 2L2, ((604) 384-7151, a large old house with character that offers good value and is thus very popular. The 53 rooms vary in size and amenities — some have private baths and some have kitchenettes. Also conveniently situated, the **Cherry Bank Hotel**, 825 Burdett Avenue, Victoria V8W 1B3, ((604) 385-5380, is a late nineteenth-century building with new extensions. The rooms are simply furnished and have no phones or television, but they are clean and adequate. You can join other guests in the Trivial Pursuit lounge, and a good breakfast is included in the price.

The **Strathcona Hotel** at 919 Douglas Street, Victoria V8W 2C2, ((604) 383-7137, is an old building that also houses a pub, a restaurant, and several nightspots. The rooms are modern with private bathrooms and lots of features that make it very good value. The **Hotel Douglas** at 1450 Douglas Street, Victoria V8W 2G1, ((604) 383-4157, is also an older building with nice, modern rooms, some of which have private baths.

Victoria has an abundance of Bed & Breakfast accommodations ranging from the basic to the luxurious. For a list of Bed & Breakfast agencies contact an Infocentre or see the British Columbia Accommodations brochure, which is available free of charge.

Victoria YM-YWCA is in the downtown area at 880 Courtney Street, Victoria V8W 1C4, ((604) 386-7511, but the accommodation is for women only. Single and double rooms are available with shared bathrooms, and there's restricted use of the swimming pool. The **Victoria Youth Hostel** downtown at 516 Yates Street, Victoria V8W 1K8, ((604) 385-4511, is a large, modern place with single-sex dormitories and good kitchen facilities.

The University of Victoria six kilometers (four miles) east of downtown offers **campus accommodation**. For details contact the University of Victoria Housing and Conference Services, Box 1700, Victoria V8W 2Y2, ((604) 721-8396. The closest campground to downtown is the **Fort Victoria Campground**, 340 Island Highway, ((604) 479-8112, about seven kilometers (four miles) northwest along Highway 1A, and it has full facilities. Many others close to town are restricted to RVs. For details of those in the parks see the listings in the British Columbia Accommodations brochure or contact the individual parks.

WHERE TO EAT

Expensive

The internationally acclaimed **Sooke Harbour House**, 37 km (23 miles) west of Victoria at 1528 Whiffen Spit Road, R.R.4, Sooke V0S 1N0, ((604) 642-3421, is one of Canada's best restaurants and offers some truly memorable dining. This is a large white house perched on a bluff overlooking a bay, with a spectacular view of the Juan de Fuca Strait and the Olympics beyond. The cuisine here is wonderfully inventive Northwestern; the couple who run the restaurant grow their own vegetables and herbs, and use only locally caught seafood and the meat of animals raised on nearby farms. The menu changes according to what is available on the day, but you can expect to find flowers liberally used in delightful salads and garnish, the freshest of fish, and free-range chicken. The presentation is pure artistry, the service knowledgeable, and the atmosphere informal.

Dinner is a far more formal affair at the distinguished **Empress Dining Room** in the Empress Hotel (see page 69). Wooden ceilings, pillars, and chandeliers create a setting that is splendidly traditional while the menu features North American cuisine and holds some pleasant surprises. Gentle piano or harp music enhances one's enjoyment of the excellent food.

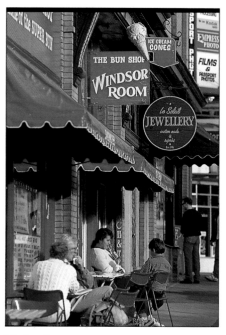

Moderate

You can sample some of the best French food in town at **Chez Pierre**, Yates Street, ((604) 388-7711, a small, attractive restaurant in the city's Old Town. It has an excellent reputation so you are advised to make reservations. **Chauney's** at 614 Humboldt Street, ((604) 385-4512, serves the most beautifully prepared seafood in gorgeously comfortable surroundings. There's also an emphasis on local seafood at the smart **Causeway Restaurant**, 812 Wharf Street, ((604) 381-2244, which has a delightful view of the Inner Harbour.

A little further north, still close to the harbor, is **Larousse**, 1619 Store Street, ((604) 386-3454, where you can admire the artworks that adorn the interior and enjoy French cuisine with a colonial, vaguely nouvelle, twist. Local produce prepared in a more traditional French manner features at **La Petite Colombe**, 604 Broughton Street, ((604) 383-3234, where there's a peaceful, intimate atmosphere.

Inexpensive

For a livelier atmosphere and live entertainment there's the Greek restaurant **Millos** at 716 Burdett Avenue, ((604) 382-4422, which also has some mouth-watering dishes on the menu. **Pagliacci's** at 1011 Broad Street, ((604) 386-1662, also offers entertainment, usually jazz, and serves dependable Italian food. There's usually a queue outside and it is very cramped inside, but everyone is fortunately very friendly, and putting your elbow in somebody else's soup can prove to be a great ice-breaker. There's a slightly Bohemian air about the **Herald Street Caffe**, 546 Herald Street, ((604) 381-1441, where you can inspect the work of local artists on display and enjoy some extremely good Italian and Californian food.

For Indian food try the **Taj Mahal**, 679 Herald Street, ((604) 383-4662, where vegetarians will find themselves well catered for. Along Fisgard Street in Chinatown a goodly number of restaurants serve Szechuan, Hunanese, and Cantonese food; for authentic Japanese food try the **Japanese Village** at 734 Broughton Street, ((604) 382-5165. For an altogether English experience go to **Old Victoria Fish 'n' Chips** at 1316 Broad Street, or on a rather more dignified note, take afternoon tea at the **James Bay Tearoom**, 332 Menzies Street, ((604) 382-8282.

HOW TO GET THERE

Victoria International Airport, ((604) 356-6600, is about 26 km (16 miles) north of downtown. The Airporter Shuttle Bus runs frequently between the airport and downtown and takes about half an hour. Victoria is served by Air Canada, Canadian Airlines, Horizon, and various provincial airlines,

ABOVE: An outdoor café in Victoria.

and there are direct connections with Seattle, Vancouver, and some major Canadian cities. Also, seaplanes run between Seattle and the Inner Harbour.

The Princess Marguerite and the Vancouver Island Princess (which also carries cars) cruise daily between Seattle and Victoria's Inner Harbour from May to September. The journey takes approximately four and a half hours and offers plenty of on-board entertainment. Contact the British Columbia Steamship Company, ℂ (604) 386-1124, for details and reservations. The *Victoria Clipper* is a jet-propelled catamaran that crosses between Seattle and Ogden Point near downtown Victoria in a mere two and a half hours. Details are available from 1000-A Wharf Street, Victoria V8W 1T4, ℂ (604) 382-8100. B.C. Ferries operate between Vancouver and Vancouver Island. The most direct route is from Tsawwassen, which is south of Vancouver on the mainland, to Swartz Bay north of Victoria. The crossing takes one hour and 35 minutes. B.C. Ferries also operate between Horseshoe Bay in Vancouver and Nanaimo. For information contact British Columbia Ferry Corporation, 1112 Fort Street, Victoria V8V 4V2, ℂ (604) 386-3431.

Black Ball Transport, 430 Belleville Street, Victoria V8V 1W9, ℂ (604) 386-2202, runs a ferry between Victoria's Inner Harbour and Port Angeles on Washington's Olympic Peninsula which takes one hour and 35 minutes. Washington State Ferries operate between Anacortes and Sidney with ports of call in the San Juan Islands. The approximate crossing time is three hours.

The Pacific Coach Line terminal is at 710 Douglas Street downtown, ℂ (604) 385-5731. They operate a frequent service from Vancouver to Victoria via the Tsawwassen-Swartz Bay crossing, with a journey time of three and a half hours. Island Coach Lines connects with other Vancouver Island towns.

The E&N (VIA Rail) Station is close to town at 450 Pandora Avenue, toll-free (800) 561-8630. A service runs to Duncan, Nanaimo, Qualicum Beach, and Courtenay, so to arrive in Victoria by train you need to take a ferry from the mainland to either Nanaimo or Courtenay where you can board.

THE REST OF THE ISLAND

WHAT TO SEE AND DO

Duncan and Vicinity

The rural town of Duncan, 60 km (38 miles) north of Victoria on the Trans-Canada Highway, is the gateway and supply center to the **Cowichan Valley**. The valley is still home to many Cowichan Indians, and some native craftsmen have collaborated with the town to produce the 20 or so totem poles that you see clustered along the roadside. This is a good place to buy one of the famous Cowichan sweaters as well as other native arts and crafts.

Highway 18 takes you 31 km (19 miles) westwards to **Lake Cowichan**, the largest freshwater lake on the island. It is known mainly for its good fishing but it is also good for swimming, camping, or canoeing, and the surrounding forest is laced with hiking trails. The valley is a lumbering area and one of the better logging roads will take you westwards from the lake to Port Renfrew on the island's west coast, the beginning of the Pacific Rim National Park's famous West Coast Trail.

About three kilometers (one and a half miles) north of Duncan the **British Columbia Forest Museum** (ℂ 604/748-9389) offers a fascinating look at the history of the forestry industry in the province through both indoor and outdoor exhibits. Here you can take a ride on a narrow-gauge steam railway, visit a reconstructed logging camp, see old equipment, and walk through the surrounding forest.

Twenty kilometers (12 miles) along the highway from Duncan lies the curious town of **Chemainus**. To avert the disaster that threatened when the town's sawmill closed down in 1983, the community set out to find itself a new source of revenue by commissioning murals to grace the town's buildings. The idea worked: visitors came to look, shops and restaurants opened, and murals depicting the town's history have spread like a rash, covering not only walls but also litter bins and anything else that stands still long enough. A ferry operates from here to nearby **Thetis** and

Kuper Islands, part of the Southern Gulf Islands.

A little further north the attractive waterfront town of **Ladysmith** actually sits right on the 49th Parallel which divides the mainland between Canada and the U.S. The old buildings here have been nicely renovated and it makes a pleasant stopping place. Just south of Nanaimo look out for **Petroglyph Provincial Park** where you can see some prehistoric carvings on the sandstone rock that were made by native Indians some 10,000 years ago.

Nanaimo

Nanaimo, 120 km (74 miles) north of Victoria, is the second largest city on Vancouver Island and a major deep-sea fishing port. Several Indian tribes lived in peaceful co-existence here until the Hudson's Bay Company discovered coal in the 1850's. Nanaimo remained a thriving coal mining area until demand dwindled with the coming of the oil-burning ships, at which point it turned to logging and fishing. Now an important B.C. Ferries terminus with a direct link to the mainland, the town has adapted itself to the tourist industry. Increased facilities, renovated buildings, smart boutiques, jolly festivals, and inhabitants renowned for their friendliness draw many visitors.

In 1853 the Hudson's Bay Company built a fortified **Bastion** as defense against possible Indian attack. Now the symbol of Nanaimo, this stout fort serves as a museum, and during the summer months its three cannons are ceremonially fired each day at noon. To find out a little more about Nanaimo's history, visit the **Nanaimo Centennial Museum** at 100 Cameron Street, ((604) 753-1821, which is open daily during the summer and from Tuesday to Saturday in the winter.

The wealth of parks and lakes in and around Nanaimo gives anglers, boaters, canoeists, hikers, and windsurfers plentiful opportunities to pursue their sports. Departure Bay at the north end of town is a popular windsurfing spot and whatever equipment you need can be hired from an outlet actu-

ally on the beach. Nanaimo has also pioneered its own rather bizarre sport: in mid-July every year people come from all around the world to take part in the famous **Nanaimo Bathtub Race**, when a motley fleet of motorized tubs set on a journey of 56 km (35 miles) across the Georgia Strait to Vancouver. Nanaimo also has its cultural side. In late June/early July it holds the **Shakespeare Plus Festival**, when drama old and new is performed. If island-hopping appeals to you, there's a regular ferry service to nearby **Newcastle** and **Gabriola Islands**. Newcastle Island is a Provincial Park inhabited only by wildlife, parkkeepers, and campers, while Gabriola Island, although home to a small artistic community, is also unspoiled, peaceful, and with some lovely beaches.

Parksville to Port Alberni

About 32 km (20 miles) north of Nanaimo, **Parksville** is well situated for a variety of outdoor activities. It lies along a coastal stretch popular for its lovely sandy beaches and waters said to be the warmest in Canada. To the west of Parksville lie wooded slopes threaded with nature trails, and in the winter months nearby Mount Arrowsmith attracts skiers. This is also where the scenic Highway 4 cuts westwards, crossing the island's central mountain range and leading to its star attraction — the magnificent Pacific Rim National Park 154 km (96 miles) away.

After a steep five kilometers (three miles) along Highway 4, a deviation of about eight kilometers (five miles) to the left will bring you to **Englishman Falls Provincial Park** where the Englishman River rushes over waterfalls down into lush, ferny forest, and brims with rainbow trout and steelhead. With beautiful clear pools for swimming, it is a delightful spot to pitch a tent. Back along Highway 4, a further 20 km (12 miles) will bring you to **Little Qualicum Falls Provincial Park**. A delightful forest trail leads to this series of waterfalls and ice-cold pools, while nearby tree-fringed **Cameron Lake** teems with trout. About nine kilometers (five and a half miles) along the road in **MacMillan Provincial Park** stands the magnificent **Cathedral Grove**, an

The handsome caboose of a vintage C.P.R. train.

awesome sight that is not to be missed. Some of the Douglas firs in this grove are 800 years old and reach heights of 76 m (250 feet). These trees were spared the chainsaw by the MacMillan Bloedel Paper Company.

Halfway across the island, **Port Alberni** sits at the head of the deep-cutting Alberni Inlet that widens into the west coast's Barkley Sound. It is a large town with a thriving lumber industry, a fact unfortunately borne out by the pungent smell that emanates from the mills. Its other main revenue comes from fishing, as anglers come here for the excellent salmon. From the harbor the stately *M.V. Lady Rose* takes passengers down the inlet to Bamfield on Tuesdays, Thursdays, and Saturdays, and to Ucluelet via the Broken Island Group on Mondays, Wednesdays, and Fridays. This cruise is a pleasant way of observing some of the wildlife of the sky and sea, and those intending to canoe or kayak around the Broken Islands are allowed to take their vessel aboard. You can hire whatever equipment you need for canoeing, kayaking, or diving from outlets in Port Alberni.

From Port Alberni, Highway 4 continues towards the west coast by **Sproat Lake**, which attracts many water sports enthusiasts and anglers. It proceeds through some beautiful mountain scenery, marred only by evidence of the extensive logging that has taken place in the area. The road follows the Kennedy River to Kennedy Lake, and then reaches the junction with the Ucluelet road where it bends sharply to the right and continues to Tofino.

The Pacific Rim National Park

This ruggedly beautiful coastal strip stretches for a dramatic 72 km (45 miles) between Tofino and Port Renfrew and is made up of three sections, each very different in character and equally rich in wildlife. The most northerly section, known as **Long Beach**, lies between the villages of Tofino and Ucluelet and is a driftwood-strewn stretch of sand and rock pounded by Pacific breakers. The weather is generally cold and

A flock of plovers takes to the air over Pacific Rim National Park.

wet here, but undeterred sportsmen and women don wetsuits to enjoy some superb surfing, swimming, canoeing, and kayaking. Hikers wrap up warmly and explore the magnificent trails through the rain forest. Porpoises, sea lions, and seals inhabit the waters. Gray whales can be spotted here, most frequently during the spring when they return from their breeding grounds in the south. **Radar Hill** with its telescope offers a good viewing point, but for a closer view there are whale-spotting boat trips that operate from Tofino. Humbler marine life

derful scuba diving with plenty of shipwrecks to be seen, not to mention the world's largest octopi.

At the entrance to Barkley Sound sits the little town of **Bamfield**, rather unusual in that its main highway is the inlet that divides it into two. A boardwalk two kilometers (one mile) long links East and West Bamfield. In recent years fishing charters, lodges, resorts, and other kinds of accommodation have appeared in response to the growing demands of tourism, but during the high season the town still

can be seen in the tidal pools along the beach — you can look but you are not allowed to remove any of the little creatures. Another interesting trip from Tofino runs to **Meares Island** where you can follow trails through unspoiled rain forest that has some ancient trees of majestic proportions.

The middle section of the park consists of the **Broken Group Islands**, 100 or so islands in Barkley Sound that can be reached by the *Lady Rose* passenger ship, by charter from Port Alberni, or by boat from Ucluelet. The islands are popular with canoeists and kayakers, and the area also offers some won-

Now you see them, now you don't: trees of British Columbia's great forests (ABOVE) are reduced to timber by the logging industry (OPPOSITE).

groans under the influx of tourists, mainly fishermen, so everything fills up very quickly.

Many of the visitors come to Bamfield to attack the third section of the park, the **West Coast Trail**, a very tough hiking trail stretching 72 km (45 miles) between Bamfield and Port Renfrew. It can take anything between five and nine days to complete. Originally constructed to allow shipwrecked sailors a chance of survival (many perished on this coastal stretch because of the impenetrable forest), this is for serious hikers only, and you have to carry all your food supplies with you. It is at times dangerous, often difficult, but rich rewards lie in the magnificent panoramas, dramatic waterfalls, verdant forest, and teeming wildlife that are to be seen. Roads run inland from both Port Renfrew and Bamfield.

Qualicum Beach to Campbell River

Slightly north of Parksville, **Qualicum Beach** is a popular spot for sunbathers, swimmers, and anglers, with plenty of accommodation and facilities geared to visitors' needs. Alternatively, there are the quiet beaches of **Denman** and **Hornby Islands**, home to small communities and accessible by ferry.

A little further north, the towns of **Comox** and **Courtenay** sit in the lovely **Comox Valley**. Both are commercial centers that also serve as bases for the surrounding recreational areas. Golf courses, fishing lodges, mountain trails, and campsites abound, and during the winter skiers flock to the nearby slopes of **Mount Washington** and Strathcona Park's **Forbidden Plateau**.

Campbell River, the gateway to Strathcona Park, is another town that is dedicated to outdoor sport, with skiing, hiking, mountaineering, and canoeing all catered for. The scuba diving here is very highly rated, but above all it is famous for its salmon fishing, which is probably the best anywhere, while its first-class fishing lodges attract enthusiasts from all around the world. It is hardly surprising, therefore, that the town's central attraction seems to be the **Discovery Pier**, a boardwalk that has shelter and facilities for anglers. From here it is well worth a trip on the ferry to historic **Quadra Island** to see the **Cape Mudge Indian Village Museum**, where there are displays of some fascinating carvings and ceremonial objects, many of which were seized by the authorities during the banning of potlatches — elaborate ceremonies involving ritual and feasting that were deemed heathen by the church.

From Campbell River Highway 28 runs west to **Strathcona Park**, the largest on Vancouver Island. It is a magnificent preserve of wilderness and wildlife that contains the **Golden Hinde**, the island's highest peak, as well as the magnificent **Della Falls**. Highway 28 cuts westwards across Strathcona Park to the small town of **Gold River**, where the *Uchuck III*, a converted mine sweeper, will take you along Nootka Sound to **Friendly Cove**, the place where Captain Cook first landed and met with the Indians in 1778.

North Island

The best reason for a stop at **Port McNeill** is to take the ferry to **Alert Bay**, an island partly populated with Kwakiutl Indians, and the home of the **U'Mista Cultural Centre**. On display here are more of the confiscated ceremonial objects that were used for the potlatch ceremonies, excellent films on aspects of Indian culture are shown, and the

Indian language is taught to local children. The island is also a good place for whale-watching.

Further north the highway ends at **Port Hardy**, where B.C. ferries ply the scenic Inside Passage to and from Prince Rupert on the mainland, a 441-km (274-mile) journey. For the intrepid, trails run from Port Hardy to the splendidly isolated **Cape Scott** and **San Josef Provincial Parks**.

WHERE TO STAY

There are many campsites throughout the island ranging from the most basic to the well-equipped. You can obtain information on camping from the Tourist Information

Centres, or get a copy of the British Columbia Accommodations brochure which carries a chart that lists campgrounds in provincial and national parks and gives details of the facilities. The same goes for Bed & Breakfast: there are many places offering this kind of accommodation and the accommodations brochure lists Bed & Breakfast associations and agencies that will help you find something suitable.

The **Best Western Cowichan Valley Inn**, 6474 Trans-Canada Highway, Duncan V9L 3W8, ((604) 748-2722, is located opposite the B.C. Forest Museum. It offers 42 comfortable rooms and suites, a dining room, and a coffee shop. Prices here straddle the mid-range and inexpensive categories. At Ladysmith the **Yellowpoint Lodge**, 3700 Yellow Point Road, R.R.3, Ladysmith V0R 2E0, ((604) 245-7422, is set in delightful parkland overlooking the sea, and inexpensive accommodation is available either in the main lodge or in rustic cottages. There is a saltwater pool, sauna, sports facilities, and a dining room.

At Nanaimo the best place to stay is the **Coast Bastion Inn**, 11 Bastion Street, Nanaimo V9R 2Z9, ((604) 753-6601, a large hotel on the waterfront with 180 rooms that all have pleasant views. The hotel has a health club, a good dining room, and a bistro. The **Dorchester Hotel**, 70 Church Street, Nanaimo V9R 5H4, ((604) 754-6835, has rooms with harbor views, a restaurant, a rooftop garden, and a library. Prices at both the Dorchester and the Coast Bastion fall into the mid-range category. Conveniently situated for the Nanaimo Ferry Terminal is the **Colonial Motel**, 950 North Terminal Avenue, Nanaimo V9S 4K4, ((604) 754-4415. The rooms have private bathrooms and telephones, and the rates are inexpensive.

There's a wide choice of motels and resorts in Parksville and several motels in Port Alberni. In the Pacific Rim National Park area most of the accommodation is to be found at Tofino and Ucluelet. Bamfield also has a few lodges, resorts, and Bed & Breakfast places. Back on the east coast there's some unusual accommodation at **Qualicum College Inn**, 427 College Road, Box 99, Qualicum Beach V0R 2T0, ((604) 752-9262, toll-free (800) 663-7306. This historic landmark building, once a boys' school, overlooks the sea and has 70 accommodations, including a few honeymoon suites. Fishing and golfing packages are available, and the prices are moderate. The **George Inn**, 532 Memorial Avenue, Box 2280, Qualicum Beach V0R 2T0, ((604) 752-9236, is a pleasant Tudor-style hotel built in the 1920s, with its own coffee shop, dining room, and pub.

Comox and Courtenay both have a large number of inexpensive motels, and at Campbell River there are also many fishing lodges. One of the most distinguished lodges in town is the **Painter's Lodge and Fishing Resort**, 1625 MacDonald Road, Box 460, Dept 2, Campbell River V9W 5C1, ((604) 286-1102, toll-free (800) 663-7090. It overlooks the ocean and guests stay either in the main lodge or in cottages, where the rooms are very well-equipped. The lodge organizes just about any kind of package you could want. Prices here range from expensive to moderate. At the **Strathcona Park Lodge** there are many kinds of accomodation to be had: campsites, hostel accommodation, apartments, cottages, and chalets. The lodge organizes packages for every kind of outdoor sport, including rock climbing, canoeing, and sailing. The lodge's address is Highway 28, Box 2160 Campbell River, V9W 5C9 ((604) 286-2008.

WHERE TO EAT

You won't be in danger of starving here, as there are plenty of snackeries, cafes, and pub-style places serving food at prices to suit the tightest budget. And of course wherever you go there's wonderful fish to be had. Chowder seems to find its way on to most menus, often served with delicious garlic bread, and there's always somewhere for fish and chips.

Needless to say, the bigger the town (or the attraction), the better the choice, and the places that seem to have the most cafes and restaurants are Nanaimo, Tofino, Campbell River, and Port Hardy.

HOW TO GET THERE

A few airlines serve Vancouver Island cities and link with Vancouver, while there are also regular seaplane flights between Nanaimo and the mainland.

B.C. Ferries run between Port Hardy in the northern part of the island and Prince Rupert on the mainland. This scenic trip along the Inside Passage takes 15 hours, with ferries operating every second day in the summer and once a week in winter. Reservations are required. B.C. Ferries also connects Horseshoe Bay in Vancouver with Nanaimo.

Island Coach Lines serves the island; you can get details of schedules from the depot at 700 Douglas Street, Victoria V8W 2B3, ℂ (604) 385-4411. Orient Stage Lines Ltd covers the run from Port Alberni to Ucluelet, Pacific Rim National Park, and Tofino. Telephone (604) 723-6924 for information.

E&N (VIA Rail), 450 Pandora Avenue, Victoria, V8W 4L5, ℂ toll-free (800) 561-8630, runs from Victoria to Courtenay, stopping at Duncan, Nanaimo, Qualicum Beach, Courtenay and waypoints. You need to make reservations for trips during the summer.

If you're traveling by car, the road that connects Victoria to the North Island is the Trans-Canada Highway. To reach Ucluelet and Tofino on the west coast you need to take Highway 4 from Parksville.

THE OKANAGAN VALLEY

This beautiful ribbon of valleys, lakes, and beaches lies in south central B.C. and stretches from Osoyoos near the U.S. border to Vernon in the north — a distance of roughly 180 km (112 miles). It is centered around the Okanagan River and a long string of lakes, the largest being the magnificent 144-km (90-mile) Lake Okanagan, which according to Indian legend is the home of the sea-serpent Ogopogo. The lakes are surrounded by arid, rolling hills, lakeside provincial parks, beautiful smooth beaches, and, inevitably, holiday resorts. Highway 97 runs the length of the valley and those who travel it can appreciate the fascinating Okanagan landscape that changes from a "pocket desert" around Osoyoos, where cactus thrives and rainfall is lightest, to the green farmlands in the north. Throughout the valley orchards

flourish, and many believe the Okanagan is at its most seductive during April and May when blossoms cover the trees and their heavy scent fills the air.

The valley averages some 2,000 hours of sunshine a year, summers are hot, winters are mild, and the rainfall is low. This congenial climate, together with the vast tract of water that makes irrigation possible, has turned the area into a major fruit-producing region with crops of apples, peaches, grapes, apricots, cherries, plums, and pears. From late June to October the roadside is

lined with stands selling these fruits. Vineyards cover the hillsides and eleven of the province's thirteen wineries are here, extending warm welcomes to the visitors who come to be shown around, to taste the wines, and to enjoy the hilltop views. The various fruit harvests are celebrated with events and festivals, and in early fall the whole valley joins in the biggest and jolliest one of all — the Okanagan Wine Festival. The valley has the largest concentration of population in the interior; its main towns are Kelowna, Penticton, and Vernon. The valley has become a popular vacation spot and attracts Canadians from colder regions who come to

A steamer on Lake Okanagan calls at Kelowna.

soak up some of the abundant sunshine. In and around the main towns holiday resorts line the lakes and spread over the hillsides. There are noisy waterslide parks and theme parks are dotted around. In the summer water sports enthusiasts flock to the lakes, and the winter brings skiers to the nearby mountainsides. If you are in search of quieter beauty spots then by far the best way to visit the valley is by car. In this way you can appreciate the variation in the scenery and have the freedom to stop your car where you please.

((604) 861-1515, or at the one that stands just outside the airport. Vernon has a Travel Infocentre at 3700 33rd Street, ((604) 545-0771, and a couple of others stationed at the northern and southern edges of the town that are open only during the high season.

WHAT TO SEE AND DO

Osoyoos

At the southern end of the Okanagan Valley, just north of the U.S. border, the little town of Osoyoos sits on the shore of Osoyoos Lake.

GENERAL INFORMATION

Apart from the information available from the provincial tourist information offices, you can get more specific information on the region from the Okanagan Similkameen Tourist Association, 104-515 Highway 97 South, Kelowna V1Z 3J2, ((604) 769-5959.

In addition, the Penticton Chamber of Commerce and Visitor's Information Centre at 185 Lakeshore Drive, ((604) 492-4103, can help with your questions, and there are two smaller Information Centres along Highway 97 both north and south of Penticton. At Kelowna you can drop in on the Travel Infocentre at 544 Harvey Avenue,

The town has cultivated a Spanish look to suit its dry, sunny climate, and as is characteristic of the Okanagan Valley, it is a fruit-growing area that celebrates its harvests with colorful festvals. Sandy lakeside beaches and warm trout-filled waters make this a popular spot for sunbathing, swimming, angling, windsurfing, boating, and the site for a variety of water sports events. Although fruit-laden orchards cluster around the lake, sagebrush and cacti grow on the arid hills that surround the town. This sandy area, which extends northwards to Skaha Lake, is often referred to as Canada's "pocket desert". It is a region that supports horned lizards, rattlesnakes, burrowing owls, and other life forms associated with the desert. Take Highway 3 slightly east of Osoyoos to **Anarchist Mountain** for views that allow you to appreciate fully the varied landscape.

West of the town Highway 3 leads into the neighboring Similkameen Valley. Highway 97 continues northwards following the Okanagan River through its valley past Vaseux and Skaha Lakes, a route that is lined with orchards and, in the summertime, with stands selling succulent fruit. Eight kilometers (five miles) south of Penticton the **Okanagan Game Farm**, ℂ (604) 497-5405, occupies

tourist-oriented with waterslide parks, motels, and other facilities lining Highway 97 as it cuts through the center of the town. The waters of the lakes are ideal for all kinds of water sports and during the high season the beaches get very busy.

The first orchards were planted here in 1874 and the town is now famous for peach-growing. In late July and August the **Penticton Peach Festival** celebrates the harvesting of the crop with sports events, music, dancing, and the extensive drinking of peach brandy. Penticton also celebrates the

a large area of scrubland above Lake Skaha. A five-kilometer (three-mile) drive through the zoo allows visitors to see over 130 species of animals from all around the world and also has some good views of the lakes.

Penticton

The town of Penticton lies along Highway 97 between Skaha Lake and the southern shore of the larger Okanagan Lake. Its name is derived from Salish Indian words meaning "place to stay forever" and the combination of a warm, dry climate and the lovely beaches of two lakes make it as appealing today as it obviously was to the Indians who named it. The town is very popular with vacationers and has become

grape harvest in September but you don't have to wait until then to enjoy a free taste of the local wine, as **Casabella Wines** at 2210 Main Street, ℂ (604) 492-0621, offers its visitors a free tour and wine sampling.

A fun way to see the magnificent Okanagan Lake is to take a cruise aboard the *Casabella Princess*, a sternwheeler that operates throughout the summer. Along the lakefront you can see the *S.S. Sicamous*, an old C.P.R. sternwheeler that was once the only transport on the lake. Also along the Okanagan lakefront the pleasant **Art Gallery of the South Okanagan** at 11 Ellis Street, ℂ (604)

Sheepish profiles in the Okanagan Game Farm: a Rocky Mountain sheep (LEFT) and a bighorn sheep (RIGHT).

492-6025, exhibits local and international works, and can be visited free of charge from Tuesday to Sunday.

About a 30-minute drive west of Penticton along Green Mountain Road lies the **Apex Recreation Area**, where there is a well-equipped ski center. Should you feel the need to escape the crowds, at the north end of town there is a road leading along the east side of the lake to the border of the untamed **Okanagan Mountain Park**. Highway 97 continues its scenic route along the west side of Lake Okanagan through or-

water sport. The largest of Kelowna's parks is the lovely **City Park** which has busy beaches, shady retreats, lawns, and tennis courts. In the summer it is sometimes the site for free outdoor concerts.

For a cruise of the lake and maybe a meal, get aboard the *M.V. Fintry Queen*, a paddle-wheeler that moors in the City Park at the foot of Bernard Road. There are also evening cruises which offer dining and dancing. For details telephone (604) 763-2780.

At the **Father Pandosy Settlement** south of downtown you can see some of the

chards, vineyards, provincial parklands, and some smaller towns.

Kelowna

About halfway along Lake Okanagan, Highway 97 crosses a floating bridge to Kelowna, the largest city in the Okanagan Valley with a population in the region of 62,000 and the center of this fruit-growing and wine-producing region. This attractive lakeside city with its many parks, gardens, orchards, and vineyards is an island of greenery set among rolling semi-arid hills. It has pleasant, sandy beaches and the lake provides plenty of scope for just about every

mission buildings that the Oblate priest founded in 1859 and which formed the first white settlement in the valley. The original church and school still stand and some other buildings of similar age have been brought to the site to give the visitor a fuller picture of life in those pioneering days. The site is open daily and admission is free. For a further look at the history of the area, return to downtown for a visit to the **Centennial Museum**, 470 Queensway Avenue, ((604) 763-2417. Here you'll find some Indian arts and crafts, an 1861 trading post complete with stock, an old stagecoach, and many other exhibits. The **Art Gallery** is housed under the same roof. It is open from Monday to Saturday during the summer

The Thompson River at Kamloops.

months and from Tuesday to Saturday during the winter.

The province's largest and oldest winery is Kelowna's **Calona Wines** at 1125 Richter Street, ((604) 762-9144, where visitors are welcome to look around and taste the wine. For a drop of something harder and to see how it's made you can join a weekday tour of the **Hiram Walker Distillery**, ((604) 763-4922, producers of Canadian Club whisky and other spirits.

During the winter there's plenty of skiing on the slopes around Kelowna. Close to the town on the other side of the lake is **Last Mountain**, which has chairlifts, a school, and something for skiers of all abilities, while about 57 km (35 miles) east of Kelowna is the **Big White Ski Area**, which is a ski resort with full facilities.

Continuing northwards along Highway 97 the scenery becomes gradually greener and cattle farming begins to take over from fruit growing.

Vernon

At the northern end of the Okanagan Valley, Vernon is surrounded by Kalamalka, Okanagan, and Swan Lakes, and has more of those pleasant Okanagan beaches that draw the holidaymakers. At the point where 25th Avenue crosses Highway 97 at the southern approach to the town stands **Polson Park**, where delightful oriental gardens offer a haven of shade and tranquility. There's also a floral clock in the park. To acquaint yourself with the history of the town you should visit the **Vernon Museum and Archives** at 3009 32nd Avenue, ((604) 542-3142, where you can see old photographs of the town, costumes, carriages, displays on the pioneering days, and a collection of Indian artifacts. It is open Monday to Saturday and admission is free.

For a fascinating peek at the past take Highway 97 12 km (seven and a half miles) north of Vernon to the **O'Keefe Historic Ranch**, ((604) 542-7868, one of the first ranches to appear in the area and one of the biggest in the entire province at the turn of the century. You can see O'Keefe's original log house, a general store, a blacksmith's shop, an early Roman Catholic church, and a fully furnished mansion house. Cornelius

O'Keefe was one of the first cattle ranchers to come to the area, after which he seems to have made a valiant effort to populate the region. With his first wife he raised nine children and after her death he remarried and had several more by his second wife. O'Keefes lived at the ranch from 1867 until 1977, and many of their furnishings and possessions remain here. The site is open daily.

Summer and winter, the **Silver Star Ski Resort**, 22 km (14 miles) east of town, has something to tempt outdoor lovers. From May to September it has some very pleasant hiking or cycling trails with views of the Coast Mountains. The resort, which has been built to look as though it's straight out of a Western, has accommodation, restaurants, and entertainment. In winter the bikes and boots are replaced by skis and snowmobiles, as the resort is awash with cross-country and downhill skiers. To get there you need to take 48th Avenue off Highway 97. En route you'll come across a turn-off (Tillicum Road) that leads to **Cedar Hot Springs**, where you can relax in warm mineral spring water in a delightful forest setting.

WHERE TO STAY

The Okanagan Valley is a popular resort area and there are masses of motels, resorts, and campgrounds that usually fall within the inexpensive and mid-range price brackets. The British Columbia Accommodations guide, available free of charge from information centers, gives details of accommodation, and the Okanagan Similkameen Campground and RV Guide, also free of charge, gives information geared towards camping. For lists of Bed & Breakfast accommodation in the area contact the **Okanagan Bed and Breakfast**, Box 5135, Station A, Kelowna V1Y 8T9, ((604) 868-2700, or the **Okanagan High Country Bed and Breakfast**, R.R.8, Site 10, Comp 12, Vernon V1T 8L6, ((604) 542-4593.

Osoyoos

There are quite a few motels around the lakeside in Osoyoos, several with their own private beach and shaded lawns which offer a cool retreat.

Penticton

At Penticton there are a few that stand out above the rest, such as the **Coast Lakeside Resort**, 21 Lakeshore Drive West, Penticton V2A 7M5, ((604) 493-8221. It stands on the shores of Lake Okanagan and offers top-line accommodation with all kinds of recreational facilities and services. The 204 rooms are attractively furnished, all have balconies, and there's a restaurant, cocktail lounge, indoor pool, and fitness center. Tennis courts and golf courses are nearby, and the beach and lake are at your disposal. Prices here range from moderate to expensive. The **Best Western Telstar Inn** is at 3180 Skaha Lake Road, Penticton V2A 6G4, ((604) 493-0311, and has 67 accommodations that include honeymoon and family suites, plus housekeeping units. There is a heated outdoor pool and sundeck, a restaurant, and the beach is close by. Prices here fall between inexpensive and mid-range.

In the inexpensive bracket there's the **Three Gables Hotel** at 353 Main Street, Penticton V2A 1K9, ((604) 492-3933, which is in the city center but only a short walk away from the beach. Rooms have private bathrooms, and there's a restaurant and a pub on the premises. The **Kozy Guest House** at 1000 Lakeshore Drive, Penticton V2A 1C1, ((604) 493-8400, is beautifully located on Okanagan Lake Beach and has 14 accommodations, some of which are housekeeping or two-bedroom family units. Just across the road from Okanagan Lake Beach the **Ti-Ki Shore**, 914 Lakeshore Drive, Penticton V2A 1C1, ((604) 492-8769, has some comfortable rooms and housekeeping units.

Kelowna and Vicinity

Seventeen kilometers (11 miles) outside Kelowna lies the **Lake Okanagan Resort,** Westside Road, Box 1321, Station A, Kelowna V1Y 7V8, ((604) 769-3511. This is an attractive lakeside resort set in landscaped gardens with luxurious condominiums, chalets, rooms and suites, two dining rooms, and a clubhouse. It is an ideal haven for sports enthusiasts as it has tennis courts (some of which are floodlit for night games), a par-3 golf course, horse riding, heated outdoor pools, and a marina where guests go to waterski, windsurf, and sail. Prices here are mid-range to expensive.

In Kelowna the **Capri Hotel**, 1171 Harvey Avenue, Kelowna V1Y 6E8, ((604) 860-6060, offers all the creature comforts you could want, with a heated pool, sauna, poolside cafe, restaurant, pub, and a cold beer and wine store. There are comfortable units and suites, all with TV and telephone. Prices here vary between mid-range and expensive. Similarly priced and similarly equipped is the **Lodge Motor Inn**, 2170 Harvey Avenue, Kelowna V1Y 6G8, ((604) 860-9711. Here accommodations include executive suites with their own jacuzzis.

The **Ponderosa Motel** at 1864 Harvey Avenue, Kelowna V1Y 6G2, ((604) 860-2218, has a warm, friendly atmosphere and low prices. It has 16 one- and two-bedroom housekeeping units, all with TV. Tea and coffee is on the house and shops and restaurants are nearby. Close to the lake and park, the **Willow Inn Hotel**, 235 Queensway Avenue, Kelowna V1Y 6S4, ((604) 762-2122, has 40 rooms with telephones and TVs, and has a coffee garden. Prices are inexpensive and include full breakfast.

Vernon

In Vernon there are plenty of motels to choose from, but for something a little different try **The Windmill House**, an inexpensive Bed & Breakfast place located about 16 km (10 miles) east of the town at 5672 Learmouth Road, R.R.1, Site 19A, Comp 2, Vernon V1T 6L4, ((604) 549-2804. It is an old Dutch windmill with four unusually shaped rooms, some with private baths, and all with lovely views. Even further east of Vernon along 48th Avenue there are several hotels and inns designed to look like something out of the Wild West at the Silver Star Mountain Resort.

WHERE TO EAT

There's no shortage of eateries in the valley — little to satisfy gourmets, but a fair amount of variety and many fast food chain outlets.

In **Penticton** you can sample Greek specialties in pleasant surroundings at **Angelinis** on Skaha Lake Road, or some hearty good-value food at the **Elite Restaurant**, 340 Main Street, where they do burgers, soups, and puddings. For Mexican food you should try **Taco Granden** at 452 Main Street.

Kelowna has the popular **Hollywood on Top** restaurant, 211 Bernard Avenue, ((604) 763-2777, a smart modern-looking place with a rooftop garden. It serves just about everything — tapas, pasta, ribs, steak, seafood and salads — and also has a busy capuccino bar. It is open for lunch and dinner daily. There are all kinds of interesting snacky items on the menu at **Jonathan L. Segals**, 262 Bernard Avenue, ((604) 860-8449, where you can enjoy lake views and, at weekends, late opening hours. At the attractive **Carmelle's Creperie**, 1862 Benvoulin Road, ((604) 762-6350, a wide choice of sweet and savory crepes awaits, and the **Old Spaghetti Factory**, Bernard Street at Bertram, maintains the chain's high standard in both its food and interesting decor.

In **Vernon, The Vernon Station Restaurant**, 3112 30th Avenue, ((604) 549-3112, has some good, inexpensive steaks, burgers, and salads, while at **The Keg and Cleaver**, 2905 29th Street, ((604) 542-0202, the menu concentrates on steaks and seafood. There are several Chinese restaurants in the town.

HOW TO GET THERE

Penticton's airport is situated at the north end of Skaha Lake, and it is served by Air BC, Time Air, and Pacific Western Airlines. Kelowna Airport is the largest in the area and is about a 20-minute drive north of the town along Highway 97. Canadian Airlines International, Time Air, and Air BC all operate flights to Kelowna, and there are daily flights to and from Vancouver, Edmonton, Calgary, and western Canadian destinations. Both Air BC and Pacific Coastal Airlines operate flights to the airport at Vernon, which is to the west of the town.

Greyhound Bus links Vancouver with Penticton, Kelowna, and Vernon. In Penticton the Greyhound station is at 307 Ellis Street, ((604) 493-4101. In Kelowna there is a station at 2366 Leckie Road, ((604) 860-3835, from which a regular service runs to Banff and Calgary; another links with Vernon, Kamloops, and Prince George. In

Vernon the Greyhound station is at 31st Avenue and 30th Street, ((604) 545-0527, and a service runs from here to Revelstoke, Golden, and Calgary.

If you're driving north from Washington in the U.S. you'll probably want to take Highway 97. It runs northwards from the U.S. border through the Okanagan Valley. At the north end of the valley the Trans-Canada Highway links with Highway 97 and 97A, and motorists coming from Vancouver can take Highway 3 then 3A to Penticton.

GLACIER NATIONAL PARK

Just before it reaches the Rockies, the Trans-Canada Highway runs through Glacier National Park, a rugged area high in the Columbia Mountains containing hundreds of glaciers, waterfalls, and rain forests. There are over 20 hiking trails — some short, some aimed at the more adventurous hiker — and there's snowshoeing and skiing in the park, although avalanches are a danger here. At the center of the park, **Roger's Pass** has some magnificent views and the **Roger's Pass Information Centre**, ((604) 837-6274, has maps of the park and pamphlets on the various trails. At the pass you'll also find the **Best Western Glacier Park Lodge**, ((604) 837-2126, and the Information Centre has details of campsites in the area.

Watch this space: a B.C. car discreetly pushes several messages.

Alberta

REACHING from the Northwest Territories to Montana, Alberta is bordered by the Canadian Rockies to the west and Saskatchewan to the east. It shares Canada's vast prairie land with Saskatchewan and Manitoba, and, covering 650,000 sq km (250,000 sq miles), it is the largest of the three Prairie Provinces. It has a population of little more than two million, half of whom live in Calgary and Edmonton, leaving vast areas of the province uninhabited by man.

Alberta has the cowboys, cattle, and wide-open spaces that epitomize prairie land, but it is also famous for the magnificent landscape of snowy peaks, sweeping slopes, and solemn lakes that characterizes Banff, Jasper, and Waterton National Parks in the Rockies to the southwest. The prairie lands of the southeast offer three different landscapes: in the southeastern corner there is an area of arid cattle-raising grassland and badlands surrounded by a larger wheat-growing belt that in turn gives way to an even larger area of parkland, trees, and mixed farming. It is in this last region that the province's major cities, Calgary and Edmonton, are located. The north of the province is a largely uninhabited region of forests and lakes.

The exploitation of the province's oil and natural gas resources sparked a period of rapid growth and prosperity in the 1970's that brought the cities of Edmonton and Calgary to the fore. The recent drop in oil and grain prices has brought an end to this boom, slowing down development and bringing hard times for some. However, Alberta has been left politically stronger, and it remains a producer of beef and grain as well as a major producer of oil and gas, with forestry and fur trapping still thriving in the north of the province. The endless outdoor opportunities that the province offers and the stunning scenery of the national parks contribute to a flourishing tourist industry.

The first white man to explore the area was Anthony Henday, who acted on behalf of the Hudson's Bay Company. Among those who eased the way for the settlement of the area was Father Albert Lacombe, who founded a mission, schools, and churches, and established good relations with the Prairie Indians. In 1869 the Hudson's Bay Company sold the land to the government and so Alberta became part of Canada. Whisky peddlers and fur traders descended on the area, and there followed a period of terrible lawlessness and bloodshed which ended with the arrival in 1874 of the North West Mounted Police.

The traders introduced guns to the Indian tribes, and the ease with which the buffalo could be slaughtered spelled the end of the massive herds that once roamed the prairie and had been the mainstay of the Indian way of life. With the herds gone, the Indians were willing to negotiate treaties, and cultivation of the prairie by the whites began in the 1880's along with immigration from Europe, Russia, and the U.S. The province of Alberta was created in 1905 and the subsequent world wars and various political upheavals brought more immigrants to the province in search of a new life.

Although the discovery of oil has brought Alberta prosperity and wealthy, modern cities, the province has steadfastly retained the spirit of its early ranching days. The picture-book image of the cowboy riding among herds on the plains is not an uncommon sight in the south of the province, while the days of the Wild West are celebrated each year with great gusto in the famous Calgary Stampede and Edmonton's Klondike Days festival.

EDMONTON

Alberta's capital city stands on the outer rim of the prairie, right at the center of the province, and is set around the deep valley of the North Saskatchewan River. Shiny modern high-rises testify to the prosperity of this oil town, a wealth that Edmonton seems to have handled wisely. The town is well-planned: streets conform to a grid system, underground and sheltered walkways protect citizens from the winter cold, and the river banks have been turned into parklands that provide winter and summer recreation.

With a population of 785,000, Edmonton is the largest city in Alberta and the northernmost major city in North America. It is Canada's oil capital, with some 2,000 wells within 40 km (25 miles) of the city, producing approximately 10 percent of Canada's oil. It deals with all the technological and scientific aspects of the oil industry, having refineries and petrochemical plants, but it leaves the administrative side of the industry to Calgary.

Edmonton is currently readjusting to the sudden deceleration in its development after a period of rapid growth. Although it remains Canada's oil center, the city is not wholly dependent on this one commodity. It is also the handling and supply center for the rich agricultural area that surrounds it.

Blackfoot confederacy of warrior tribes who together with the Cree then inhabited the land.

In 1870 the Hudson's Bay Company sold the land to the Canadian government and the area opened to settlers. Here as elsewhere in Alberta there followed a very wild and lawless period during which the town of 600 inhabitants was incorporated. Law and order finally arrived with the North West Mounted Police in 1875. In 1891 the railroad reached Edmonton, increasing its importance as a transportation center and

Its situation also makes it the main distribution center for the mineral-rich North Alberta, and for northern Canada as a whole.

BACKGROUND

In the late eighteenth century two fur trading posts were established in the area, one belonging to the Hudson's Bay Company and the other to its rival the North West Trading Company. When the two companies merged in 1821 the fort that had been established in 1795 by the Hudson's Bay Company, known as Edmonton House, became the trading and administrative center of the northwest and the jewel in the company's crown. The fort traded with the

triggering an influx of settlers. The discovery of gold in the Klondike in 1898 brought Edmonton its first boom period as prospectors flooded to the town to prepare for the long trek, increasing the population to around 4,000 and bringing prosperity to the merchants. This period of Edmonton's history is affectionately remembered every year in the town's annual Klondike Days celebrations.

When the province of Alberta was created in 1905, Edmonton, then with a population of 8,000, was elected its capital, much to the disappointment of the rival town of Calgary. It continued to grow in size with a further surge of immigration during the construction of the Alaska Highway. The biggest boom of all started with the discovery of oil in 1947 at Leduc, to the south of Edmonton. The discovery of further oil fields followed and by 1965 the population had quadrupled. The 1960's and '70's brought a period of great prosperity and frantic urban development, which in the 1980s declined with the drop in oil prices. However, as with the Gold Rush boom, Edmonton seems to have kept its head and to have profited greatly from its good fortune.

GENERAL INFORMATION

For brochures and a road map to help you on your travels through the province drop in on Travel Alberta at 10055 102nd Street, Edmonton, ((403) 427-4321, toll-free (800) 661-8888, or write to Alberta Tourism, Box 2500, Edmonton, Alberta T5J 2Z4. Alberta Tourism also publishes the very useful brochures Accommodation in Alberta and Campgrounds in Alberta.

For information on Edmonton contact the Edmonton Tourism Visitor Centre at N° 104, 9797 Jasper Avenue, Edmonton, Alberta T5J 1N9, ((403) 422-5505 or 988-5455, which is open seven days a week throughout the summer months, and from Monday to Friday during the rest of the year. There are also two tourist offices that are open during the summer along Highway 16, one at the eastern end of the city and the other in the western section.

WHAT TO SEE AND DO

Sights

The North Saskatchewan River snakes its way east-west through the city with a long green belt of parkland running along both banks. This is Canada's largest stretch of city parkland, one long recreation area strewn with cycling paths and trails. To get your bearings and an excellent view of the region take a trip up to **Vista 33**, an observation deck on the 33rd floor of the Alberta Telephone Tower building at 10020 100th Street, ((403) 493-3333. While you're there take a look at the small museum of telecommunications equipment which is also on the 33rd floor and features some interesting hands-on displays. Open daily from 10 am to 8 pm

Close to the tower the modern steel and glass **Convention Centre** steps down the riverbank on four levels. It houses the **Aviation Hall of Fame**, where exhibits include a flight simulator, films, and displays about people who have contributed to the advancement of Canadian aviation. The Convention Centre is at 9797 Jasper Avenue, ((403) 424-2458. It is open daily and admission is free.

In the heart of the downtown area lies Sir Winston Churchill Square, site of the Civic Centre which contains the **Edmonton Art**

Gallery. The gallery holds temporary exhibitions of works from its own collection or visiting exhibitions, usually of quite a high standard. The gallery is at 2 Sir Winston Churchill Square, ((403) 422-6223, and is open daily. Admission is free on Thursdays between 4 pm and 8 pm.

The **Legislature Building**, home of the provincial government, is a dignified building of yellow sandstone, fronted with a columned portico and capped with a stately dome. Built between 1907 and 1912, it occupies the site of the original Fort Edmonton,

OPPOSITE: The little steam train chugs its way across Fort Edmonton Park. ABOVE: The West Edmonton Mall is not just for shopping.

overlooking the river and surrounded by landscaped grounds with fountains, pools, formal gardens, and lawns. Below ground, the Government Centre Pedway links the Legislature Building to other government buildings and has an exhibition area where there are displays on various aspects of Alberta. The Legislature Building is at 109th Street and 97th Avenue, ☎ (403) 427-7362, and there are free tours daily throughout the year.

Over on the south side of the river close to Macdonald Bridge is the unmistakable **Muttart Conservatory**, 9626 96A Street, a group of four striking glass pyramids. Three of the structures simulate different climatic zones — tropical, arid, and temperate — and contain plants indigenous to each particular climate. The fourth pyramid houses changing displays. Open daily. ☎ (403) 428-2939 or (403) 428-5226 for recorded information.

West of downtown the **Provincial Museum**, 12845 102nd Avenue, ☎ (403) 427-1730, is pleasantly situated in parkland that overlooks the riverbank. This modern building contains four galleries, each devoted to a different aspect of Alberta's natural and cultural heritage. The Habitat gallery has displays that re-create the various aspects of Albertan countryside such as the mountains, the forests of the north, and the grasslands, complete with animal and plant life. The Natural History gallery deals with the geology of the area, its fossils, and the days of the dinosaurs, while the History gallery looks at the white settlement of the province. The Indian gallery describes the life and rituals of the Plains Indians, with a particularly interesting section devoted to the Sun Dance Ritual. Open Tuesdays to Sundays.

For a particularly enjoyable history lesson visit one of Edmonton's top attractions, the **Fort Edmonton Park** on the south bank of the river just west of Whitemud Freeway and close to Quesnel Bridge. This is an ambitious project that aims to recount the history of the white settlement of Edmonton in the most vivid terms. It has a detailed reconstruction of the palisaded Fort Edmonton, the 1846 Hudson's Bay Company trading post complete with "inhabitants" who are

happy to chat to you about their life in the employ of the company. Outside the fort there is a re-creation of village life in Edmonton during 1885 before the coming of the railroad, an Edmonton street in 1905 when the town was an expanding capital city, and a 1920 street scene showing Edmonton as a prosperous business city. Meticulous attention is given to detail, and there are shops that carry stock appropriate for the period as well as schools, churches, and offices. To complete the experience you can ride in a restored streetcar, a steam train, a stagecoach, or a horse wagon. Special events are held here throughout the year. It is open daily. Ring (403) 428-2992 for information.

Local history will tell you that to the south of the river lies an area that was once

the town of Strathcona, which joined with Edmonton in 1912. In the **Old Strathcona Historic Area** between 101st and 106th Streets, and Saskatchewan Drive and 80th Avenue, many of the buildings predate the union and have been restored. Pick up a walking tour brochure from an Information Centre and enjoy a stroll along these Victorian streets.

Coming back to modern times with a jolt, over at 170th Street and 87th Avenue lies the **West Edmonton Mall**, to date the world's largest mall, which covers a staggering 500,000 square meters (five and a half million square feet). Devoted to shopping and recreation, it holds about 800 stores, over 100 restaurants, 34 cinemas, a vast water park, a large amusement park with roller coaster,

and a mini-golf course. There are caged animals and performing dolphins for your entertainment, and much more besides. Like it or hate it, it's there and worth a visit for the experience alone.

The **Space and Sciences Centre** northwest of the city center in Coronation Park, 11211 142nd Street, ((403) 452-9100, is a suitably spaceship-like building containing Canada's largest planetarium, an IMAX theatre, displays on astronomy and science, and a nearby observatory. Open daily except for Mondays between September and June, admission is free but a charge is made for the star and laser shows.

A ride in one of Fort Edmonton Park's horse-drawn wagons.

Over to the east of the city, the **Strathcona Archaeological Centre**, ℂ (403) 427-2022, in the Strathcona Science Park off 17th Street just south of Highway 16, offers a fascinating insight into native Indian life 5,000 years ago. Recent archaeological excavation has unearthed a settlement that dates from from around 3,000 BC and an interpretive center has been set up to explain the history of the site. Open daily between May 15 and Labor Day, with guided tours available.

On a far more frivolous note, Edmonton really lets its hair down every year around

unspoiled wilderness of forests and lakes which is a wildlife reserve, only 35 km (22 miles) east of Edmonton on Highway 16 (the Yellowhead Highway). Elk, plains bison, wood bison, moose, and deer roam here, and hundreds of species of birds can be seen. The park has hiking and cross-country skiing trails, golf courses, swimming, and camping. The Astotin Interpretive Centre (ℂ 403/922-5790) tells you all about the park, and there is a **Ukrainian Pioneer Home** here which is open between mid-May and September, Fridays to Tuesdays.

mid-July when it celebrates **Klondike Days**. Not to be outdone by Calgary's successful Stampede celebration, Edmonton introduced this 10-day knees-up in honor of the 1898 gold rush that brought prospectors to the city on their way to Dawson City. There are parades, silly competitions, music, dancing, parties, and breakfasting in the open air. Northlands Park becomes Klondike Village, and everyone from the bank manager to the shopkeeper joins in by dressing up in period costume, making this one of Canada's favorite festivals.

Excursions

If you hear the call of the wild it could be coming from **Elk Island National Park**, an

Further east along Highway 16 and about 50 km (31 miles) east of Edmonton lies the **Ukrainian Cultural Heritage Village**, ℂ (403) 662-3640, a reconstruction of an early settlement of these immigrants who arrived in Alberta in droves during the 1890's and contributed greatly to the cultural development of the province. A reception area has exhibitions on the lives of these pioneers and on the story behind their immigration. Open daily between May and Labor Day.

Sports

The National **Hockey** League Edmonton Oilers, four times winners of the Stanley Cup in the 1980's, play at the Edmonton Northlands Coliseum at 115th Avenue and

73rd Street, ((403) 471-2191, from October to May. **Baseball** fans can see the Pacific Coast League Edmonton Trappers play at John Ducey Park, close to the city center, ((403) 429-2934, and the Edmonton Eskimos play their **Canadian Football** League opponents at the Commonwealth Stadium, 11000 Stadium Road, ((403) 429-2881, a structure that is part of the legacy left by the 1988 Winter Olympics. The Edmonton Northlands is also the site of a racetrack where you can watch **thoroughbred and harness racing,** ((403) 471-7210.

((403) 428-7970, Mill Wood's Recreation Centre, 7207 28th Avenue, ((403) 428-2888, and the Commonwealth Stadium, 11000 Stadium Road, ((403) 428-5555.

Golf enthusiasts have a choice of 30 municipal and private courses. Among the best of the municipal courses are the Riverside Golf Course at Rowland Road and 86th Street, ((403) 428-5330, the Victoria Golf Course and Driving Range, River Road and 120th Street, ((403) 428-5349, and Rundle Park, 2902 118th Avenue, ((403) 428-5342, all of which are 18-hole courses.

The City Recreation Park that stretches along both banks of the North Saskatchewan River has all kinds of facilities, including networks of **jogging, running,** and **cycling** trails. In the winter there are **cross-country skiing** trails here and also at Elk Island Park, which is located approximately 35 km (22 miles) east of town along Highway 16. In the summer Elk Island National Park is also a pleasant spot for **swimming.** There are both private and public **tennis** courts throughout the city, some of which can be found at the city's recreation centers. These centers also offer **racquetball, volleyball,** and **squash** courts, **skating** rinks, and gyms. They include the Kinsmen Sports & Aquatic Centre, 9100 Walterdale Road,

Shopping

Edmonton's downtown area is a major shopping district under which walkways link malls with the railway station, hotels, and major buildings. At the center of this district lies the **Edmonton Centre** at 100th Street and 102nd Avenue. Just west of downtown along 124th Street is a rather upmarket shopping district, and to the southwest of downtown lies the **West Edmonton Mall,** the world's largest shopping complex, containing over 800 shops and 11 department stores. This is situated at 170th Street and 87th Avenue, but you have to brace yourself

Children splash (LEFT) while adults (ABOVE) shop at the West Edmonton Mall, the world's largest shopping complex.

for a visit here as it's also a vast amusement park.

Nightlife
To check what's on, pick up a copy of The Edmonton Bullet, a free paper that carries entertainment listings. The city has dozens of bars and eateries that double as nightclubs and feature a wide range of music, so check the listings to find something that suits your mood.

You'll find Edmonton to be particularly well-endowed with theaters and theatrical

companies. The **Citadel Theatre,** 9828 101A Avenue, is a major Canadian performing arts center. This impressive glass-and-brick complex houses five theaters where a variety of first-rate stage and musical productions are performed, and there is also a pleasant indoor garden where you can while away some time. The **Jubilee Auditorium,** 1415 14th Street, ((403) 427-9266, is another venue for theater, ballet, and concerts, and is home to the Edmonton Symphony Orchestra and the Edmonton Opera. There are also many other theater venues scattered throughout Edmonton. **Yuk-Yuk's** at The Point, 7103 78th Avenue, ((403) 466-2131, is part of a Canadian chain of stand-up comedy venues, and there are a couple of theater-restaurants in town. Edmonton holds a Fringe Theatre Festival for 10 days in late August when alternative theater productions crop up all over the city, both indoors and outdoors.

There's no shortage of cinemas either, with 34 of them situated in West Mall alone and some more in the Calgary Tower complex. But if you want to see something other than mainstream, go to the excellent **Princess Theatre,** 10337 82nd (Whyte) Avenue, ((403) 433-0979, or the **National Film Theatre** situated within the Citadel (see above for address).

For jazz music, there's the **Yardbird Suite,** 10203 86th Avenue, ((403) 432-0428, and there are occasional jazz concerts at the **Jubilee Auditorium,** 1415 14th Street, ((403) 427-9266. You can hear rhythm and blues at **Blues on Whyte** in the Commercial Hotel, 10329 Whyte Avenue, ((403) 439-3981, and at the **Sidetrack Cafe** 10333 112th Street, ((403) 421-1326, where you can also enjoy some excellent food, and sometimes there's jazz or rock music playing. Edmonton's **Jazz City** festival is held for ten days during late June/early July, and in August there is a **Folk Music Festival**.

WHERE TO STAY

Luxury
Located in downtown on the river bank's parkland, **Château Lacombe**, 101st Street at Bellamy Hill, Edmonton T5J 1N7, ((403) 428-6611, toll-free (800) 268-9411, is a circular high-rise hotel. Rooms and suites are attractively decorated, with views of the river, a very plush lobby, a revolving restaurant, and a pleasant bar. Also downtown, the superb **Hilton International Edmonton**, 10235 101st Street, Edmonton T5J 3E9, ((403) 428-7111, toll-free (800) 268-9275, has some of the best accommodation in town and is conveniently connected to a major shopping mall. The hotel has two good restaurants, a beautiful lounge set amid an indoor garden, a pub, and an indoor swimming pool. The rooms are elegantly furnished and the well-equipped bathrooms add to the sense of luxury. The **Westin Hotel** at 10135 100th Street, Edmonton T5J 0N7, ((403) 426-3636, toll-free: (800) 228-3000, is another first-rate hotel. It has 413 rooms and suites, all beautifully decorated and luxuriously furnished. It houses the excellent Carvery Restaurant,

an attractive lounge, an exercise room, an indoor swimming pool, and a sauna. The **Ramada Renaissance Inn** at 10155 105th Street, Edmonton T5J 1E2, ℂ (403) 423-4811, toll-free (800) 268-8998, is another large downtown hotel with around 300 rooms and suites. It has plenty of in-house entertainment and recreation, with restaurants, indoor pools, and an exercise room. All rooms are spacious and thoughtfully furnished, many have balconies, and some have mini-bars. Prices here fall between the high end of the mid-range and the low end of the luxury category. The **Sheraton Plaza Edmonton** at 10010 104th Street, Edmonton T5J 0Z1, ℂ (403) 423-2450, toll-free (800) 228-3000, offers 138 lovely rooms with private balconies, and the usual good facilities. Prices here also fall between the low end of the luxury and the mid-range.

If you feel like being really frivolous, take one of the themed rooms at the **Fantasyland Hotel & Resort** over in northwest Edmonton in the larger-than-life West Edmonton Mall at 17700 87th Avenue, Edmonton T5T 4V4, ℂ (403) 444-3000, toll-free (800) 661-6454. There is a Polynesian room, a Roman room, a Hollywood room, an Arabian room, and a truck room (sic), to name but a few, all with whirlpools, and some with steam baths. Prices vary between mid-range and luxury.

Mid-range

The **Edmonton House All Suite Hotel**, downtown at 10209 100th Avenue, Edmonton T5J 4B5, ℂ (403) 424-5555, toll-free (800) 661-6562, is exactly that. There are 294 attractive suites with balconies and kitchens, and a very good range of facilities and services that include an exercise room, and a bar. Also in downtown, the **Alberta Place Suite Hotel**, 10049 103rd Street, Edmonton T5J 2W7, ℂ (403) 423-1565, toll-free (800) 661-3982, has 86 apartments comfortably furnished with compact but well-equipped kitchens. The hotel has an exercise room, a sundeck, and most things you need for self-catering on the premises. There is the added touch of complimentary coffee, fruit juice, and morning paper. Weekly, monthly, and corporate rates are available. The **Renford**

Inn at Fifth, 10425 100th Avenue, Edmonton T5J 0A3, ℂ (403) 423-5611, toll-free (800) 661-6498, has 107 accommodations, including honeymoon and executive suites, all smartly decorated, and services that cater for most needs.

Northwest of downtown near the airport, the **Edmonton Inn**, 11830 Kingsway Avenue, Edmonton, T5G 0X5, ℂ (403) 454-9521, toll-free (800) 661-7264, has airy and very comfortable rooms, some family units, and executive suites. The service here is very good, and the hotel has a piano lounge, a restaurant, and several function rooms. It also runs a complimentary shuttle service to the airport.

Inexpensive

Downtown the **Edmonton Centre Travelodge** at 10209 100th Avenue, Edmonton, T5J 0A1, ℂ (403) 428-6442, toll-free (800) 255-3050, is very good value with 73 nicely furnished rooms, all with TV and telephone. There's a pub, a cocktail lounge, and a restaurant on the premises. The **Mayfair Hotel**, 10815 Jasper Avenue, Edmonton T5J 2B1, ℂ (403) 423-1650, is a smart blue-and-white building that is another downtown bargain. The lobby is large and comfortable, there are 126 simply-furnished rooms and suites, and complimentary coffee and fresh fruit are supplied. It is a lively spot to stay as the hotel contains a casino, various eateries, and a restaurant/theatre. Also downtown, the **Château Louis Motor Inn** at 11727 Kingsway Avenue, Edmonton T5G 3A1, ℂ (403) 452-7770, toll-free (800) 661-9843, has rooms and suites, 24-hour room service, and a French ambience.

Northwest of the city center, the **Continental Inn** at 16625 Stony Plain Road, Edmonton T5P 4A8, ℂ (403) 484-7751, is a large modern building with 60 comfortable accommodations. There's just about everything you could want here: night club, pub, lounge, dining room, coffee shop, conference facilities — and it's close to the West Edmonton Mall. For accommodation in one of Edmonton's few older establishments, try **La Bohème**, 6427 112th Avenue, Edmonton, T5W 0N9, ℂ (403) 474-5693. Known primarily as a very good French restaurant, it now offers a few characterful suites that, along with the service, are continental in style and quite charming. Breakfast is included in the price.

There's a **YMCA** at 10030 102A Avenue, Edmonton T5J 0G5, ((403) 421-9622, close to the Edmonton Centre and conveniently placed for the train station. It has accommodation for men, women, couples and families, and there are a few rooms with private bathroom. Guests have use of the fitness facilities. The **YWCA** at 10305 100th Avenue,Edmonton, T5J 3C8, ((403) 429-8707, has accommodation for women only, and there are a few rooms available with private bath. Again, guests get to use the fitness facilities.

For Bed & Breakfast accommodation you should contact one of the agencies listed in the back of the Alberta Hotel Association's Accommodation in Alberta brochure, which is available free of charge from Tourist Information Centres. Farm and ranch accommodation is another popular option in Alberta. A list of some of these places can also be found in the above brochure. For fuller lists write to Alberta Tourism, P.O.Box 2500, Edmonton, T5J 2Z4.

WHERE TO EAT

Edmonton's cultural mix makes for a healthy restaurant scene with a wide choice of cuisines, but as a prairie town it has its own specialty: some of the best beef in Canada. You will find concentrations of restaurants in the Old Strathcona district between 101st and 106th Streets, the downtown area, and the Boardwalk Market at 103rd Street.

Moderate
La Bohème at 6427 112th Avenue, ((403) 474-5693, is housed within an older building close to downtown and is decidedly French in both cuisine and ambience. You'll find some of the best French fare in town here, and there is a wine cellar to match. It is open throughout the week; reservations are recommended. The menu is also French at **La Ronde**, the revolving restaurant at the top of the Château Lacombe hotel, 101st Street at Bellamy Hill, ((403) 428-6611. Unlike many of its counterparts, it is not only a feast for the eyes: the food and the service are also

of a high standard. Situated within a downtown hotel is the excellent Carvery, Westin Hotel, 10135 100th Street, ((403) 426-3636. This is a good place to sample some of the province's first-rate beef. For more of that wonderful meat make a reservation at **Hy's Steak Loft**, 10013 101st Street, ((403) 424-4444, one of the best steak houses in town.

The **Un-Heard-Of** at 9602 82nd Avenue, ((403) 432-0480, offers two prix-fixe menus featuring excellent international cuisine prepared with the freshest of ingredients, and includes desserts to die for. The acclaimed **Sushi Tomi** at 10126 100th Street, ((403) 422-6083, serves both innovative and traditional dishes prepared with beautifully fresh seafood, and there's more good traditional Japanese food served at **Shogun**, 121st Street and Jasper Avenue, ((403) 482-5494.

Inexpensive
The family-run **Smokey Joe's Hickory Smokehouse** at 156th Street and 87th Avenue, ((403) 489-3940, serves hickory-smoked ribs, poultry, and sausages in large helpings and in a warm, friendly atmosphere. There's also a homey atmosphere at the much-loved **Mother Tucker's**, 10184 104th Street, where baked chicken, fish, and some of that prairie beef appear in generous portions. **Uncle Albert's Pancake House**, at 10370 Whyte Avenue, ((403) 439-6609, is another very popular spot where the food fits even the tightest of budgets and fills the emptiest of stomachs. One of Edmonton's oldest restaurants is **The Silk Hat** at 10251 Jasper Avenue, ((403) 428-1551, which has retained its old jukeboxes and booths, and where the prices don't seem to have changed much either. It is a good place for breakfast or lunch.

For a flavor or two of the east, the **Mongolian Food Experience** at 10160 100A Street, ((403) 426-6806, is a good bet. Here you'll find several eastern cuisines in evidence on the mouth-watering menu. Reservations are necessary. Nearby, the **Bistro Praha** at 10168 100A Street, ((403) 424-4218, offers tasty central European fare in relaxing and attractive surroundings. It is a good place to take tea or coffee and indulge yourself with some of the delightful pastries. The stylish **Russian Tea Room**, 10312 Jasper Avenue, ((403) 426-0000, does indeed serve Russian tea along with wonderful cakes and pastries, but it also has a restaurant menu where you'll find traditional Russian dishes.

HOW TO GET THERE

Edmonton International Airport is served by several major airlines and also by some regional carriers. It is 16 km (10 miles) south

of the city along Highway 2 and the drive takes about 45 minutes. A Grey Goose Airporter bus runs between some of the big downtown hotels and the airport. The Municipal Airport is slightly north of downtown and is used by smaller craft that tend to run to other Albertan destinations.

Edmonton is very well served by rail services, lying at the center of the network and along the C.N.R. (Canadian National Railway) transcontinental line. The VIA Rail Station is at 10004 104th Avenue at 100th Street, ((403) 429-5431, toll-free (800) 665-8630.

The Greyhound bus terminal is at 10324 103rd Street at 103rd Avenue, ((403) 421-4211, and operates services that run to the west and to the east of Edmonton, to

Yellowknife in the Northwest Territories, and south to Calgary. Coachways operates from the same terminal and runs a daily service to Whitehorse in the Yukon and on to the Alaskan border.

Motorists will find that the inter-provincial Yellowhead Highway (Highway 16), which runs from east to west and passes through Edmonton is easy to join, whatever direction you're coming from. Highway 2 runs from the U.S. Montana border via Calgary to Edmonton and continues northwards.

CALGARY

Calgary sprawls over prairie land that seems to stretch ever eastwards, but it lies in the foothills of the Canadian Rockies and so to the west of the city you can see the magnificent snow-tipped mountains some 80 km (50 miles) away. Originally a small settlement at the confluence of the Bow and Elbow Rivers, Calgary now spreads over the largest land area of any Canadian city, and has become a high-powered city of mirrored high-rises, malls, and other modernities. The climate here is generally dry and sunny with hot summers, and winters that can get bitterly cold but are tempered by the warming Chinook winds from the mountains. These winds can raise temperatures quite dramatically within hours and also have the delightful effect of creating some of the most dramatic sunsets that you'll see anywhere on the prairie.

The character of the city also has its contrasts: on the one hand it is undeniably an oil boom town, with glittering skyscrapers and busy traffic, but it also retains the identity of the cowtown it once was, and this is the image that the residents are anxious to nurture. The people behave in a way you don't quite expect of citizens of an oil-rich city of glass and steel: they are almost aggressively nice, whatever you do, and they love to lay on the welcome for visitors. And of course it's almost impossible to think of

Calgary's Olympic Park, main site for many events of the 1988 Winter Olympics.

Calgary without the word "Stampede" springing to mind. This annual festival held in early July seems to get the whole of Canada reaching for cowboy hats and boots. Visitors and cowboys pour in from all over the world to join in the yeehah-ing and the explosion of rodeos, chuckwagon races, dancing, parades, and general merrymaking. This is when the city indulges its cowboy alter ego, with everybody dressing themselves and their city up for the occasion and wallowing in riotously good fun.

BACKGROUND

In 1875 the newly-formed North West Mounted Police were sent here to restore peace to an area where whisky traders and fur trappers had generally been cooking up trouble and fanning wars between the Indians. They set up a fort at the point where the Bow and Elbow Rivers meet; the commander of police named it after Calgary Bay in his native Scotland. Settlers clustered around the post almost immediately, and in 1877 a treaty was signed, without bloodshed, in which the Indian tribes who roamed the area relinquished the land to the government in return for certain provisions and rights.

The Canadian Pacific Railway came to Calgary in 1883, and this together with the offer of free land to settlers brought about rapid population growith. The excellent grazing lands of the prairie brought the ranchers and their huge herds from the U.S., so the town continued to expand, becoming an important meat-packing center and the hub of the farming and ranching region. By 1891 the population was around 4,000; in 1893 the city was granted a charter.

In 1914 the discovery of oil in the Turner Valley just southwest of Calgary brought prosperity to the area, but it was the big strike in Leduc in 1947 and subsequent discoveries in the Edmonton area that triggered the meteoric rise in Calgary's fortunes. The city has become the administrative center for Canada's petroleum industry and now over 500 oil and gas companies have their headquarters here. In the late 1960's there began a 20-year period of frantic development with skyscrapers breaking out like a rash, dramatically changing the face of the city and turning it into a perpetual building site while the population exploded to around 640,000. The decrease in the demand for oil in recent years has slowed down the pace of development, allowing Calgary to clear away the dust of its construction work and to get its breath back.

When Calgary hosted the 1988 Winter Olympics it had the opportunity to extend some of its famous hospitality to the whole world, and the Games brought the city to the attention of millions of television viewers everywhere. The event proved to be a successful PR exercise: people liked what they saw. Realizing there was more to Calgary than oil and the Stampede, they began to come and see for themselves this city of contrasts.

GENERAL INFORMATION

For information on the province as a whole, contact the Alberta Tourism Information Centre, McDougall Centre, 455 6th Street S.W., Calgary, ((403) 297-6574, toll-free in Alberta (800) 222-6501. It is open from Monday to Friday during summer months.

For information specifically on Calgary and the surrounding area get in touch with the Calgary Convention & Visitors Bureau at 237 8th Avenue S.E., Calgary T2G 0K8, ((403) 262-2766 or toll-free (800) 661-1778. There's also an Information Office in the Calgary Tower in Palliser Square at the junction of 9th Avenue and Centre Street, ((403) 261-8616.

The Calgary Convention & Visitors Bureau also offers a free accommodation service, ((403) 263-8510.

WHAT TO SEE AND DO

Sights

Calgary is divided into northwest, southwest, southeast, and northeast sections, and this is important to note as you'll find N.E., S.E., S.W., or N.W. forming part of the addresses here. The east and west dividing line is Centre Street, and the Bow River separates north from south. Streets follow a grid system, and virtually all of them in the downtown section are one-way. Getting around the city is easy if you use the network of enclosed walkways called "Plus 15's" (because they are a minimum of 15 feet (4.5 m) above the ground) and the efficient transport system of buses and streetcars that are known as C-Trains.

Begin your tour of the downtown section with a trip up **Calgary Tower** at 9th Avenue and Centre Street South, ((403) 266-7171. A high-speed lift will whisk you to the observation deck close to the top of this 191-m (626-ft) landmark where you can see seemingly endless prairie land stretching to the east and the magnificent Canadian Rockies to the west. The tower contains the almost statutory revolving restaurant and there's a cocktail bar at the very top. The Olympic flame atop the tower is lit on occasion. The observation deck is open until 11:30 pm Monday to Saturday and until 10:30 pm on Sundays so you can enjoy nighttime views of the city.

Over the road from the tower is the **Glenbow Museum**, 130 9th Avenue S.E., ((403) 264-8300/237-8898, which has an art gallery on one floor with permanent and temporary exhibitions, a floor devoted to the history of Western Canada, and another to an extensive military and weaponry collection that spans medieval to modern times. One of the

most noteworthy sections here is the excellent collection of Indian and Inuit art. The museum is open daily except Mondays, and admission is free on Saturdays.

If you feel like a respite from the concrete jungle, take yourself up to the fourth level of the nearby Toronto Dominion Square at 317 7th Avenue S.W., where you'll find a one-hectare (2.5 acres) **indoor garden** with fountains, pools, waterfalls, a stage for lunchtime entertainment, and, we are told, some 20,000 local and Californian tropical plants. There are a few snack bars here and

it makes a very agreeable meeting place. It is accessible daily except for times when it is hired out for a private function. Another unusual and very commendable feature of downtown is the **Lunchbox Theatre**, at the second level of Bow Valley Square, 205 5th Avenue S.W., where you can watch free lunchtime theatre given by professional performers. The shows change regularly — sometimes a short play, sometimes a musical — and are kept to a length of around 50 minutes, allowing local workers to spend

ABOVE: Public art in downtown Calgary.
OPPOSITE: A replica dinosaur in the Prehistoric Park attached to Calgary Zoo.

Alberta

their lunch hour here. Plays are performed between September 25 and mid-May.

To understand a little more about what made Calgary rich, visit the **Energeum** at the West Lobby of the Energy Resources Building, 640 5th Avenue S.W., ((403) 297-4293. The formation, exploitation, and uses of Alberta's energy resources are described through fascinating displays that involve models, computer games, hands-on presentations, and even hands-in (you can feel the oil with gloved hands). Open Monday to Friday all year and on Sundays between June and August.

Turning from the ground to the heavens, slightly to the west is the **Alberta Science Centre and Centennial Planetarium** at Mewata Park, 11th Street and 7th Avenue S.W., ((403) 221-3700, where there are star shows and hands-on displays that help you understand the laws of physics. There's also a small observatory where you can star-gaze through telescopes. Walking distance away and to the north of downtown, **Prince's Island Park** in the Bow River offers a very pleasant and shady retreat. It makes a good picnic spot, with cycling and jogging trails, and is accessible by footbridge from both banks of the river.

Fort Calgary Park, 750 9th Avenue S.E., lies at the east end of the city center at the confluence of the rivers. This was once the site of Fort Calgary, established by the North West Mounted Police in 1875. It was the birthplace of the city. Little remains of the fort but an Interpretive Centre offers a very vivid picture of life in the days of the early settlers and traces the history of the city. Open daily during the summer and from Wednesday to Sunday during winter.

From Fort Calgary, cross the bridge to St. George's Island to see the excellent **Calgary Zoo**, ((403) 232-9300. Here some 300 species of creatures great and small are represented by over 1,400 animals in environments that simulate their natural habitats. Glass panels allow visitors to observe the seals, polar bears, penguins, and others in the water. A large conservatory filled with thousands of tropical plants also provides an ideal setting for exotic birds and butterflies. Attached to the zoo is the **Prehistoric Park**, where a group of life-size replica di-

nosaurs are set in a prehistoric landscape. The zoo is open throughout the year and the Prehistoric Park is open between Victoria Day and November 11th. There's yet more wildlife to be seen at the **Inglewood Bird Sanctuary**, about two and a half kilometers (one and a half miles) from the zoo and southeast of the city center at 9th Avenue S.E., ((403) 269-6688. In this forested reserve on the west bank of the Bow River there have been sightings of over 245 species of birds.

Stampede Park, southeast of downtown at 14th Avenue and Olympic Way S.E., is where the real action takes place during the Calgary Stampede. It's worth a trip even when the Stampede isn't in progress just to see the stunning **Olympic Saddledome**, a

sports arena with a roof in the shape of a gigantic saddle. The Saddledome is the home of the Calgary Flames, the city's National Hockey League team. While you're in the park you might like to visit the **Grain Academy** on the upper floor of the Round-Up Centre, ((403) 263-4594, a museum where models and a miniature railway show how grain is transported from the prairies to the Vancouver docks. Open Monday to Friday all year and on Saturdays from April to September.

Southwest of downtown at the Canadian Forces Base, the **Museum of the Regiments**, 4225 Crowchild Trail South, ((403) 240-7002, presents military uniforms, weapons, and other memorabilia belonging to four regiments: the Lord Strathcona Horse, Princess

Patricia's Light Infantry, the King's Own, and the Calgary Highlanders.

For a full reconstruction of life in pioneer times and other periods of Calgary's history, you must go to **Heritage Park**, 16 km (10 miles) southwest of town at the Glenmore Reservoir. Many original buildings have been brought here from various parts of Alberta, and an early-1900's village has been reconstructed with a working bakery, a mill, a newspaper office, stocked-up stores, and housing. You can take a trip on a restored steam train or go out onto the reservoir aboard the old sternwheeler the *S.S.Moyie*. There are places to snack or dine here. Open

A polar bear in Calgary Zoo.

daily. For information telephone (403) 255-1858.

Continuing south along the Macleod Trail, then left along Bow Bottom Trail S.E., you'll come to **Fish Creek Park** which spreads out along eight kilometers (five miles) at the edge of the city boundary. This parkland, through which Fish Creek runs, is a wildlife sanctuary but is also where people come simply to escape from city life. It is open daily and there is no admission charge. A visitor center is open throughout the year, ((403) 297-5293.

amusement park that features a large maze (1,653 sq m or 18,000 sq ft), a petting farm, rides, shows, and much more. Open daily in summer.

The Calgary Stampede
Billed as "The Greatest Outdoor Show on Earth", this 10-day celebration of Calgary's Wild West days takes place every July and has been going since 1912. Everyone gets into the spirit of it, donning stetsons, jeans, and boots. There is a big parade with dancing in the streets, while hearty breakfasts are

The impressive facilities which Calgary built for the 1988 Winter Olympics are still in use, and the **Olympic Park**, ((403) 247-5404, which was the main site for ski jumping, luge and bobsled events, stands to the west of town, a 10-minute drive along Highway 1 (the Trans-Canada Highway) from downtown. You can explore the site for yourself or join a guided tour and see the courses from the perspective of the Olympic athletes who tackled them. The **Olympic Hall of Fame** has three floors stacked with enough Olympic memorabilia, photographs, and films to make you feel that you had actually been at the Games. A few minutes' drive further west along Highway 2 will bring you to **Calaway Park**, a large

served up around town. The inhabitants use the Stampede as an excuse to be extra nice to people. Southeast of the town at Stampede Park there are bands, more dancing, food, livestock shows, and the real business of the Stampede: the rodeo and the chuckwagon races. For the professional cowboys who take part in the rodeo and make their living from the sport, this is very serious business with big prize money awaiting only the first-prize winner in each of seven main events. To enter the events they have to prove they have earned a certain annual income from rodeos and must pay to participate. Visitors need to reserve their tickets and accommodation in advance. For details of the event contact the Calgary Exhibition and Stampede, P.O. Box 1060, Station M, Calgary T2P 2K8, toll-free (800) 661-1260.

Excursions

The small town of **Fort Macleod** is approximately a two-hour drive south of Calgary, and is one of Alberta's earliest settlements. It is the site of the first North West Mounted Police post, and is named after their first commander, Colonel James Macleod. This force (now the Royal Canadian Mounted Police) was formed in 1873 to enforce law and order in the west, where at that time the whiskey traders were wreaking havoc, and their first action was to set forth on a gruelling march from Manitoba through the Northwest which brought them here in 1874. The **Fort Macleod Museum**, ((403) 553-4703, is built in the fashion of a police post, with log buildings surrounded by a wooden palisade, but it is not a replica of the original Fort Macleod. The log buildings contain displays on the way of life of the Mounties, of the province's pioneers, and of the native Indians. Throughout July and August there are Royal Canadian Mounted Police musical parades performed four times daily. The **town center** is itself worth a visit as it contains many old buildings and has been declared a provincial Historical Area.

The luridly-named **Head-Smashed-In Buffalo Jump** lies 153 km (95 miles) south of Calgary and 16 km (10 miles) west of Fort Macleod along Highway 2 and Secondary Highway 785. For over 5,000 years Indians stampeded herds of buffalo to their deaths over the edge of this steep cliff. These hunts were an important part of the Indian culture, involving hundreds of men, precision planning, and religious rituals. The hunt would provide the Indians with everything they needed: food, hides, and bone. Archaeological digs at the foot of the cliff have uncovered bones, village-sites, and Indian artifacts. In 1987 a multi-million-dollar **Interpretive Centre** opened here which describes the culture of the Plains Indians and the business of the hunt itself through films, displays, and guided tours of the site. The Centre is open daily throughout the year. Telephone (403) 553-2731 for details.

A one-and-a-half-hour drive northeast of Calgary will bring you to the strange, lunar-like landscape of the **Red Deer River Valley Badlands**, characterized by gullies and columns of rock known as **hoodoos**. This area was once a sub-tropical marshland where dinosaurs roamed, and there have been many discoveries of fossils and skeletons in the area. Located in this strange valley is the small city of **Drumheller**. The **Drumheller Dinosaur and Fossil Museum**, 335 First Street East, ((403) 823-2593, has displays on the geology of the valley and dinosaur re-

mains, including that of the nine-meter (30-ft) long Edmontosaurus. There is a Tourist Information Centre at the museum.

Drumheller is the starting point of the **Dinosaur Trail**, a 48-km (30-mile) circular driving route taking you to various places of interest in the area and offering some good views of the badlands. Along the trail, six kilometers (four miles) northwest of Drumheller, the **Royal Tyrrell Museum of Palaeontology**, ((403) 823-7707, offers a fascinating account of evolution. The building itself blends perfectly with the surrounding landscape, and it contains an extensive fossil collection. It has the largest display of dinosaurs in the world, some of which are careful reconstructions, some of which are fossils, and there's a garden of plants that are closely related to those that grew here in the age of the dinosaurs.

OPPOSITE: "Old-timers" in Heritage Park's turn-of-the-century village. ABOVE: This old-timer is at home in the Royal Tyrrell Museum of Paleontology near Drumheller.

Computers, videos, and hands-on displays help you understand the process of evolution.

Those who have caught the dinosaur bug may want to extend their journey to the **Dinsoaur Provincial Park**, 140 km (87 miles) southeast of Drumheller, an area of the Red Deer Valley badlands that has been declared a UNESCO World Heritage site. It is one of the most extensive dinosaur graveyards in the world and throughout the park skeletons are on view exactly in the position that they were discovered. In the park you can visit the **Field Station** where you can see the

1989 Stanley Cup, the Calgary Flames, play at home in the splendid Olympic Saddledome at Stampede Park, ((403) 261-0455. The Saddledome is also home to the 88's, Calgary's **basketball** team. The Grandstand in Stampede Park is the scene of **harness and thoroughbred horse racing**, ((403) 261-0214, and there are international **show jumping** trials and other equestrian events held at Spruce Meadows, southwest of the city, ((403) 254-3200. You can watch **stock car racing**, **drag racing**, and **motorcycle racing** at the Race City Speedway, 114th Avenue and

palaeontologists working on finds. There's an interpretive display here, and it is also the starting point for a bus tour of the park and guided walks. Open daily from Victoria Day to Labor Day and from Wednesday to Sunday during the rest of the year. To reach the park from Drumheller, take Route 56 to Brooks then Highway 873 and follow the signs.

Sports

The Calgary Stampeders are contenders in the Canadian **Football** League championships and can be seen in action at the McMahon Stadium from June to November, ((403) 284-1111. **Hockey** enthusiasts can see the winners of the National Hockey League's

68th Street S.E. ((403/251-6955 for recorded message).

There are **cycling**, **hiking**, and **jogging** trails in the pleasant Prince's Island Park, which is accessible by footbridge from downtown, and also at Fish Creek Provincial Park at Calgary's southern border. The Glenmore Reservoir, situated southwest of downtown by Heritage Park, is a pleasant spot for **boating**. The Bow and Elbow Rivers are popular for **canoeing**, particularly at Bowness Park at 48th and 90th Street N.W. There's world-class fly fishing and trout fishing in the section of the Bow River between Carseland and east Calgary, and lists of the many places that offer float fishing trips are available from Information Centres. The Bow and Elbow Rivers are too cold for **swimming**, but you can take a dip at Fish Creek Provincial Park at the southern end of the city and also at the various leisure centers. The closest to downtown is the Lindsay Park Sports Centre, 2225 Macleod Trail S.W., ((403) 233-8619.

Golf players are well catered for with six city-run courses and a number of private clubs that visitors can use. The closest public course to downtown is the 18-hole McCall Lake, 1600 32nd Avenue N.E., ((403) 250-5677, and the nearest private one is probably the Inglewood course, ((403) 272-3949, close to the Inglewood Bird Sanctuary at 9th Avenue S.E. There are **tennis** courts throughout the city, both private and public, and there are **squash** as well as **racquetball** courts in the city's leisure centers.

The Fish Creek Riding Stables in Fish Creek Park, ((403) 251-6955, give riding lessons and also operate guided or unguided trail rides. If **kart racing** appeals you should go to the Kart Gardens International, 9555 Barlow Trail N.E., ((403) 250-9555, just north of the airport where there are a variety of tracks to choose from. Open April to October daily, and on warm weekends only during winter.

In winter there's **skating** on the lagoon at Bowness Park, 48th Avenue and 90th Street N.W., also at Fish Creek Provincial Park, and all year round in the covered speedskating track at the Olympic Speed Skating Oval at the University of Calgary, ((403) 220-7890, which is open for public use. The downhill **ski** slopes at the Olympic Park are open to the public, and there's cross-country skiing at Fish Creek Provincial Park.

Shopping

As is the trend with modern cities, Calgary tends towards shopping malls that are linked to various facilities, partly by the "Plus 15" system of protected walkways. Although this all makes for a somewhat characterless shopping scene, it provides welcome protection from the bitter cold of the winters. Furs and cowboy gear are Calgary's specialties.

The central section of 8th Avenue is a pleasant pedestrianized shopping mall with a variety of shops, including a few

department stores and eateries. There is also quite a smart shopping area along 17th Avenue between 5th and 9th Streets S.W., with boutiques, cafes, specialty shops, and the **Mount Royal Village Shopping Center**, which has some upmarket fashion shops, antiques shops and galleries.

Nightlife

For entertainment listings you should check the local daily and weekly newspapers. Several large hotels have nightclubs, and offer quite a variety of entertainments.

Calgary's cultural life centers around the **Centre for the Performing Arts** at 205 8th Avenue S.E., ((403) 294-7444 for information and (403) 266-8888 for tickets. This excellent arts complex comprises the Jack Singer Concert Hall, which is home to the Calgary Philharmonic Orchestra, the Max Bell Theatre, the Martha Cohen Theatre, and the One Yellow Rabbit Theatre. The Southern Alberta Opera Association and the Alberta Ballet Company are some of the companies that perform at the **Jubilee Auditorium**, 14th Avenue and 14th Street N.W. The

OPPOSITE: The race track in Stampede Park. ABOVE: The center of Old Calgary remains the quiet eye of the building storm that hit the city in the sixties.

Pumphouse Theatre, 2140 9th Avenue S.W., ((403) 263-0079, has a program that features a variety of theatrical companies.

For jazz music go to **Marty's Cafe** on 17th Avenue S.W., and for Country & Western there's **Ranchman's Steak House**, 9615 Macleod Trail S., ((403) 253-1100, where there's also beer swilling and dancing. There's a section of 11th Avenue known as **Electric Avenue** that consists of a stretch of bars, clubs and pubs, or there's the less noisy and older neighborhood of **Kensington** centered around Kensington Road and 10th

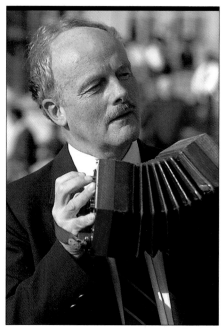

Street N.W. — a good area for pubs, bars, restaurants, and nightlife.

WHERE TO STAY

Luxury

Downtown, **The Palliser Hotel** at 133 9th Avenue S.W., Calgary T2P 2M3, ((403) 262-1234, toll-free (800) 268-9411, was built by the C.P.R. in 1914, and is situated over the station. With its pillars, stately staircases, and crystal chandeliers, it remains an oasis of old-fashioned splendor in a city of high-rises. It has 405 rooms and suites, with just about every comfort provided for. There are excercise facilities, a splendid dining room, a cafe, and a lovely bar. For a more modern

kind of elegance there's the centrally located **Skyline Plaza Hotel** at 110 9th Avenue S.E., Calgary T2G 5A6, ((403) 266-7331, toll-free (800) 648-7200, which is within the Convention Centre complex. Part of an excellent hotel chain, it is luxurious without being brash, and the service echoes this quality with its understated excellence. There are 386 rooms and suites with all kinds of special features, an indoor pool and garden, two dining rooms, a lounge, and a bar with live entertainment.

Also downtown, the **Westin Hotel**, 320 4th Avenue S.W., Calgary T2P 2S6, ((403) 266-1611, toll-free (800) 228-3000, offers modern luxury with 525 attractive bedrooms and suites, and lots of nice complimentary touches. The lobby is large and sumptuously decorated, there is a beautiful indoor swimming pool, and the hotel has several dining spots including the city's famous Owl's Nest restaurant. The **Delta Bow**, 209 4th Avenue S.E., Calgary T2G 0C6, ((403) 266-1980, toll-free (800) 268-1133, is another large top-rated downtown hotel which has 398 rooms, exercise facilities, and a restaurant. The **International Hotel**, 220 4th Avenue S.W., Calgary T2P 0H5, ((403) 265-9600, toll-free (800) 661-8627, is a modern high-rise that oozes luxury. It has 247 attractive suites. All have balconies and are extremely comfortable. It also has a health spa, a gym, a restaurant, and a piano bar.

Mid-range

The **Sandman Hotel**, 888 7th Avenue S.W., Calgary T2P 3J3, ((403) 237-8626, toll-free (800) 663-6900, is centrally situated and offers an excellent range of facilities. It has 300 attractively furnished rooms, some with good views, with all kinds of comforts and conveniences. There is a fitness center, a glass-roofed swimming pool, and a lovely restaurant. The **Prince Royal Inn All Suite Hotel**, downtown at 618 5th Avenue S.W., Calgary T2P 0M7, ((403) 263-0520, toll-free (800) 661-1592, has 300 accommodations, some of which are one- or two-bedroomed suites, and all with kitchens, making it good value for families. The hotel has a laundry, a health club, a swimming pool, and a dining room. Complimentary continental breakfasts are served.

The **Hotel Calgary Plaza**, 708 8th Avenue S.W., Calgary T2P 1H2, ℓ (403) 263-7600, toll-free (800) 661-8684, is in the town center and has 200 large and pleasant rooms, including some that are set aside for female travelers. It has an attractive garden terrace, outdoor swimming pool, two restaurants, and a cocktail lounge.

In southwest Calgary there's a **Best Western Hospitality Inn** at 135 Southland Drive S.E., Calgary T2J 5X5, ℓ (403) 278-5050, toll-free (800) 528-1234, which has rooms and suites, some with mini-bars. There's an indoor pool, a pleasant sheltered courtyard, a tavern, three restaurants, and three lounges.

Conveniently placed for the airport is the **Marlborough Inn & Convention Center** at 1316 33rd Street N.E., Calgary T2A 6B6, ℓ (403) 248-8888, toll-free (800) 661-1464. It has 250 accommodations with some floors geared to business travelers. Facilities are good, and there are squash and racquetball courts. It has a nightclub called Jimmy Dean's where you can enjoy some 1950's and '60's music.

Inexpensive

Downtown is the **Lord Nelson Inn**, 1020 8th Avenue S.W., Calgary T2P 1J3, ℓ (403) 269-8262, with 55 rooms and suites that have bathrooms, refrigerators, TVs, and telephones. There are also some bridal and executive suites. The hotel has a warm and attractive lobby, a dining room, and a pub. The **York Hotel**, 636 Centre Street South, Calgary T2G 2C7, ℓ (403) 262-5581, is also among the few hotels offering good low-price accommodation downtown. Rooms are reasonably-sized, comfortable, clean, with bathrooms and TVs, and there is a dining room and lounge.

Near downtown in southeast Calgary, the **Elbow River Inn & Casino**, 2720 Glenmore Trail S.E., Calgary T2G 4S1, ℓ (403) 269-6771, toll-free (800) 661-1463, sits on the banks of the Elbow River and is connected by an underpass walkway to Stampede Park. All its rooms have bathrooms, some have kitchenettes, and there is a dining room with pleasant riverfront views.

There is a cluster of motels along Macleod Trail which runs through the southwest of the city. Among them is the **Stanley Park**

Inn, 4206 Macleod Trail South, Calgary T2G 2R7, ℓ (403) 287-2700, toll-free (800) 661-1889, which is conveniently near an L.R.T. station and offers comfort in pleasant surroundings. All rooms are equipped with telephones and TV, and room service is available. There's also a restaurant and an indoor swimming pool. The **Flamingo Motor Hotel**, 7505 Macleod Trail South, Calgary T2H 0L8, ℓ (403) 252-4401, is set in pleasant grounds and has 60 good-sized rooms and suites with bathrooms, some with kitchenettes. The **Stampeder Inn** at

3828 Macleod Trail S.W., Calgary T2G 2R2, ℓ (403) 243-5531, has nicely appointed rooms and suites, meeting facilities, shops, a pub, cocktail bar, and a dining room that lays on an excellent buffet.

In northwest Calgary there is another motel strip along Banff Trail, near the point where Crowchild Trail crosses the Trans-Canada Highway. Along this strip, the **Sun Bow Inn**, 2359 Banff Trail N.W., Calgary T2M 4L2, ℓ (403) 289-1973, has one of the best ranges of facilities. The suites and rooms have telephones and TVs, and there is a poolside dining room as well as a cocktail lounge.

OPPOSITE: A street musician entertains.
ABOVE: Calgary's skyline and "saddleline".

Calgary has a very nice **YWCA** at 320 5th Avenue S.E., Calgary, T2G 0E5, ((403) 263-1550, which offers accommodation for women and their children. There's also a dining room, and lots of sports facilities. The **University of Calgary** has some good accommodation during the summer months, and also a few rooms available during term-time. For details contact the university at 2500 University Drive N.W., Calgary T2N 1N4, ((403) 220-3210.

For guest ranch accommodation in the area contact **Homeplace Guest Ranch & Trail Trips**, Mac Makenny, Box 6, Site 2, R.R. 1, Nanton, Alberta T0L 1W0, ((403) 931-3245. Rooms come with private bathrooms, family meals are provided, riding lessons and trips are organized, and horse pack trips up into the Rockies with tepee accommodation are also available.

WHERE TO EAT

Moderate

La Chaumière at 121 7th Avenue S.E., ((403) 228-5690, offers traditional French cuisine prepared to gourmet standards and excellent service in a charming, intimate setting. The **Owl's Nest** in the Westin Hotel, 320 4th Avenue S.W., ((403) 267-2823, is one of Calgary's best-known and finest dining spots. It is a splendidly decorated place serving European food, with some of the region's excellent beef featuring largely on the menu. **Traders** is another well-known hotel restaurant. It is at the Skyline Plaza Hotel, 110 9th Avenue S.W., ((403) 266-7331, and serves gourmet food in a distinguished wood-panelled setting.

Sky's Rôtisserie and Wine Bar, situated at the foot of the Calgary Tower, 9th Avenue at Centre Street, ((403) 266-7177, is a modern, glassy bistro where the dishes are prepared in a nouvelle way — but served in large portions. Some wonderfully inventive dishes feature on the menu; try the delicious chicken and duck cooked over an oak fire rotisserie. The innovation also extends to the irresistible dessert menu. The **Three Greenhorns**, 505 4th Avenue S.W., ((403) 264-6903, has adopted a nautical look that gives a below-deck coziness to the surroundings. The food is of a very high standard, with steak and seafood forming the basis of the menu.

The Green Street Cafe, 815 7th Avenue, S.W., ((403) 266-1551, is a popular downtown spot, with a glass wall affording good views of the nearby park. The surrounding greenery, a restful color scheme, and the spaciousness make for a very relaxing atmosphere. There are Cajun, French, and Italian dishes, steaks and seafood — in short a bit of everything — on offer. Prices here range between moderate and inexpensive.

Inexpensive

4th Street Rose at 2116 4th Street S.W., ((403) 228-5377, is a trendy place where you can get very good pizzas, salads, pasta, and snacky foods. There are several other eateries around this section of 4th Street. Along 17th Avenue S.W. you'll find another such cluster of restaurants, among which is the **Greek Village**, 1212 17th Avenue S.W., ((403) 244-1144, an attractive restaurant that serves traditional Greek food.

Hearty is the word that springs to mind when describing **Franzi's Gasthaus** at 2417 4th Street S.W., ((403) 228-6882. It brings a little bit of Germany to the town, with costumed waitresses and musicians, a variety of beers, and large helpings of good German fare. The **Unicorn Pub** at 304 8th Avenue S.W., ((403) 233-2666, is a busy but snug place that serves traditional pub grub. Over in the Kensington neighborhood the **Take Ten Cafe**, 304 10th Street, ((403) 270-7010, has German food and lots of home baking on the menu, and near Prince's Island The Cafe 1886 serves all kinds of omelettes for breakfast and lunch.

Calgary's small **Chinatown** is located at the downtown end of the Centre Street Bridge and has plenty of Chinese restaurants to choose from, some of which serve dim sum.

HOW TO GET THERE

The Calgary International Airport, ((403) 292-8477, is about 15 km (nine miles) northeast of downtown and is served by many

OPPOSITE: A Plains Indian in full regalia.
OVERLEAF: Telephone poles march single-file across the prairies of eastern Alberta.

international airlines as well as regional carriers operating a local service. Canadian Airlines International runs a frequent Air-bus service between Calgary and Edmonton. To get you to the town there's the Air-porter Bus (℃ 403/291-3848) which runs every 20 minutes from the airport to some of the main downtown hotels.

The VIA Rail station is located under the Calgary Tower, ℃ toll-free (800) 665-8630, and the transcontinental service links Vancouver, Banff, Winnipeg, Toronto, and Montreal with Calgary.

Greyhound operates bus services to Calgary from all directions, with frequent services running to and from Edmonton, Vancouver, Banff, and Drumheller. The station is at 850 16th Street S.W., ℃ (403) 265-9111.

The Trans-Canada Highway (Highway 1) runs through Calgary, linking it with British Columbia to the west and Saskatchewan to the east. West of Calgary the TCH runs through Banff National Park and through Glacier National Park in British Columbia Highway 2 runs north from the U.S. Montana border to Calgary, continuing north to Edmonton and beyond.

BANFF AND JASPER NATIONAL PARKS

Banff and Jasper National Parks lie deep in the Canadian Rockies along the border with British Columbia, joining to form 17,518 sq km (6,800 sq miles) of some of the most breath-takingly beautiful scenery on earth. In this vast nature preserve, white mountain peaks and glaciers tower over turquoise and emerald lakes, rivers and waterfalls rush through forested valleys, and wild animals run free. This is beauty on such an awesome scale that it almost overwhelms the senses.

Banff National Park, the more famous and popular of the two, is about 113 km (70 miles) west of Calgary along the Trans-Canada Highway. It has two resorts that attract visitors from all around the world: Banff and the smaller Lake Louise, both of which have splendid castle-like hotels built by the Canadian National Railway and superbly located. The town of Banff is the park's main center for entertainment, accommodation, and restaurants, and is also the starting point for tours and trails into the park.

Banff's counterpart in Jasper National Park is the town of Jasper, 292 km (181 miles) north of Banff and 362 km (225 miles) from Edmonton along the Yellowhead Highway. The two towns are linked by the Icefields Parkway, a 233-km (144-mile) stretch of road between Lake Louise and Jasper town which is one of the world's most scenic drives. Although it is possible to complete this journey in four hours, you should really set aside at least a whole day for it, to allow for sightseeing along the way and for the stops you may have to make because of animals wandering into the road.

In July and August it gets extremely busy, especially in Banff, and some believe the best time to visit is in the spring or fall when the towns and roads are emptier. Jasper Park is generally quieter than Banff and is consequently a better spot for animal watching. Both parks present a wealth of opportunities for outdoor enthusiasts, with trails to be walked, mountains to be climbed, lakes or rivers to be fished and sailed, and in the winter a thick coat of snow turns it all into a skiers' paradise. Here in the mountains the temperature varies quite a lot, and the higher you are, the colder it is, making warm clothes an essential part of holiday luggage, even in July.

ABOVE: Wintry landscape at Lake Louise.
OPPOSITE: Moraine Lake, a few kilometers east of Lake Louise.

The population of the two parks is around 8,000, but that's just people. Other inhabitants include moose, black and grizzly bears, bighorn sheep, mountain goats, and chipmunks, to name but a few. Throughout your visit you will be constantly reminded not to feed the animals, both for their good and for your own, and to keep your distance. Some of these animals are wild and, despite their apparent ease around people, they retain the unpredictability of the wild. To drive the message home, the park authorities have imposed

area, and in 1888 the C.P.R. opened the magnificent Banff Springs Hotel, a summer resort that was the last word in luxury. A beautiful golf course was laid, trips and expeditions were organized for its guests, and every whim was catered for. People came from far and wide, the town developed, the boundaries of the park were expanded and its name was changed to Banff National Park. Today it covers an area of 6,640 sq km (2,600 sq miles).

Jasper National Park, the larger of the two parks, developed later than Banff. In the

heavy fines on those caught feeding or touching the animals.

BACKGROUND

Banff was the first national park to be established in Canada. The area had been explored in 1841 by the governor of the Hudson's Bay Company, but it was in the 1880's with the coming of the Canadian Pacific Railway that word of the area's great beauty began to spread. During the laying of the tracks three workers discovered some hot sulphur springs, and as soon as word of them got out, visitors began to arrive. In 1885 the government created the Rocky Mountain Park around the springs to preserve the

early nineteenth century the Athabasca River and Pass were part of the overland fur trading route, and at one time a trading post existed not far away from the present town of Jasper. Apart from these traders and some gold prospectors on their way to the Cariboo, the area was unvisited until the national park was created in preparation for the transcontinental railway that was to cross the Rockies at Yellowhead Pass. The railway brought with it visitors, and the opening of the Icefields Parkway in 1940 made Jasper Park even more accessible. Although Jasper is today a major tourist attraction, it remains quieter and wilder than its older neighbor, although equally well served by road and rail.

GENERAL INFORMATION

The Park Information Centres are a vital source of information for visitors to either park. They carry maps, pamphlets, and brochures, which include details of the various trips and trails throughout the area. They also give valuable advice on how to protect yourself against attack from animals, on weather conditions, and on basic survival tactics.

For information specifically on Banff,

to sign in at the Centre if you're planning an overnight hike in the park. For information on accommodation and restaurants contact the Jasper National Park Chamber of Commerce, Box 98, 632 Connaught Drive, Jasper T0E 1E0, ((403) 852-3858.

WHAT TO SEE AND DO

Sights
BANFF

Sixteen kilometers (10 miles) beyond the park gates, the town of Banff lies in the Bow

you can contact the Superintendent, Banff National Park, Box 900, Banff T0L 0C0, ((403) 762-3324, or Banff Park Information Centre at 224 Banff Avenue, ((403) 762-4256. For information on accommodation and restaurants in the park, contact the Banff/Lake Louise Chamber of Commerce, Box 1298, 93 Banff Avenue, Banff T0L 0C0, ((403) 762-3777. If you're planning on an overnight hiking trip, you must sign in at the Information Centre.

Over in Jasper, the Visitor Information Centre is at 500 Connaught Drive, ((403) 852-4401; information is also available from the Superintendent, Jasper National Park, Box 10, 632 Patricia Street, Jasper T0E 1E0, ((403) 852-6161. As in Banff, it is necessary

River valley, nestling close to the base of Cascade Mountain and shadowed by snowy peaks on all sides. It is the hub of the Banff National Park and Canada's favorite year-round resort. You'll find everything you need here. It is the starting point for scores of trips, some on horseback, some in the bicycle saddle, some on coaches, and others tailored for other outdoor pursuits. There are all kinds of walking trails to places that cars cannot reach, and the most timorous and the most intrepid of hikers will find something to suit them. But unless you are prepared to hike long distances, you will

OPPOSITE: The Num-ti-Jah Lodge in Banff National Park. ABOVE: The elegant Banff Springs Hotel.

require transport to take you at least part of the way to many of the top attractions.

The town is small, however, and during the peak season of July and August it gets jam-packed, parking becomes a problem, and it can get quite claustrophobic — especially along Banff Avenue, the town's busy main street lined with shops and restaurants.

A Victorian wooden building houses the **Banff Park Museum**, 93 Banff Avenue, ((403) 762-3324, where you can see old-fashioned displays of stuffed animals and birds from the park: the only place where you can

work. The **Whyte Museum of the Canadian Rockies** at 111 Bear Street, ((403) 762-2291, has a gallery devoted to paintings and sculptures of the mountains. It also houses the Banff Library, archival material, and some historical log cabins. Tea is served on weekend afternoons at the fireside. The museum is open daily from mid-May to mid-October, and is closed on Mondays and on Thursday mornings during the rest of the year.

Banff's cultural life revolves around the **Banff Centre**, which is near downtown at St. Julien Road, ((403) 762-6300. It is one of the

study some of them at close quarters. There is also a reference library where you can read up on the area. A little further along the road, the **Natural History Museum**, 112 Banff Avenue, ((403) 762-4747, deals with the geological formation of the Rockies and the early life forms that inhabited them. There are audio-visual displays, exhibits on dinosaurs, and a model of the Sasquatch, the Rockies' version of the abominable snowman. Open daily.

At the southern end of the town close to the Bow River, a fortified log building houses the **Luxton Museum**, 1 Birch Avenue, ((403) 762-2388, where there are displays on the various Indian tribes of Alberta, featuring photographs, clothing, and craft-

top North American schools for the arts, where theatre, dance, writing, music, and the visual arts are taught. Throughout the year it serves as an entertainments center and from June to August it is the setting for the **Banff Festival of the Arts**, a lively and varied arts program presented by both students and professionals.

South of downtown along Cave Avenue you can see the original hot sulphur spring that first brought tourism to the area. The **Cave and Basin Hot Springs** were discovered by railway workers in 1883 and the spa building that surrounds them has been rebuilt in the original 1914 style. Here at the **Cave and Basin Centennial Centre**, ((403) 762-4900, you can relax in the pool or visit the interpretive center that details the history of the area. It is open daily throughout the year and the pool is open from mid-June to Labor Day. For even warmer spring water (about 40°C), go to the **Upper Hot Springs Pool** outside the town at the top of Mountain Avenue, ((403) 762-2056. Here visitors can enjoy a dip in the outdoor pool and soak up the glorious mountain views.

About four kilometers (two and a half miles) south of the town and next to the Upper Hot Springs, the **Sulphur Mountain Gondola Lift** will take you 2286 m (7500 ft)

For some bird's-eye views of the area you can take the gondola lift up **Mount Norquay** which is a short drive north of the town, or you can travel 23 km (14 miles) south of town along the Trans-Canada Highway and Sunshine Road to take a gondola up to **Sunshine Village**. This resort lies at an altitude of 2,215 m (7,267 ft) and has hiking trails that lead through alpine meadows. The other mountains around the town also have hiking trails, and one of the more gentle climbs close to downtown is up **Tunnel Mountain** along the Tunnel Mountain Road, where

to the top of Sulphur Mountain. Once at the top you can feast your eyes on the wonderful views from an observation deck, enjoy a repast at the Summit Restaurant, or follow one of several hiking trails.

Following the discovery of the springs, the C.P.R. built the **Banff Springs Hotel**, a magnificently-located tourist resort close to the springs. So great was its success that in 1910 the hotel was rebuilt to accommodate the growing number of visitors, and a majestic Scottish baronial-style structure emerged from the pine-covered slopes. If you're not staying at Banff Springs during your visit, you should at least make sure to have a meal there so you can take a look around it and admire the beautiful setting.

you can see the strange column-like rock formations known as **hoodoos**.

For a different angle on the landscape take a trip to **Lake Minnewanka** 11 km (seven miles) west of the town where you can take a two-hour cruise across the waters or take advantage of the excellent trout fishing. Nearby, **Two-Jack Lake** is a popular spot for rowing and canoeing.

Northwest of Banff, 28 km (17 miles) along Highway 1A, there's a lovely one and a half hour hiking trail leading from **Johnston Canyon** that takes you by waterfalls and pools. If you feel a little more adventurous you can extend the hike by a couple of miles

OPPOSITE: Downtown Banff. ABOVE: The view from the Château Lake Louise.

into a lovely meadow where there are some deep-colored underground springs known as the Ink Pots.

LAKE LOUISE

Just off the Trans-Canada Highway, 56 km (35 miles) northwest of Banff, lies this exquisitely beautiful emerald-green lake surrounded by mountains and dominated by the magnificent Victoria Glacier. At the lakeside stands another palatial railway hotel, the **Château Lake Louise**, that was built in 1924. The **Lake Louise Gondola** takes you

THE ICEFIELDS PARKWAY

This highway linking Lake Louise with Banff is one of the most beautiful drives anywhere, offering those who travel it a spectacular overview of the two national parks. It follows the continental divide along a route lined with glaciers, lakes, valleys, and mountains, where wildlife roams — sometimes into the middle of the road, so you must beware. You should set aside at least a day for traveling the Parkway to allow time for stopping and enjoying the views.

up Mount Whitehorn for another perspective on this wonderful scene. There are trails around the lake, some leading to neighboring lakes, and there are a couple of teahouses open during the summer. Supplies and other accommodation can be found nearby at Lake Louise Village.

Over the other side of the Trans-Canada Highway, 13 km (eight miles) east of Lake Louise, lies Moraine Lake, another beautiful and improbably-colored lake that is surrounded by the Wenkchemna Peaks or Ten Peaks and makes an idyllic spot for canoeing or hiking.

Some 16 km (10 miles) north of Lake Louise along the Parkway you'll see the bright waters of **Hector Lake** fringed by dark green forest. Eighteen kilometers (11 miles) further along the road, the glacial waters of **Bow Lake** reflect the surrounding peaks, and a few miles beyond a trail leads to **Peyto Lake** where the waters change from green to blue as the year advances — a phenomenon caused by the presence of glacial silt. Other sights along the way include the **Mistaya Canyon** and the **Weeping Wall**, where melting snow streams down the cliff face at the bottom of Cirrus Mountain.

At the **Sunwapta Pass**, 122 km (76 miles) north of Lake Louise and 108 km (67 miles) south of Jasper town, you enter Jasper

ABOVE: Athabasca Glacier in Banff National Park. OPPOSITE: Maligne Lake in Jasper National Park.

National Park. This is the edge of the huge **Columbia Icefield**, an area of glaciers and snow that covers 310 sq km (120 sq miles) of the Canadian Rockies. An Interpretive Centre here has a scale model of the icefield and shows a short film about it. Close by, the toe of the **Athabasca Glacier** stops just short of the Parkway, so close in fact that you can wander up to its edge. Between May and late September snowcoach tours will take you right out on to the glacier for a closer look. They operate from the Interpretive Centre, ((403) 762-6736, toll-free (800) 661-1152. Guided icewalk tours of the glacier will safely shepherd you over the surface, away from the deep and treacherous crevasses that thread through the ice.

Continuing towards Jasper, there are two spectacular waterfalls to be seen. The first is the **Sunwapta Falls** 175 km (108 miles) north of Lake Louise and 55 km (34 miles) south of Jasper, which is reached via a short access road off the Parkway, and further along the Parkway there's access to the **Athabasca Falls** where the river rushes over a ledge and down into a narrow gorge.

JASPER

The town of Jasper sits in a broad valley at the point where the Icefields Parkway crosses the Yellowhead Highway. It is smaller than Banff, less spectacular in its setting, but quieter and considerably less congested during the summer season. The main street is Connaught Drive and along it stands the C.N.R. railroad station that links the town with Edmonton to the east and Vancouver to the west. The town is the starting point for many excellent hiking trails, riding treks, rafting tours, and various other excursions into the beautiful wilderness beyond that teems with wildlife.

One of the most popular features of the park is the **Jasper Tramway**, seven kilometers (four miles) south of Jasper, which whizzes you up **Whistlers Mountain** for panoramic views of the icefield and of **Mount Robson** — the highest mountain in the Canadian Rockies. At the top terminal you'll find a restaurant, a cafe, an interpretive center, and hiking trails that lead up to the very top of the mountain. Once at the top you may discover for yourself the reason for

the name of the mountain when you hear the whistling noises made by the little animals there, known as hoary marmots. The tramway operates from mid-April to early October.

There are several lakes within easy reach of the town that make lovely spots for outdoor sports and general relaxation. Just seven kilometers (four miles) northwest of town at Pyramid Lake Road, the **Patricia** and **Pyramid Lakes** make fine places to picnic, boat, or canoe, and three kilometers (two miles) east of town at Lodge Road **Lake**

Edith and **Lake Annette** both have beaches and trails. Closer still to town is **Lake Beauvert**, where the famous **Jasper Park Lodge** spreads out along the shore, offering some of the area's best accommodation and catering for all kinds of activities.

To the east of the town lies **Maligne Valley**, which is reached by the Yellowhead Highway and then Maligne Valley Road. The first sight it has to offer is **Maligne Canyon**, which is about 10 km (six miles) outside Jasper. The water has worn away the limestone to create this deep, but in parts very narrow, slash across the landscape which can be explored by means of paths and bridges. Fourteen kilometers (nine miles) further along Maligne Road lies the

beautiful and mysterious **Medicine Lake**, where the water level changes throughout the year, causing it virtually to disappear during the autumn, although water is seen to enter continually. The reason behind this phenomenon is that the water constantly seeps away through holes in the bedrock, but during summer the water level is maintained because melting snow increases the amount of water entering the lake.

The crowning glory of this valley trip — some might say of the entire tour of the parks — is **Maligne Lake**, which lies a further 21 km (13 miles) along Maligne Road. This delightful lake stretches a length of 22 km (14 miles) and the amount of Kodak film that

has been shot here would probably cover that distance several times over. Snow-capped mountains rise up from the deep blue glacial waters, and at its center lies the magical **Spirit Island**, a tiny island crowned with trees. A boat trip will take you along the lake and to Spirit Island between mid-May and the end of September. Rowing boats, canoes, and fishing tackle can be rented here, and it makes a lovely place for horse riding. There are hiking trails all around and in winter it draws cross-country skiers.

For a relaxing treat, maybe after a hard day's hiking, visit the **Miette Hot Springs** which lie 60 km (37 miles) northeast of the town off Highway 16. The springs are the hottest in these mountains, and their soothing properties can be enjoyed in outdoor

Skiers at Lake Louise.

Sports

Both Banff and Jasper Parks have a wealth of **hiking** trails of all lengths. Some are little more than short walks, while others are wilderness expeditions that take several days to complete. The Canadian Parks Service produces two brochures detailing the trails, and copies of these can be picked up from the Information Centres. If you're planning an overnight hike into the back country you will need to get a permit from either an Information Centre or a park warden, but it is free of charge. There are also numerous **cycling** trails which must be strictly adhered to. A few companies operate cycling tours, and there's no problem renting bikes in either town. Several companies offer **heli-hiking**, which involves a helicopter trip out to remote spots high on the mountaintops or on to glaciers for some extra-special hiking. If you intend to do a spot of **fishing**, and there certainly are some ideal opportunities in both parks, you must get a national park fishing license, which can be bought either from an Information Centre or an outfitter. Several places run fishing trips and rent out tackle.

Rivers throughout both parks offer opportunities for **whitewater rafting** and Information Centres can supply you with lists of the companies who operate guided trips. If you're interested in **boating** or **canoeing**, there are many beautiful lakes to choose from, most of which have places that rent out a variety of vessels, including **motorboats**, which are allowed on most lakes.

Horse riders or would-be horse riders have a choice of many treks of all lengths and designed for all abilities. There are several stables in both parks, including one at the Banff Springs Hotel and another at the Jasper Park Lodge. The Information Centres have details of where the stables are and what they have to offer.

At Banff, **golf** enthusiasts have a special treat in store at the Banff Springs Hotel, where the old 18-hole course and a new nine-hole course are set against some of the world's most spectacular scenery, with a smart new clubhouse. Although primarily for guests at the hotel, it is open to the public. Telephone (403) 762-6801 to book. In Jasper

pools that are set against a stunning alpine backdrop. The pools are open to the public from mid-May until Labor Day.

To the south of the town **Mount Edith Cavell** looms magnificently. For a closer look, take a 30 km (18 miles) trip south of Jasper along Highway 93A, turning onto an access road which will bring you to the foot of the mountain. It was named in honor of the heroic British nurse shot by the Germans in 1915 for helping Allied soldiers, and such a majestic sight makes a fitting memorial. A trail will take you to **Angel Glacier**, a wing-shaped tongue of ice that clings to the north-eastern slopes of the mountain. There's another path that will take you into the alpine meadows, and further back along the access road a trail leads to **Cavell Lake**.

Park, the Jasper Park Lodge has an excellent 18-hole course which is open to the public. To make a reservation or to find out more about it telephone (403) 852-3301 or 852-6090.

During the winter there's excellent **skiing** throughout the parks. Particularly good places in Banff include the slopes of Mount Norquay only five kilometers (three miles) away from town, the well-equipped Sunshine Village Resort west of the town, and around Lake Louise. In Jasper Park there's excellent skiing at Marmot Basin near the town. Here there are slopes to suit beginners and experts, and cross-country trails sweep through the stunning scenery surrounding Maligne Lake. Jasper Park Lodge offers good skiing packages.

Nightlife

At the **Banff Centre** at St Julien Road, you'll usually find there's a play, a concert, or a film on, and between June and August it's the venue for the Banff Festival of Arts, when a program of theatre, music, and dance is presented by students and professionals (ring 403/762-6300 for information). There are several busy bars in Banff, mostly around Banff Avenue, some in the hotels, and several have live musical entertainment.

Jasper doesn't exactly have a vibrant nightlife. What drinking and dancing goes on there tends to take place in the hotel lounges, sometimes to the accompaniment of live music.

WHERE TO STAY

For Bed & Breakfast accommodation in the Banff, Lake Louise, and Jasper areas you should contact the Bed & Breakfast Bureau, P.O. Box 369, Banff T0L 0C0, ((403) 762-5070. The area has plenty of camping grounds, details of which you'll find in the camping brochure produced by the Alberta Tourist Authority, available from Information Centres. There is a privately-run room reservation service for the Banff and Jasper areas that charges fees. For details contact Jasper Experience, P.O. Box 1570, Jasper T0E 1E0, ((403) 852-5656 and 852-4242.

Banff and Environs

The most delightful accommodation in the area is at the **Banff Springs Hotel** on Spray Avenue, P.O. Box 960, Banff T0L 0C0, ((403) 762-2211, toll-free (800) 268-9411, a splendid château overlooking the Spray Valley and surrounded by towering peaks. It was here in 1882 that the Canadian Pacific Railway built the first resort hotel, to encourage tourism in the area. It was so popular that it had to be replaced by this larger structure, which was completed in 1928 with no expense spared. It remains a resort with riding stables, skiing and fishing packages available, almost every kind of sports facility, including one of the most spectacular golf courses anywhere. There are 841 beautiful rooms and suites, three dining rooms, a library, shops, and services. Now that it is open all year round, it makes a particularly lovely place to spend Christmas. The prices vary between mid-range and expensive.

For luxury in more contemporary surroundings, try the **Banff Park Lodge**, 222 Lynx Street, P.O. Box 2200, Banff T0L 0C0, ((403) 762-4433, toll-free (800) 661-9266. This attractive lodge is just a couple of blocks away from the town's main street, and elegantly decorated throughout, with 210 balconied rooms. There is a sauna, jacuzzi, indoor swimming pool, restaurants, and a lounge. Prices mostly fall within the luxury bracket. **Inns of Banff Park**, 600 Banff Avenue, P.O. Box 1077, Banff T0L 0C0, ((403) 762-4581, toll-free (800) 661-1272, is an attractive resort-style hotel, where the rooms have balconies and lots of luxurious touches. It has an indoor swimming pool, a squash court, a good dining room, and a lovely lounge. The hotel offers special winter skiing packages. Prices vary from inexpensive to the low end of the luxury bracket.

The **Mount Royal Hotel**, 138 Banff Avenue, P.O. Box 550, Banff T0L 0C0, ((403) 762-3331, is a busy and pleasant place with its own health club and spacious and comfortable rooms at mid-range prices. The **Rundle Manor Apartment Hotel**, 348 Marten Street, P.O. Box 1077, Banff T0L 0C0, ((403) 762-5544, toll-free (800) 661-1272, is an attractive stone building which has 24 large units with kitchenettes, including some one- and two-bedroomed suites, all very well-equipped. Prices vary from inexpensive to mid-range, depending on the size of the unit you take. The **Red Carpet Inn**, 425 Banff Avenue, P.O. Box 1800, Banff T0L 0C0, ((403) 762-4184, is a chalet-style building offering good, comfortable accommodation, and the **Swiss Village Lodge**, 600 Banff Avenue, P.O. Box 1077, Banff T0L 0C0, ((403) 762-4581, toll-free (800) 661-1272, has 49 units, some of which are self-catering. The hotel also offers ski packages. Prices vary from inexpensive to mid-range.

For low-budget accommodation there's a **YWCA** at 102 Spray Avenue, Banff T0L 0C0, ((403) 762-3560, which welcomes women, men, couples, and families; the **Banff International Hostel**, three kilometers (two miles) outside downtown on Tunnel Mountain Road, (403) 762-4122, is an attractive building with good facilities and accommodation for 154 people.

Lake Louise

The aptly-named **Château Lake Louise**, Lake Louise T0L 1E0, ((403) 522-3991, is another spectacular railway hotel, overlooking the beautiful emerald waters of the lake and overshadowed by the imposing Victoria Glacier. There are 515 attractive rooms and suites with spectacular views. The hotel boasts a good restaurant, evening entertainment, riding stables, fitness facilities, indoor pools — and there's canoeing on the lake. The **Post Hotel**, P.O. Box 69, Lake Louise T0L 1E0, ((403) 522-3989, toll-free (800) 661-1586, is a lovely alpine-style building with 93 rooms and suites, some of which have lofts or fireplaces while some have self-catering facilities. The hotel has a swimming pool and sauna, a very good dining room, a cocktail lounge, and a tavern. Prices at both hotels vary between mid-range and luxury.

The **Lake Louise Inn**, P.O. Box 209, Lake Louise T0L 1E0, ((403) 522-3791, toll-free (800) 661-9237, is just a short distance from the lake. There are 186 accommodations, including some self-catering apartments, all with beautiful views of the surrounding woods. It has tennis courts, fitness facilites, and swimming pool. Prices here vary between inexpensive and mid-range.

Jasper

Canadian Pacific's **Jasper Park Lodge**, P.O. Box 40, Jasper T0E 1E0, ((403) 852-3301, toll-free (800) 642-3817, sprawls along the pine-clad shores of Lake Beauvert. This famous resort hotel has entertained many celebrities since it opened in 1922, and between the main lodge, cabins, and outbuildings it has 440 accommodations — all with beautiful views, lots of character, sitting rooms, and creature comforts. The lodge has a golf course, tennis courts, stables, a health club, two restaurants, a nightclub, and some good shops. It also offers fishing, boating, and skiing packages. Prices vary according to the type of accommodation and the setting, but there are some that fall within the mid-range and others that are high in the luxury bracket. **Château Jasper**, 96 Geikie Street, P.O. Box 1418, Jasper T0E 1E0, ((403) 852-5644, toll-free (800) 661-9323, is another first-rate hotel. Elegantly furnished throughout, it has 121 rooms and suites, all with large bathrooms and luxury touches. It has an attractive dining room, a rooftop sundeck, a fitness center, and an indoor pool. The prices fall within the luxury bracket.

Lobstick Lodge, close to the center on the corner of Geikie and Juniper Street, P.O. Box 1200, Jasper T0E 1E0, ((403) 852-4431, toll-free (800) 661-9317, has 138 comfortable motel units and lots of home-from-home comforts, making it an ideal choice for families. Prices are mid-range. The **Whistlers Motor Hotel**, 105 Miette Avenue, P.O. Box 250, Jasper T0E 1E0, ((403) 852-3361, toll-free (800) 282-9919, is a busy hotel with 41 nicely furnished rooms and suites, all with bathrooms, televisions, and telephones. It has a sauna, a cocktail lounge, and a dining room, and prices vary between mid-range and inexpensive. The **Jasper Inn**, 89 Geikie Street, P.O. Box 879, Jasper T0E 1E0, ((403) 852-4461, toll-free (800) 661-1933, has pleasant accommodations, some of which are on two levels and have kitchens. There's an indoor pool and sauna, two restaurants, and honeymoon and winter ski packages are available. Rates vary from inexpensive to mid-range.

South of the town, **Tekkara Lodge** offers some cozy and peaceful self-catering cabins with fireplaces at prices that vary between inexpensive and moderate. In the town itself, the inexpensively-priced **Athabasca Hotel**, 510 Patricia Street, P.O. Box 1420, Jasper T0E 1E0, ℂ (403) 852-3386, has simply-furnished rooms, about two-thirds of which have bathrooms. There's a pub on the premises, an attractive dining room, and a cocktail lounge.

WHERE TO EAT

Banff

There are quite a few dining places in Banff, mostly inexpensive, and several of the hotels have good dining rooms.

The **Drifter's Inn**, Sundance Mall, Banff Avenue, ℂ (403) 762-4525, serves steak and seafood in pleasant surroundings, and steak also features on the menu along with burgers at **Melissa's** on Lynx Street. For good Italian fare try **Giorgio's** at 219 Banff Avenue, ℂ (403) 762-5114, where there's a warm, intimate atmosphere, or if a pizza will do, you could go to **Aardvark's**, 304 Wolf Street, ℂ (403) 762-5500. At **Grizzly House**, 207 Banff Avenue, ℂ (403) 762-4055, fondue figures largely and there's always music playing. For English-style food try the **Rose and Crown**, 202 Banff Avenue, ℂ (403) 762-2121, and for pan-European dining try the **Paris Restaurant**, 114 Banff Avenue, ℂ (403) 762-3554.

Jasper

The Jasper Park Lodge on Lake Beauvert has a French restaurant called the **Moose's Nook**, which is moderately priced, and in the town **The Beauvallon** at 96 Geikie Street, ℂ (403) 852-5644, serves continental cuisine. The **Something Else Greek Taverna**, 621 Patricia Street, ℂ (403) 852-3850, has some good traditional dishes and suitably Greek decor. For sushi and other Japanese dishes go to **Tokyo Tom's**, 410 Connaught Drive, ℂ (403) 852-3780. **L & W** at Hazel and Patricia Street, ℂ (403) 4114, has the look of a conservatory and serves spaghetti, pizza, and an assortment of non-Italian dishes, while **Villa Caruso** on Connaught Drive, ℂ (403) 852-3920, offers good Italian food in more upmarket surroundings, although the prices remain inexpensive.

HOW TO GET THERE

The nearest major airport to Banff is at Calgary, which is served by national and international airlines. At the airport you can hire a car from one of several car rental companies if you wish to drive the 113 km (70 miles) to Banff. Jasper is 292 km (181 miles) north of Banff along the Icefields Parkway, making Calgary Airport 405 km (255 miles) away from Jasper. Edmonton International Airport is 411 km (225 miles) away from Jasper along the Yellowhead Highway. If you're aiming for Jasper during the winter the drive from Edmonton is generally safer via the Calgary route, as weather conditions along the Icefields Parkway can get bad.

In Banff the VIA Rail station is on Elk Street, ((403) 762-3722 or 852-3168, and from here trains run west to Vancouver and east to Calgary and Montreal. At Jasper it's at 314 Connaught Drive, ((403) 852-4102, toll-free (800) 561-8630, and trains run west to Vancouver, eastwards to Edmonton, Winnipeg and beyond.

In Banff the Greyhound bus station, ((403) 762-2286, is by the train station and operates a frequent service to and from Calgary. Another service links Banff with Edmonton, and there's a bus to Lake Louise that continues on to Vancouver. Brewster Transportation, ((403) 762-6767, which uses the same depot as Greyhound, runs a once-daily service to Jasper and also operates tours of the area. In Jasper the Greyhound station is at 314 Connaught Drive, ((403) 852-3926, and regular services operate to Vancouver via Kamloops, to Edmonton, and to Banff.

The Trans-Canada Highway (Highway 1) runs through Banff National Park, linking it with Calgary in the east and with Vancouver in the west. The Yellowhead Highway runs through Jasper from Edmonton in the east and to Prince George in the west, also linking with Vancouver via Kamloops.

The spectacular Icefields Parkway linking Lake Louise with Banff.

Saskatche-
wan

OF the three Prairie Provinces, Saskatchewan contains the largest area of Canada's prairie, and it lies sandwiched between Manitoba in the east and Alberta in the west. It is the country's major wheat producer, and has become a byword for the endless, treeless plain that in the minds of many typifies the word "prairie". This is unfortunate and somewhat unfair, as Saskatchewan does have quite a varied landscape, both within the prairie and beyond it. Besides, that vast, flat, and treeless wheat-growing belt with its endless rippling fields of gold and dramatic skies has its own kind of beauty.

In the south of the province lies the large semi-circular portion of the prairie known as the badlands, a mixture of semi-arid grasslands and desert-like areas. This section is surrounded by a wheat-growing belt in which the provincial capital of Regina lies, and beyond that strip is the outer section of the prairie, known as the parkland, an area of gently rolling hills and trees, through which the North and South Saskatchewan Rivers flow. Beyond the prairie, Prince Albert National Park stands at the edge of the remote North Country, a wilderness of forests and marshlands, criss-crossed with a latticework of lakes and rivers, much of which is Canadian Shield country. Here the roads peter out, and it is very sparsely populated — mainly by the Metis — but the wide-open spaces, ideal for fishing and canoeing, attract adventurers and urban refugees nevertheless.

When in 1858 John Palliser led an expedition through the southwest of the province, he deemed the land unsuitable for agriculture, but subsequent irrigation proved his assessment wrong, turning Saskatchewan into North America's largest wheat-growing region. Sixty percent of Canada's crop is produced here, while the grasslands of the south have made good cattle-raising country. The mineral wealth of the province has also proved profitable; oil is now an important part of the the economy. The favorable summer weather and hundreds of parks attract outdoors lovers, making the tourist industry a newer strand in an economy that is still developing.

Saskatchewan has a population of around one million and an area of 651,901 sq km (251,700 sq miles), leaving a lot of empty space, and the citizens of its two major cities revel in the opportunities that their parklands provide. The relaxed character of the people masks a fighting spirit and a willingness to work together for the common good that has brought them through some very difficult times. They are also unafraid of change: in 1944 Saskatchewan elected the first Socialist government in North America and embarked upon a series of innovative social programs. The people are proud of their pioneering past, which they commemorate in many museums — Saskatchewan has the most per capita of all the provinces. There are frequent reminders of the remarkable contribution made by the North West Canadian Mounted Police in the development of the area, and also of the bitter Northwest Rebellion that once shook the province and still seems to send out shock waves.

Saskatchewan has quite a colorful history. The first white man to explore the territory was Henry Kelsey in 1690, acting on behalf of the Hudson's Bay Company. Trading posts were then established in the region, and throughout the nineteenthth century the fur trade flourished here. As a result the Metis people came into being, children of French fathers and Indian mothers who lived the native way of life but followed Roman Catholicism.

In 1870 the Canadian government, seeing the agricultural potential, bought the land from the Hudson's Bay Company and began to negotiate treaties in preparation for the settlement of the area. The government advertised free land to settlers, and ranchers began to move their herds into the southwest. In 1873 the North West Mounted Police was formed to enforce law and order in the Northwest Territories. But it was the coming of the Canadian Pacific Railway in 1882 that began to reel in settlers from the United States, Britain, and Europe.

The arrival of the settlers and the surveying of the land in preparation for further immigration caused great consternation among the Metis, who stood to lose rights to the lands they already inhabited. As their pleas to the government went unheeded, they turned to the leadership of a young man named Louis Riel. They set up their own provincial government in an attempt to establish their rights, but the English Metis did not lend their support to this faction, and conflict arose between Riel's people and some of the settlers. This resulted in Riel having one of them killed following an attempt on his life. The Metis were eventually granted some land for settlement and Riel was forced into exile, but when the Metis and the Indians again found

themselves about to be dispossessed, Riel returned to lead them in the Northwest Rebellion of 1885. This was a bitter conflict that ended with a hopeless but noble stand by the rebels at Batoche, against government troops using Gatling guns. Riel surrendered, was brought to trial in Regina, and was hanged for treason there.

Subsequently the Metis received the land rights they had sought, but the death of Riel had other political repercussions. For many it came to represent the French-English conflict, and to this day it remains an emotive subject. Saskatchewan does much to keep the memory alive, and each year in Regina the trial of Riel is re-enacted.

In 1905 Saskatchewan was incorporated, with Regina as its capital, and immigration to the province steadily continued along with prosperity and growth. The Depression of the 1930's hit Saskatchewan particularly hard, and to add to the misery 10 years of drought brought crop failure, creating a depressing brown landscape dotted with starving cattle. The spirit of the people and their sense of community brought them through this terrible time and they have emerged strong, still united, and unafraid of the future.

REGINA

Saskatchewan's capital is one of Canada's sunniest cities, and as befits its name Regina rises regally from the center of the flat prairie wheat fields. With the Canadian Pacific Railway and the Trans-Canada Highway running through the city, it is the financial, industrial, and agricultural center of Saskatchewan, with a population of 179,000. Although those looking for excitement won't find too much of it here, it has a healthy cultural life with a good number of theatre and dance companies, as well as Canada's oldest symphony orchestra and one of her top concert halls. Regina is home to the Royal Canadian Mounted Police training school, which adds a splash of red color and some ceremonial pomp to the town. The museum that traces the development of the force and other museums throughout the city afford visitors a fascinating window on the province's past.

Once a miserable, muddy, and unpromising site along the banks of the Wascana, Regina has been transformed into a dignified and serene city of parklands, carefully planted trees, and well-considered public facilities, offering travelers welcome respite from the vast plains that surround it. The core of the city, and the buildings that house some of its major attractions, lie in a pleasant parkland of trees and gardens surrounding a man-made lake — a triumph over the once inhospitable terrain and testimony to the pioneering spirit of the people of Saskatchewan.

BACKGROUND

When the Canadian Pacific Railway was planning its route across the plains, the government, realizing that the erstwhile capital of the Northwest Territories would be nowhere near the railway, entered into discussions with the C.P.R. to decide on a site for a new settlement that would lie along the line. The place they settled upon was a far from obvious choice. It lay along the banks of an almost dried-up creek with a few stagnant pools — a place that was either too muddy or too dusty. The banks had been used by the Cree Indians for slaughtering buffalo and drying the skins, and because of the large numbers of buffalo skeletons there, they had given it the inauspicious name Oskana, meaning "Pile of Bones". However, settlement was soon under way, and in 1882 the first train chuffed into the station. The Princess Louise, wife of Canada's Governor-General, bestowed upon it the more dignified name of Regina in honor of her mother, Queen Victoria.

The North West Mounted Police set up headquarters here, and in 1885 Regina became the focus of attention when, following the Northwest Rebellion, it was the scene of the trial of the Metis leader, Louis Riel. Opinion was divided over Riel, as many believed his cause to be a just one that highlighted the French-British conflict in Canada, but Riel was found guilty of treason and hanged in November of that year.

When the province of Saskatchewan was incorporated in 1905, Regina was its capital city and immigrants began to flood in. Gradually the problems of the location were solved: the creek was dammed to create an artificial lake, the surrounding parkland was landscaped, the dignified Legislative Building was planned, and present-day Regina began to take shape.

GENERAL INFORMATION

For information on Saskatchewan as a whole you should contact Tourism Saskatchewan at the Saskatchewan Trade & Convention Centre, 1919 Saskatchewan Drive, Regina S4P 3V7, ((306) 787-2300, toll-

free (800) 667-7538 within the Regina area or (800) 667-7191 from elsewhere in Canada. The U.S. Saskatchewan Parks and Renewable Resources is another valuable source of information, and has an office in Regina which is open between mid-May and the end of August, ((306) 787-2700, or toll-free (800) 66-PARKS.

For information specifically on Regina and vicinity contact Tourism Regina, which is located on the Trans-Canada Highway at the eastern edge of the city at Highway 1 East, P.O. Box 3355, Regina S4P 3H1, ((306)

789-5099. A more central information office is located in the old streetcar at Scarth Street Mall, ((306) 527-4685, open from Monday to Saturday. The Chamber of Commerce is another good source of information and can be found at 2145 Alberts Street, ((306) 527-4685.

WHAT TO SEE AND DO

Sights
Along the banks of Wascana Creek lie several parks, but Regina's pride is the **Wascana**

OPPOSITE: The iron-and-wood stitchery that since 1885 has sewn Canada together. ABOVE: A car decorated for Regina's Buffalo Days.

Centre, a 930-hectare (2,300-acre) park that forms the heart of the city. Once an ugly, muddy area with an uncertain water supply, settlers dammed the creek here to create Wascana Lake and a water reserve. It is now a beautiful park where trees have been planted and flower beds cultivated. Around the lake a pleasant marina has been built where you can take a ferry over to Willow Island, a lovely spot for a picnic. With canoeing, sailing, boating, windsurfing, and many picnic areas, it is a place of recreation, but the art gallery and science center located

frieze. If you intend visiting the Saskatchewan that lies beyond the cities, this is an excellent introduction to the flora and fauna you will encounter. There are dioramas of various regions, complete with wildlife and sound effects that add to the realistic effect, and displays on the biology of the wildlife. The Earth Sciences Gallery traces the province's geological history and features some hands-on displays, while another gallery deals with native American history. A popular feature of the museum is "Megamunch", a full-size ani-

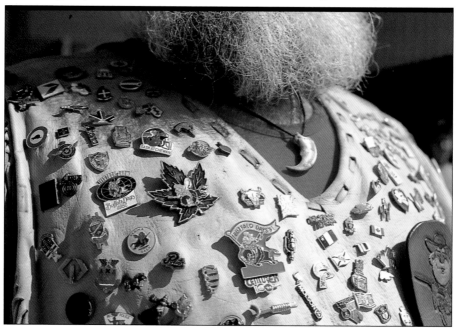

here also make it a place of culture and education.

On the western side of the park stands the stately domed **Legislative Building**, ℂ (306) 787-5358, built between 1908 and 1912 in the style of the English Renaissance Revival, lavishly decorated within, and set in pleasant gardens. It is open to the public and frequent tours take visitors around the huge library, the Legislative Chamber, and the art galleries on the lower levels. Admission is free.

Over on the north bank of Wascana Lake at the corner of College Avenue and Albert Street stands the **Museum of Natural History**, ℂ (306) 787-2815/2818, a low building built in Tyndall stone and decorated with a

mated dinosaur. The museum is open daily and admission is free.

Close by stands the **Norman Mackenzie Art Gallery** at Albert Street and 23rd Avenue, ℂ (306) 522-4242. This began as a private collection bequeathed to the University of Regina, and it now includes both contemporary and older works from a variety of countries, but with an emphasis on Canadian art. It is open daily and admission is free. In August a theatre company re-enacts the trial of Louis Riel here from court transcripts, which never fails to stir up controversy.

Also on the north shore of the lake the old city power station has been converted to house the **Saskatchewan Science Centre**, ℂ (306) 791-7900, where hands-on exhibits help to explain some of the laws of physics. There's also an observatory and an IMAX theatre that shows films specially made for the enormous screen. During the summer the Centre is open Tuesday to Sunday, and in the winter it is open between from Tuesday to Friday.

Over on the south side of the lake along Lakeshore Drive you can visit the **Diefenbaker Homestead**, ((306) 522-3661/565-2742, the childhood home of John Diefenbaker, Prime Minister of Canada from 1957 to 1963. This pioneer dwelling was moved

of Broad Street, ((306) 522-3661. As well as the information center there's a gift shop and a small art gallery. Open daily.

Close to the Legislative Building stands **Government House**, Dewdney Avenue at Connaught Street, ((306) 787-5717/5726. This served as the residence of the Lieutenant-Governors between 1891 and 1945. The rooms have been beautifully restored and contain period furnishings. Admission is free.

North of the Wascana Centre, the famous Royal Canadian Mounted Police, or

here from Borden, Saskatchewan, and is furnished in the style of the early 1900's with some items that belonged to the family. It is open daily and admission is free.

Also within the Wascana Centre on Lakeshore Drive you'll find the **Saskatchewan Centre of the Arts**, ((306) 565-0404, housing an excellent concert hall among other facilities. Nearby on the lakeshore is the **Waterfowl Park** where you can see Canada geese, swans, pelicans, and many other species. There's a naturalist on hand to answer questions and to arrange guided tours. Within the park there is also a **Speaker's Corner** and a **bandshell** for summer entertainment. For information on the park and its facilities call into **Wascana Place** on Wascana Drive west

Mounties, have their training academy and also the **RCMP Centennial Museum** at Dewdney Avenue West, ((306) 780-5838. The museum traces the colorful history of the Mounties and the vital role they played in Canada's development — a role that far exceeds that normally fulfilled by a police force. Archival material, uniforms, weaponry, artifacts, and a wealth of memorabilia recall the famous and gruelling march that the newly-formed force made through the west to establish law and order. Various other events in the force's history are also recalled, including

OPPOSITE: Pinning down enthusiasm for Buffalo Days. ABOVE: The Legislative Building in Regina.

Saskatchewan

some of their more bizarre projects. There are some curiosities on display here, such as Chief Sitting Bull's tobacco pouch, while some exhibits add a lighter touch, such as the Hollywood representations of those who "always get their man". Open daily and admission is free.

For lovers of military drills, the **Sergeant Major's Parade** takes place daily at noon, and from July to mid-August the colorful **Sunset Retreat Ceremony** draws the crowds on Tuesday evenings when the flag is lowered.

entertainment in Wascana Park and the live-stock exhibitions, music, shows, sporting events, and parades held in the Regina Exhibition Park.

Excursions

Seventy-one kilometers (44 miles) west of Regina along the Trans-Canada Highway lies **Moose Jaw**, an industrial city that is the scene of many annual events, including the **Saskatchewan Air Show** held in July. The city has two tourist attractions, one of which is the **Wild Animal Park**, Seventh

For an insight into what life was like for the early settlers, pay a visit to the **Regina Plains Museum** located on the fourth floor of one of downtown's historic buildings at 1801 Scarth Street, ((306) 352-0844/352-0861. The museum traces the history of the Indians and the pioneers who lived on the plains. Exhibits include a primitive hut and some reconstructed interiors. The museum is open daily during the summer and from Wednesday to Sunday during winter months.

At the end of July/early August each year, Regina returns to the days of the Wild West for a week of celebration known as **Buffalo Days**. Citizens dress themselves and the town up in pioneer style to enjoy free

Avenue S.W., ((306) 691-0111, with around 50 species of animals, mainly North American. The other attraction is the **Western Development Museum**, 50 Diefenbaker Drive at the junction of the Trans-Canada Highway and Highway 2, ((306) 693-6556/693-5989. There are four Western Development Museums throughout Saskatchewan, each dealing with a different area of provincial history. This branch covers the history of transportation, with displays on aviation, the railway, plus land and water transportation. Exhibits include vintage cars and aircraft, an old C.P.R. train, a reconstructed railway station, wagons, and old snowmobiles. Open daily during summer, closed on Mondays during winter.

Northeast of Moose Jaw in the Qu'Appelle Valley you can see some more wildlife at the **Buffalo Pound Provincial Park**, ((306) 693-2678/694-3659. This is a large area of parkland where a herd of buffalo roam; the park also has hiking trails, a beach, tennis courts, a lake for fishing, and horse-trekking trails.

The **Qu'Appelle Valley** cuts through the prairie from Lake Diefenbaker to the northwest of Regina up to the Manitoba border to the east, a route that stretches across roughly two-thirds of the province.

students of the Saskatchewan Summer School of the Arts present their work to the public.

Sports

Regina's contenders in the Canadian **Football** League are the Saskatchewan Roughriders, who can be seen in action at Taylor Field on Albert Street at Dewdney Avenue. There's year-round **horse racing** at Queensbury Downs in the Exhibition Park west of the city center at Elphinstone Street and Lewvan Drive.

This long, green valley of trees and lakes was a favorite place for fur traders and Indians as it offered welcome respite from the prairie and was a valuable source of wood. Today it is as green as ever and is lined with parks, villages, and resorts. Route 10 from Regina will bring you to **Fort Qu'Appelle**, some 70 km (43 miles) away, which is a good place to buy local craftwork. In this stretch of the valley there are a series of lakes that are excellent for fishing and swimming. **Echo Valley Provincial Park**, which lies between Pasqua and Echo Lakes, and **Katepwa Point Provincial Park** are both pleasant recreation areas comprising beaches, golf courses and other facilities. On the northern shore of Echo Lake at **Fort San**,

There are pleasant, paved **running** trails through the parks, which are also suitable for **cycling**, **jogging**, or **walking**. There are places that rent bicycles at the Wascana Centre. **Golf** enthusiasts have a choice of several golf courses around Regina, one of the newest ones being the 18-hole Emerald Park Golf and Country Club east of the town. Information on courses in the area can be obtained from the Saskatchewan Golf Association based in Saskatoon, ((306) 975-0834.

If you'd like to do some **riding**, either as a beginner or a more experienced rider, there are a few places around Regina that give

OPPOSITE: Regina's skyline as seen from the Wascana Centre. ABOVE: Youngsters enjoying Buffalo Days.

Saskatchewan

lessons and offer trail rides. The Dude Ranch, a few minutes' drive east of town along Dewdney Avenue, offers year-round riding, and has overnight trail packages that include supper and breakfast. ℂ (306) 757-5462 for details. Northeast of Regina, the string of lakes in the Qu'Appelle Valley (see Excursions) are popular with **boaters** and **water-skiers**. These are also ideal **fishing** lakes, but make sure to get a license first. Outfitters, resorts, and the Parks offices sell them, and you should carefully read the copy of the regulations that you get with your license.

Shopping and Nightlife

There are quite a few galleries and craft shops selling local work, Indian and otherwise, and there are several pleasant shopping malls around the town.

Along Lakeshore Drive in the Wascana Centre, the **Saskatchewan Centre of the Arts**, ℂ (306) 565-0404, contains two theatres, the larger of which serves as an excellent concert hall where you can hear the Regina Symphony Orchestra play. The Centre presents operas, theatrical productions, dance, and other musical presentations. At the **Globe Theatre** at the old City Hall, 1801 Scarth Street, ℂ (306) 525-9553, a variety of productions ranging from the classics to contemporary drama are performed.

If you like the idea of dinner and a show, **Stage West** in Regina Inn Mall, ℂ (306) 800-8162, has professional acts which you can sit back and enjoy after a good meal. Dinner and a rather different kind of entertainment are on the menu at **Celebrations**, 669 Albert

Street, ℂ (306) 525-8989, where the waiters are characters in the play. There are several bars and nightclubs in town, some of which are located in hotels.

WHERE TO STAY

There are a few places around Regina that offer farm accommodation, mainly in the Qu'Appelle Valley. For details of these and of campsites in the area check the Saskatchewan Accommodation brochure that is available free of charge from Information Centres. It also lists some Bed & Breakfast places in the town.

Luxury to Mid-range

The **Regina Inn**, 1975 Broad Street, Regina S4P 1Y2, ℂ (306) 525-6767, toll-free (800) 667-8162, is a top-rank modern hotel in the heart of downtown. It has 239 rooms, most of which have balconies, and good facilities. There is an indoor swimming pool, a sundeck, fitness facilities, two attractive dining spots, and a popular nightclub. There are similarly high standards at the **Sheraton Inn Regina**, 1818 Victoria Avenue, Regina S4P 0R1, ℂ (306) 569-1666, toll-free (800) 325-3535. It has particularly attractive public areas and 250 rooms and suites, all very well-equipped. There's a lovely indoor swimming pool, a restaurant, a lounge with nighttime entertainment, and a pub. Prices at both hotels vary between luxury and mid-range.

For first-class accommodation in older surroundings, book into the **Hotel Saskatchewan**, 2125 Victoria Avenue, Regina S4P 0S3, ℂ (306) 522-7691, toll-free (800) 667-5828, a grand building that dates from 1927. The public areas have an old-fashioned sense of grandeur, and the generously proportioned rooms are furnished in modern style and with many creature comforts. There are 233 accommodations including suites and the "Royal Suite", which has indeed housed royalty. There is a cocktail lounge, a pub, a coffee shop, and a restaurant. Prices here vary widely between inexpensive and luxury.

Situated downtown, the **Chelton Inn** at 1907 11th Avenue, Regina S4P 0J2, ℂ (306) 569-4600, toll-free (800) 667-9922, has 56 large rooms and suites, attractively deco-

---

ABOVE: Projecting Buffalo Days.

Saskatchewan

rated and equipped with fridge and wet bar. A particularly good and popular restaurant, a friendly atmosphere, and prices that vary from inexpensive to mid-range make this good value.

South of downtown, the **Regina Travelodge**, 4177 Albert Street, Regina S4S 3R6, ((306) 586-3443, toll-free (800) 255-3050, has 164 modern rooms, all with telephone and TV, and some deluxe suites that feature jacuzzis. It has a waterslide, a coffee shop, a pub, and a restaurant geared to family dining, making it an excellent choice if you have children with you. Prices dip down into the inexpensive bracket from the lower end of the mid-range. North of downtown, the **Seven Oaks Motor Inn**, 777 Albert Street, Regina S4R 2P6, ((306) 757-0121, toll-free (800) 667-8063, offers a similar range of facilities. It is another modern hotel with 156 rooms and an executive floor. Prices vary between inexpensive to the upper end of the mid-range.

Inexpensive

The **Plains Motor Hotel**, downtown at 1965 Albert Street, Regina S4P 2T5, ((306) 757-8661, has 60 rooms with bathrooms, a pub on the premises, and a dining room. Slightly to the north of the center the **Inntowner Motor Inn**, 1009 Albert Street, Regina S4R 2P9, ((306) 525-3737, toll-free (800) 667-7785, has 43 rooms, some with waterbeds, a dining room, and a cocktail lounge.

South of downtown the **Landmark Inn**, 4150 Albert Street South, Regina S4S 3R8, ((306) 586-5363, is virtually a resort hotel incorporating a large recreational complex with a waterslide and a fitness center. There are 188 rooms, all well-equipped, two good restaurants, one of which serves French food, a pub, and a cafe. Not far away, the **Sandman Inn**, 4025 Albert Street, Regina S4S 3R6, ((306) 586-2663, toll-free (800) 663-6900, has attractive rooms in hotel and motel units, a large indoor pool — the largest in the province, they claim — a poolside restaurant and bar, a coffee shop, and a gift shop. The **Imperial 400 Motel**, 4255 Albert Steet, Regina S4S 3R6, ((306) 584-8800, is very good value for money with smart and comfortable rooms, good recreational facilities that include an indoor pool, sauna and waterslide, and in-house entertainment.

Away from downtown, the **North Star Motel**, Sub 35, 2052 Park Street, Regina S4N 0T0, ((306) 352-0723, has 25 rooms with kitchen facilities, and also a two-bedroom cottage. There's a trusty **Journey's End** at 3221 East Eastgage Drive, Regina S4N 0T0, ((306) 789-5522, toll-free (800) 668-4200, with 100 rooms, all with the usual good facilities.

Close to Wascana Park, the **Turgeon International Hostel**, 2310 McIntyre Street, Regina S4P 2S2, ((306) 522-4200, is a restored heritage house with lots of character, offering dormitory-style rooms, good self-catering facilities, and a lovely old sitting room. There's a **YWCA** downtown at 1940 McIntyre Steet, Regina S4P 2R3, ((306) 525-2141, with just 32 rooms and a **YMCA** close to downtown, 2400 13th Avenue, Regina S4P 0V9, ((306) 757-9622.

WHERE TO EAT

Moderate

Most of the restaurants in this section fall into the lower end of the moderate category, bordering on inexpensive.

For innovative continental food in delightful surroundings be sure to visit **Mieka's** at 1810 Smith Street, ((306) 522-6700. Mieka prides herself on an imaginative menu that she puts together with great panache, and vegetarians will find much more than the obligatory nut roast or omelette to cater for their tastes. The interior displays equal flair and creates an intimate atmosphere with its graceful modern decor. There's a completely different kind of setting at the aptly-named **Upstairs Downstairs**, 2305 Smith Street, ((306) 525-1496, a Victorian house with a warm, old-fashioned interior. The menu has a slight English accent with steaks, seafood, and Yorkshire pudding on the menu. **The Diplomat**, 2032 Broad Street, ((306) 359-3366, is probably the place to go for steaks, though poultry and other dishes are also featured. The setting is one of traditional elegance.

Roxy's Bistro at 1844 14th Avenue, ((306) 352-4737, is another excellent eatery, with an interesting and wide-ranging menu that has a French touch, and some glorious desserts. The setting is modern and sophisticated, and it makes a pleasant spot for an intimate dinner. Good continental cuisine is served at **C.C. Lloyd's Dining Room** in the Chelton Inn, 1907 11th Avenue, ((306) 569-4650.

Inexpensive
Bartleby's at 1920 Broad Street, ((306) 565-0040, is a popular dining spot and bar, with a menu that has a United Nations feel, but it's the decor that they really come here for. Heaps of Victorian curiosities adorn the place and just about every corner has some piece of memorabilia or hardware poking out of it. For English-style pub grub go to the **Elephant & Castle** in the Cornwall Centre at 11th Avenue and Scarth Street, ((306) 757-4405. **Vien Dong** at 1841 Broad Street serves good Vietnamese food.

HOW TO GET THERE

The airport is a 15-minute drive west of the city center, and flights arrive there from all over eastern and western Canada. An airbus will take you from the airport to the major downtown hotels.

The VIA Rail station is on the northern edge of downtown along Saskatchewan Drive at Rose Street, ((306) 359-1822, toll-free (800) 665-8630. There are services linking Regina with Vancouver and Calgary, Saskatoon and Prince Albert, and Toronto and Montreal.

Greyhound buses run to Regina from Calgary and Vancouver, Winnipeg, Toronto, and Montreal, while the Saskatchewan Transportation Company operates services between Regina and other Saskatchewan towns. The bus station is close to downtown at 2041 Hamilton Street, ((306) 787-3340.

The two main highways into Regina are the Trans-Canada Highway (Highway 1) that runs east and west of the city, and Highway 6 that runs from the U.S. Montana border to the south through the town, continuing northwards beyond Melford. Just north of the city, Highway 11 from Saskatoon links

with Highway 6, just north of Regina, which runs into the city center.

SASKATOON

Saskatoon sits in the center of the prairie parkland, an area of trees and farmland that lies to the north of the wheat-growing belt and south of the forested northern wilderness. It is a small, pleasant city of around 200,000 people that lies along both banks of the South Saskatchewan River, which runs northeast to southwest through the city. The river is crossed by several bridges, and its banks are lined with parks offering peaceful retreats and recreation. There is a mixture of old and new buildings, generally low-rise,

Royal Canadian Mounted Police at their training academy in Regina.

and there are wide downtown streets that die out around the edges of the town.

The city doesn't have many tourist attractions, but it can offer its visitors some decent accommodation, several interesting eateries, and a warm, friendly welcome, making it a good stopover if you are on your way to the wild North Country. The east bank of the river is dominated by the Saskatoon University campus, the city's largest employer. Although the university has been at the forefront of medical technology development, the city has still not shaken off the aura of a frontier town.

While Saskatoon's economy is still bound up with agriculture, as it is an important distribution center, this is something that looks set to change as the area's rich mineral deposits attract more industry. Nearby lies one of the world's largest potash deposits and a large uranium mine, so the development of mining in the region could lead to the rapid growth of the city.

BACKGROUND

Saskatoon was founded as a temperance colony in 1882 by a group of Methodists from Ontario. They christened it after the purple berries that grew plentifully in the area. Temperance seems to have been unpopular, for at the turn of the century there were only 113 inhabitants, and even the coming of the railroad in 1890 didn't tempt new settlers here. However, in the early 1900's the agricultural potential of the area began to attract settlers from Europe and the Ukraine and in 1906 the city was incorporated. A year later Saskatoon University was founded.

GENERAL INFORMATION

Tourism Saskatchewan offers information on the province, and is situated in the Bank of Montreal building at 2103 11th Avenue. For information on the city you can contact the Saskatoon Visitor's Bureau just outside the city center at 304 Spadina Crescent, ((306) 242-1206, or Tourism Saskatoon at 102-310 Idylwyld Drive North, P.O.Box 369, Saskatoon S7K 3L3, ((306) 242-1206. The Visitor and Convention Bureau is another valuable source of information and can be found at 345 Third Avenue South, ((306) 242-1206, open Monday to Friday. In addition there are several information booths in the city during the summer.

WHAT TO SEE AND DO

Sights
The downtown core lies along the west bank of the South Saskatchewan River and is a fairly small area, so most of the main attractions, with a few exceptions, are all within walking distance of one another. The streets conform to a grid system, and 22nd Street cuts across the city dividing it into north and south, while Idylwyld Drive forms the east-west dividing line.

The river banks are lined with pleasant parks, trees, and recreation areas. One of the most distinguished landmarks on the west bank is the Bessborough Hotel, a 1930's railway hotel built in the grand château style favored by the railway companies of that time. Just by the Bessborough Hotel lies Kiwanis Park, a pleasant picnicking spot, where you can rent a canoe if you fancy paddling your way through the valley. If you like the idea but don't feel quite that enegetic, you can take a riverboat trip with W.W. Northcote River Cruises, ((306) 665-1818. Their riverboats leave from behind the park's bandstand, and you get a running commentary and refreshments on board. The trips run from June to the end of September.

A little further north along the river bank, the Ukrainian Museum of Canada, 910 Spadina Crescent East, ((306) 244-3800, preserves examples of the culture of these peasant immigrants who settled in the region during the late nineteenth and early twentieth centuries. There are displays of costumes, arts and crafts, artifacts, textiles, and photographs documenting the history of their immigration. The gift shop here sells Ukrainian cookery books, arts, and crafts. The museum is open daily from June to September and closed on Saturdays during the rest of the year.

Continuing northwards along the riverbank, the Mendel Art Gallery and Civic Conservatory is housed in a modern building at 950 Spadina Crescent East, ((306) 975-7610. The gallery has a permanent collection of contemporary and older works from Europe and Canada, and also hosts visiting exhibitions. The building contains a small but pleasant conservatory and an interesting gift shop. Open daily and admission is free. Behind the Gallery is a departure point for W.W. Northcote River Cruises.

Looking across the river from the gallery you'll see the attractive graystone buildings of the University of Saskatchewan campus. Tours of the campus start from Place Riel Campus Centre; places of interest here include the Biology Museum, the Museum of Antiquities, the Gordon Snelgrove Gallery, and the Observatory. The university's John Diefenbaker Centre houses the papers and memorabilia of this Canadian Prime Minister who held office in 1957–1963, and also on the campus stands the Little Stone School House, Saskatoon's first schoolhouse, dating from 1887. Tours of the campus run from May to the end of August. For further information telephone (306) 966-5788.

The main tourist attraction in Saskatoon is the Western Development Museum at 2610 Lorne Avenue South, ((306) 931-1910. It is one of four such museums in Saskatchewan (the others are in Moose Jaw, North Battleford, and Yorkton), each of which is devoted to a different aspect of the province's history. The subject dealt with by this museum is "Boomtown 1910", and the museum brings that period of Saskatchewan's history very much to life in an impressive indoor reconstruction of an entire street of that year, complete in every detail. Care has been taken to represent the period not only in visual terms but also in smells and sounds, creating a very vivid impression of life at that time. As you stroll along the wooden sidewalks, past the horse-drawn buggies and automobiles, you can peruse the remedies on display at the pharmacy, look in the windows of the stores, and even see a silent movie at the picture house. The street also has a fully-equipped Chinese

areas, making it a nice spot for a family outing. It is open daily throughout the year. Telephone (306) 975-3382 for details.

Every July Saskatoon stages the **Exhibition**, a week of agriculturally-based events. There are livestock shows, competitions involving agricultural equipment old and new, live music, parades, racing, dances, and much more entertainment for children and adults alike. Other Saskatoon events include a **Folkfest** held over an August weekend which celebrates the cultures of the various ethnic groups that settled in the

laundry, a bank, a railway station, and a school.

Other areas of the museum have collections of old cars, aircraft, and farming equipment. There's also a display on the mail order services that were an important part of life for many families until quite recently. The N° 1 bus will take you from Second Avenue downtown to the museum.

Eight kilometers (five miles) northeast of downtown along Attridge Drive lies the **Forestry Farm Park and Zoo**. The zoo stands at the north end of this pleasant area of trees and flowers, and contains around 300 animals and birds, mainly those indigenous to North America. There are recreation areas in the park along with picnic and barbecue

province, and in June there is another ethnic celebration, **Vesna Festival**.

Excursions

The **Batoche National Historic Park,** ((306) 423-6227, lies 88 km (55 miles) northeast of Saskatoon along the banks of the South Saskatchewan River, and is a must for anyone interested in the history of the Northwest Rebellion. Batoche was the site of a major Metis settlement in the nineteenth century and was the headquarters for Louis Riel's Provisional Government, which was set up to fight for the lands of the Metis people. At the park you can see the remains

The campus of Saskatoon University.

of the Metis village, the church of St Antoine de Padoue, and a rectory. Batoche was the site of the final battle of the Northwest Rebellion, and the trenches that were used by the victorious army can still be seen. The Interpretive Centre has displays on the Metis culture and the rebellion, and altogether the park pays a moving tribute to Metis people and their plight. The park is open from mid-May until mid-October and admission is free. To get there, take Highway 11 from Saskatoon, turn on to Highway 312 at Rosthern, then north on

Historic Park, Central Avenue, ((306) 937-2621, you can see the restored fort which has been fitted with authentic artifacts and furnishings. Within the palisades there are five buildings, including the Officers' Quarters, the Commanding Officer's Residence, and the Barracks. The Interpretive Centre provides some good displays on the 1885 rebellion.

Across the bridge, North Battleford was created because the C.N.R. ran its line along the north shore of the river, and it contains another **Western Development Museum**

to Highway 225, which brings you to the park.

There are more history lessons in store, quite fun ones too, at the **Battlefords,** the two communities of Battleford and North Battleford, divided from one another by the North Saskatchewan River and lying 140 km (87 miles) northwest of Saskatoon. Battleford sits on the south side of the river and was once the capital of the Northwest Territories, but it lost this status when the C.P.R. laid their line further south. It was the site of a North West Mounted Police fort built in 1876, and at **Battleford National**

located at the junction of Highways 16 and 40, ((306) 445-8033. This one takes the "Heritage Farm and Village" as its theme and there are extensive displays on agricultural equipment and techniques, as well as a reconstruction of a small village of 1925 vintage. The village includes pioneer homes, a Ukrainian Orthodox church, and a railway station. It is open from the beginning of May until the end of October, and to get to the Battlefords from Saskatoon, the most direct route is along the Yellowhead Highway (Highway 16) to North Battleford.

Sports

There's **thoroughbred horse racing** between early May and mid-October at the

OPPOSITE and ABOVE: Scenes from the Forestry Farm Park and Zoo in Saskatoon.

Marquis Downs Racetrack in the Saskatoon Exhibition Center off Ruth Street and Herman Avenue, ℂ (306) 242-6100.

For those who fancy doing some **horse riding** themselves, the Sandhills Stable 10 km (six miles) south of town along Lorne Avenue, ℂ (306) 955-4311, has trail riding and suppers around the campfire. There are good **cycling** trails running through the parks along the riverbanks which double as **jogging** paths. In the winter there are **cross-country skiing** trails at the Forestry Farm Park, eight kilo-

meters (five miles) northeast of downtown, ℂ (306) 975-3382.

Shopping and Nightlife

The downtown center is bounded by the river south and east, and is bordered by First Avenue to the west and 25th Street to the north. There are several shopping malls in this area, and Eatons, Sears, and The Bay all have stores here. Several galleries and shops downtown sell arts, crafts, and antiques, and some other outlets can be found on the east side of the river, particularly along Victoria and Broadway Avenues. Both the Ukrainian Museum and the Western Development Museum have good gift shops that sell a selection of local arts and crafts.

Saskatoon does not have a scintillating nightlife, but it does have a few theatres and some annual cultural events. The **Saskatoon Centennial Auditorium** downtown at 35 22nd Street East, ℂ (306) 975-7777, has a good theatre where you can hear the **Saskatoon Symphony** play, see some ballet companies perform, and also catch some top-name entertainers. During July and August the **Shakespeare on the Saskatchewan Festival** is held. Innovative and enjoyable interpretations of Shakespeare's plays are performed in two tents, one of which is erected on the riverbank. For details of the festival telephone (306) 653-2300.

There are a couple of pubs in the town and some pleasant hotel lounges where you can while away an evening, maybe to the tinkling of piano keys. The **Samurai Lounge** in the Bessborough Hotel is a particularly attractive spot. There are a few country and western clubs, among them the **North 40 Inn** on 20th Avenue West at Sixth Street and the **Texas "T"** at 3331 Eighth Street East, ℂ (306) 373-8080.

WHERE TO STAY

For details of camping grounds and country vacation farms, pick up a free copy of *Saskatchewan Accommodation* available from Information Centres.

Luxury to Mid-range

The **Sheraton Cavalier**, 612 Spadina Crescent East, Saskatoon S7K 3G9, ℂ (306) 652-6770, toll-free (800) 325-3535, is a modern downtown hotel that has just about all the facilities you could wish for, including special executive facilities. There are 250 rooms, with lots of comforts such as fridges and mini-bars, and enough recreational features to keep all the family happy. There are two indoor waterslides, a sundeck, fitness facilities, an attractive dining room, a cafe, and a nightclub. Prices here vary from luxury to the lower end of the mid-range.

Close to the airport, the **Saskatoon Inn**, 2002 Airport Drive, Saskatoon S7L 6M4, ℂ (306) 242-1440, toll-free (800) 667-8789, has 257 quite sumptuously decorated rooms with sitting areas. The hotel has a lovely courtyard filled with tropical plants, a pleasant indoor pool and whirlpool, a smart restaurant, and a more casual dining spot. There's nightly entertainment and dancing in the hotel lounge.

The **Delta Bessborough**, 601 Spadina Crescent East, Saskatoon S7K 3G8, ℂ (306) 244-5521, toll-free (800) 268-1133, is Saskatoon's most distinguished hotel, built in the grand chateau style of railway hostelries and set in attractive gardens overlooking the river. The hotel retains its 1930's splendor while incorporating modern conveniences. There are 221 rooms, all slightly different but quite spacious with old-style furnishings. There is both an indoor and outdoor swimming pool, a fitness center, an excellent seafood restaurant, a pleasant lounge, and a coffee shop. The hotel also has special business facilities. Also on the riverbank is the **Ramada Renaissance**, 405 20th Street East, Saskatoon S7K 6X6, ℂ (306) 665-3322, toll-free (800) 268-9889, a new 18-story building with an ornate lobby and 291 well-decorated rooms. There are luxury suites available and the hotel offers guests an excellent range of recreational facilities, including two indoor water slides and a sauna. There are also several dining spots to choose from.

The **Holiday Inn**, 90 22nd Street East, Saskatoon S7K 2A9, ℂ (306) 244-2311, toll-free (800) 465-4329, is another high-rise hotel which is conveniently close to the Centennial Auditorium and the shops. All rooms and bathrooms have a number of thoughtful extras and come up to the high standards of this hotel chain. It has an indoor swmming pool, an excellent restaurant, and a nightclub.

Inexpensive

The **King George Hotel**, 157 2nd Avenue North, Saskatoon S7K 2A9, ℂ (306) 652-4672, toll-free (800) 667-1234, is conveniently located downtown opposite The Bay. The building dates from 1905, but all 104 rooms are equipped with modern facilities. There's a restaurant and a bistro on the premises. The **Senator Hotel** is of a similar vintage and is also in the downtown area at 243 21st Street East, Saskatoon S7K 0B7, ℂ (306) 244-6141. The hotel retains a rather grand style throughout, and the 45 rooms are all slightly different but with the same modern amenities. The dining room has lots of character

and an English-style pub. Breakfast is included in the price. Also centrally located, the **Parktown Motor Hotel**, 924 Spadina Crescent East, Saskatoon S7K 3H5, ℂ (306) 244-5564, toll-free (800) 667-3999, has 109 newly renovated and attractive rooms all with TVs and telephones, and offers guests the use of an indoor pool and a sauna.

Near the airport, the **Journey's End Motel**, 21255 Northridge Drive, Saskatoon S7L 6X6, ℂ (306) 934-1122, toll-free (800) 668-4200, is good value, and the **Travelodge Hotel**, 106 Circle Drive West, Saskatoon S7L 4L6, ℂ (306) 242-8881, toll-free (800) 255-3050, also has bargain accommodation, with well-equipped rooms, an indoor pool with waterslide, a sauna, and a choice of places to dine.

The **YWCA Residence and Youth Hostel**, 510 25th Street East, Saskatoon S7K 4A7, ℂ (306) 244-0944, has basic accommodation for women only, conveniently situated in the downtown area.

WHERE TO EAT

Moderate

This is prairie land and consequently there are some excellent steak houses in town. **John's Prime Rib**, 401 21st Street East, ℂ (306) 244-6384, serves good quality steaks and seafood in attractive surroundings. **Cousin Nik's**, 1110 Grosvenor Avenue, ℂ (306) 374-2020, also specializes in surf and turf, but adds a Greek touch, both in the food and the decor. The attractive outdoor courtyard makes a particularly appealing dining spot. The splendid Bessborough Hotel, 601 Spadina Crescent East, ℂ (306) 244-5521, houses **Aerial's Cove**, a highly-rated seafood restaurant which also has meat dishes on its menu. For French cuisine, go to **Whiteside's** at the Ramada Renaissance, 405 20th Street East, ℂ (306) 665-3322. You'll find elegant continental dining at the Holiday Inn's **R.J. Wiloughby**, 90 22nd Street East, ℂ (306) 244-2311. For good Italian food you should try **Lucci's** at 117 Third Avenue South.

Inexpensive

The **St Tropez Bistro**, 243 Third Avenue South, ℂ (306) 652-1250, is a pretty and popular spot for snacking or dining, while at

Adonis, 103B Third Avenue South, ((306) 652-9598, there is Middle Eastern cuisine and al fresco dining in the summer. **Fuddruckers**, 2910 Eighth Street East, ((306) 955-7777, serves good home-made hamburgers, and the **Ambassador**, 2318 Eighth Street East, ((306) 373-4888, has a wide selection of Cantonese dishes. The **Artful Dodger**, 119 Fourth Avenue South, ((306) 653-2577, is a pub-like place with Old English decor, traditional British pub fare, and beer.

HOW TO GET THERE

Saskatoon International Airport, ((306) 975-4754, is about a 10-minute drive west of downtown and is served by Air Canada, Canadian Airlines International, and Time Air.

The VIA Rail terminal, ((306) 384-5665, is at the western edge of the city on Chappell Drive, and trains link Saskatoon with Regina in the southeast; Edmonton, Jasper, and Vancouver in the west; and Winnipeg and Toronto in the east. A bus runs between the station and downtown.

The Greyhound bus station is at 50 23rd Street East, ((306) 933-8000, and it handles services between Saskatoon and Regina, Winnipeg, Calgary, Edmonton, and Jasper.

If you're driving to Saskatoon from Regina, you'll arrive on Highway 11, and if you're coming from Manitoba in the east or Alberta in the west, you'll probably need to take the Yellowhead Highway (Highway 16) which becomes Idylwyld Drive within the city limits. If you're driving from Prince Albert National Park or La Ronge Provincial Park further to the north, you need to take Highway 2 and then pick up Highway 11 south of Prince Albert which will bring you to the northern edge of Saskatoon.

ELSEWHERE IN SASKATCHEWAN

PRINCE ALBERT NATIONAL PARK

Lying at the center of Saskatchewan, where the prairie parkland meets the forested northern territory of Saskatchewan, this million-acre wilderness reflects both landscapes. The park lies 200 km (124 miles) north of Saskatoon and 56 km (35 miles) north of

Prince Albert, and is a paradise for lovers of the Great Outdoors. It is a preserve of lakes, streams, hills, and forest, where grizzlies and black bears, coyotes, elk, moose, beavers, and many others roam free. It offers its visitors hiking trails that range from easy walks to backpacking hikes that last for days, as well as fishing, riding, camping, canoeing, and in the winter cross-country skiing.

Just inside the eastern entrance of the park lies **Waskesiu Lake**, and along its shores the Waskesiu townsite. With accommodation of all descriptions, cafes, and shops, it

makes an excellent base from which to explore the park. Waskesiu has a beach, a golf course, tennis courts, stables, boat rentals, and you can take a leisurely cruise along the lake aboard a paddlewheeler. The **Nature Centre**, ((306) 663-5322, gives interesting and entertaining presentations on the park, telling the story of Grey Owl, the self-styled naturalist who lived in the park during the 1930's and spoke out for the cause of conservation. For further information contact Prince Albert National Park, P.O. Box 100, Waskesiu Lake S0J 2Y0, ((306) 663-5322, and the Waskesiu Chamber of Commerce, ((306)

ABOVE: There is superb fishing to be found in the many lakes of central Saskatchewan.

922-3232, which has information on accommodation in the area.

LAC LA RONGE PROVINCIAL PARK

Deeper into the Saskatchewan north, 148 km (92 miles) beyond Prince Albert National Park lies Lac la Ronge Provincial Park, 340,500 hectares (841,035 acres) of lakes and forests. Over 100 lakes, including the huge Lake la Ronge, plus waterfalls and rapids, make this an ideal place for canoeing and fishing. The town of La Ronge on the southwestern edge of the lake has accommodation and places that offer canoeing and camping package trips. For information on the park telephone (306) 425-4234.

MEADOW LAKE PROVINCIAL PARK

Northeast of Prince Albert National Park lies this horizontal strip of parkland that surrounds a string of lakes. Like Prince Albert, it is an area of forests, lakes, and rivers that marks the transition between the northern Saskatchewan wilderness and the prairie parkland area. Visitors come here to enjoy its beautiful lakeside beaches and its wildlife, and to canoe, fish, and hike. There are tennis courts, stables, and in the winter cross-country skiing trails. There are campsites in the park and cabins for rent. For information on the park ring (306) 236-3382.

THE WESTERN DEVELOPMENT MUSEUM AT YORKTON

If you're keen to complete a tour of all four of the Western Development Museums, then you need to travel to Yorkton, which is 331 km (205 miles) east of Saskatoon along the Yellowhead Highway (Highway 16) or 189 km (117 miles) northeast of Regina along Highway 10. Yorkton is a major distribution center with a population of 16,000, and it has some decent accommodation to offer. If you visit in May or early June, you can catch the **Yorkton Short Film and Video Festival**.

The museum, ((306) 783-8361, is on the west side of town along Highway 16, and its theme is the "Story of People". The museum depicts daily life in Saskatchewan during the eighteenth and nineteenth centuries, with displays of tools and machinery both old and new. The interiors of early homes are re-created, reflecting the style of the various ethnic groups, such as the Plains Indians, the English, French, Ukrainians, and Swedes.

CYPRESS HILLS PROVINCIAL PARK

In the southwest corner of Saskatchewan, and stretching into southern Alberta, Cypress Park comes as something of a surprise. It is an area of hills, valleys, lakes, streams, and forests that rise out of the prairie plains to heights of almost 1,500 m (5,000 feet). There are pine forests (which were mistaken by the French explorers for cypresses, hence the name), rare flowers, birds, and animals. An area of the park is set aside for a resort with campsites, cabins, tennis courts, golf courses, a beach, and riding stables.

This is also an area of historical significance. In 1873 it was the scene of a massacre when Assiniboine Indians were killed by some Montana wolf hunters who mistakenly believed the Assiniboines were responsible for stealing their horses. The illegal trading of whisky in the area had played its part in the affair, and the massacre spurred the creation of the North West Mounted Police. In 1878 they set up headquarters at Fort Walsh, now the center of the **Fort Walsh National Historic Park**, ((306) 662-3590. It is located 55 km (34 miles) southwest of Maple Creek along Highway 271. The fort has been restored both inside and out, so that visitors can see for themselves the tough living conditions that the men endured. The interpretive center here shows films and has displays on the fort and the history of the police force. Among the more difficult tasks assigned to them was that of trying to persuade Chief Sitting Bull and his 5,000 braves to return to the U.S. after they had fled here following their defeat of Custer at Little Big Horn.

A bus from the fort will take visitors to **Farewell's Trading Post**, where costumed guides take you through the buildings and help re-create the lawless days of the whisky traders.

OPPOSITE: Images, from a distance and in close-up, of life on the prairies.

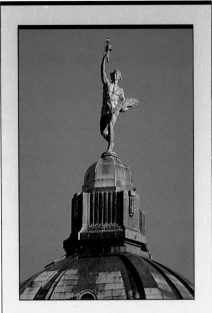

Manitoba

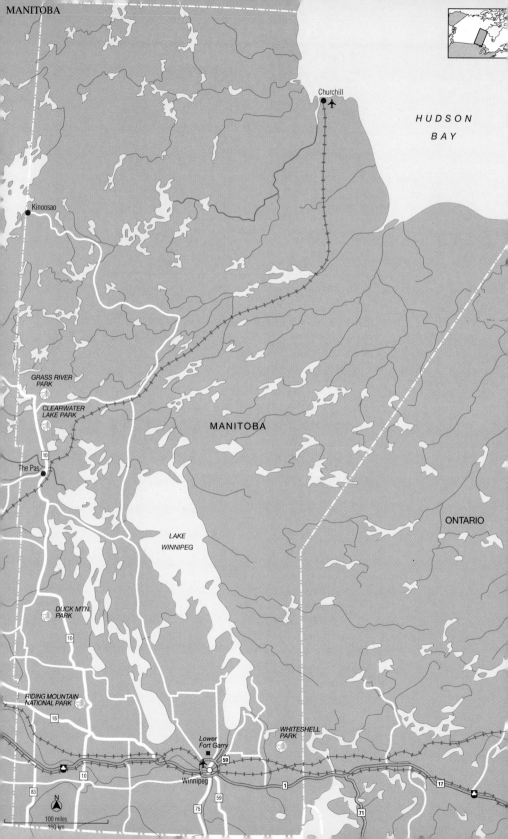

OFTEN referred to as Canada's "keystone province" because of its central position, Manitoba is the most easterly of the Prairie Provinces. It is bordered by the U.S. states of North Dakota and Minnesota to the south, by the province of Saskatchewan to the west, Ontario to the east, the Northwest Territories and Hudson Bay to the north. It stretches over a vast 650,088 sq km (251,000 sq miles), approximately one-sixth of which is covered with rivers and lakes. It has a population of just over one million, half of whom live in the capital city of Winnipeg, the province's only major city.

Of all three Prairie Provinces Manitoba has the smallest portion of prairie land, with the wheat-growing belt intruding only into its southwest corner. Beyond the prairie parkland strip lie the great lakes of Winnipeg, Manitoba, and Winnipegosis; beyond them a vast, rugged, rocky wilderness of forests, bogs, and lakes stretches northwards to the Arctic coastline of Hudson Bay, covering approximately half the country. With the Northern Lights and polar bears of Hudson Bay, around 100,000 lakes, the desert-like landscape of Spruce Woods Provincial Park, and numerous parks offering escape routes into the wilderness, there is a lot more to Manitoba than wheat fields.

Agriculture, however, has always played an important role in the province's growth and economy. Wheat is the major crop, with other grains and cattle-raising also important sources of revenue. Food processing and manufacturing are the province's main industries, and the rich mineral deposits of the Canadian Shield form the basis of several others. The tourist industry is developing and outdoor enthusiasts are attracted to the province by the wonderful opportunities that the lakes and forested wilderness have to offer. The climate, however, is a limiting factor for adventurers: it varies between hot summers, when the temperature often soars into the 90's, particularly in the southwest, and bitterly cold winters, when it's often well below freezing.

In 1612 an Englishman named Thomas Button sailed into Hudson Bay and spent the winter at the mouth of the Nelson River. He came in search of the fabled Northwest Passage to the Orient, but the disappointment at coming up against the mass of mid-Canada was diminished by the discovery that it was a hunter's paradise, teeming with furry animals and cut by rivers that brimmed with fish. In 1668 the ketch *Nonsuch* sailed from England to Hudson Bay and returned laden with furs. As a result, the Hudson's Bay Company was formed and was granted the vast territory, then known as Rupertsland, by Charles II, and trading posts were established around the province.

In 1738 the Frenchman Pierre Gaultier de la Verendrye established a trading post in the south of Manitoba, at the confluence of the Red and Assiniboine rivers, an area that is now the center of the city of Winnipeg. French trappers were the first white settlers in the prairie and they were the fathers of the Metis race, a half-French, half-Indian people who held with the Catholic faith but led the Indian way of life. The fur trade continued to flourish and eventually the French posts were surrendered to the British. In 1812 it served the interests of the Hudson's Bay Company to grant land for settlement in the Red River valley to Lord Selkirk, who brought some of his poorer compatriots from the Scottish Highlands to settle there, thus creating a supply center for the fur traders.

Because of the success of trade and transportation in the area, the province began to open up, but this success brought with it a threat to the Métis way of life.

In 1870 the Hudson's Bay Company sold its lands to the Dominion of Canada, which immediately commissioned surveys of the area in preparation for land allotment to new settlers. This prompted the Métis people to rise up in defense of their land rights, and, under the leadership of the young Louis Riel, they set up their own provisional government. As a result of their action and negotiations, a small area around the Red River valley was declared the province of Manitoba with land allocated to the Metis, and in 1870 Manitoba was incorporated into the Dominion of Canada.

In 1873 the government formed the North West Mounted Police to enforce law and order throughout the lands.

The coming of the C.P.R. in the 1880's heralded a period of great change, bringing with it immigrants from Ontario, Iceland, Eastern and Western Europe, and the Ukraine. By 1912 the ever-growing province had been extended to its present-day boundaries, farming was flourishing, and good communications increased the province's supply lines, thus strengthening the economy.

WINNIPEG

Halfway across Manitoba at the very center of Canada, the city of Winnipeg rises out of the vast flat prairie land rather like a mirage, so far away is it from any other city. It lies at the junction of the Assiniboine and Red rivers, 2,093 km (1300 miles) west of Toronto, and 572 km (355 miles) east of Regina, connected by rail and the Trans-Canada Highway. It is Manitoba's only major city. Around 650,000 people live in it, over half the entire population of the province. It is also Western Canada's oldest city, and its nucleus is, and always has been, the junction of Main Street and Portage Avenue, streets that stretch out for miles across the prairie, following the direction of the city's two rivers.

Winnipeg is a very likeable city, quite cosmopolitan in character and very cultured. It has pleasant parks, lovely riverside walks, wealthy suburbs with old mansion houses, and at the northeastern end of the city an old area of warehouses and depots reminds visitors of its early importance as a distribution center. The buildings along the wide, flat downtown streets testify to a policy of urban development that has respect for the city's stately older buildings, while remaining unafraid of change and innovation.

The famous corner of Portage Avenue and Main Street has benefitted from such innovation, with an underground mall and linkways now offering shelter from what is billed as the windiest and coldest spot in Canada. The summer temperatures in the city can hit the high 80's, but the winter sees temperatures of minus 4°F with snow and blizzards that chill to the bone. Winnipeggers seem to take pride in their ability to withstand the bitterness of these long winters, and they will boldly go forth in search of an evening's entertainment. The combination of this harsh weather and Winnipeg's isolation from other urban centers may be the reason why it has created such a gloriously rich cultural scene for itself. It boasts the world-famous Royal Winnipeg Ballet, a widely-acclaimed symphony orchestra, the Manitoba Opera Company, the excellent Theatre Centre, and one of the country's finest museums.

Another enriching factor in Winnipeg's cultural life is the diverse ethnic mix of its population. It started out with a mixture of Indians, British, French, and Metis, but the coming of the C.P.R. added more to the melting pot. Chinese came as laborers working on the construction of the railway, then came other Western and Eastern Europeans, Ukrainians, Mennonites, and Icelanders. The various nationalities tended to settle in ethnic-based communities around the city, and though this arrangment has to a large extent broken down, certain districts still retain a strong cultural identity. The downtown area has a sizable Chinatown, while the St Boniface district to the south of the river has a large French-speaking community, and the southern part of town generally tends to be British in origin. Each August the city celebrates its ethnicity with the Folklorama festival.

Winnipeg's skyline.

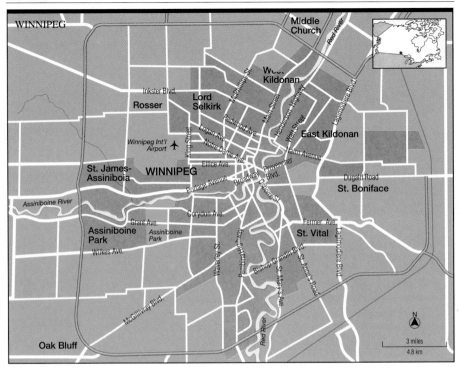

Maybe it is again the city's isolation and self-sufficiency that underlies its strong character. Even the cityscape, with its cast-iron buildings, huge stockyards, warehouses, and mansion-like houses, has solidity and a sense of security about it. Winnipeggers are themselves a resilient bunch, proud of their city, whose feelings of intense loyalty bind them to it wherever they wander.

BACKGROUND

This was once a region where the Cree and Assiniboine Indians roamed, but change began when the first white man set foot in the area in 1738. He was the French explorer and fur trapper Pierre Gaultier de la Verendrye, and he established a fort near the confluence of the Red and Assiniboine rivers. The fur trade flourished in the area, albeit with a good deal of friction between rival factions, and in 1812 the Hudson's Bay Company gave land in the Red River valley to Lord Selkirk, allowing him to establish a Scottish settlement, thus creating a supply center for the traders.

These Scottish Highlanders came here in search of a more prosperous life, and they

began to farm the area, slowly at first, as regular flooding and pestilence made for a difficult start. To the Metis people who lived by hunting buffalo, the settlement and farming of the area was a threat to their survival, and in 1816 they attacked the settlement, killing 20 of the Scots in what has become known as the Seven Oaks Massacre. The colony spluttered, but continued to grow slowly. A commercial center developed around the junction of the two rivers that served as trading trails, with river and road transportation linking it to the U.S.

In 1870 the province of Manitoba was created, and by 1873 the city of Winnipeg was incorporated. The C.P.R. arrived in 1886, sparking the rapid expansion of the city and bringing large numbers of immigrants to the city. The agricultural industry flourished, and Winnipeg's position as a distribution center and financial capital was strengthened. Today it has a thriving manufacturing industry, and it remains a major financial and distribution center with a large Commodity Exchange. The junction of Portage Avenue and Main Street, shadowing the two old trade routes, remains at the center of the city's financial district, a reminder of its past.

GENERAL INFORMATION

For general information on the province contact Travel Manitoba at Department 8231, 155 Carlton Street, Winnipeg R3C 3H8, ((204) 945-3777, toll-free (800) 665-0040. They have a main Travel Information Centre in the Legislative Building at Broadway and Osborne Street, ((204) 945-3777, toll-free (800) 665-0040. The Winnipeg Convention and Visitors Bureau is another useful source of information. It is located on the second floor of the Convention Centre, 375 York Avenue, Winnipeg R3C 3J3, ((204) 943-1970, and during the summer there are information kiosks dotted around the town. For recorded tourist information call (204) 942-2535.

WHAT TO SEE AND DO

Sights
The **Exchange District** lies at the very heart of Winnipeg, a 20-block area stretching from Portage Avenue and Main Street to the Centennial Centre, and incorporating the famous Canadian cold spot at the corner of Portage Avenue and Main Street. Today the large buildings that stand here are all linked together by an underground shopping mall. This area has always been the commercial hub of the province and many of its beautiful old buildings still stand. The **Winnipeg Commodity Exchange**, ((204) 949-0495, after which the district is named, is still located here. Originally the world's largest grain exchange, it has expanded into other commodities and now occupies the fifth floor of a tower block at 360 Main Street. Visitors can watch the action on the trading floor from a gallery and join a guided tour. Trading takes place between 9:30 am and 1:15 pm. One particularly attractive building in the area is the ornate **Electric Railways Chambers Building**, which is a reminder of the importance of the railway in Winnipeg's development.

This is not purely a business district, however, as many of the restored buildings now house restaurants and boutiques. The **Market Square** at King Street and Bannatyne Avenue is a popular gathering place

where there are shops, market stalls, trendy restaurants, and street entertainment during the summer months. The Exchange District is also a lively nighttime spot when the theatres, clubs, and restaurants open up.

On the edge of the Exchange District at Main Street stands the **Centennial Centre**, a complex comprising several buildings, including the **Centennial Concert Hall**, the **Planetarium**, and the **Manitoba Museum of Man and Nature**. As its name suggests, this splendid museum is devoted to the development of the province in geological,

natural, historical, and cultural terms. There are realistic dioramas of Manitoba's various natural regions — combining sight, sound, and smell — and there's a gallery devoted to the prairie lands with reconstructions of pioneer dwellings and displays describing the native way of life, while the Arctic-Subarctic Gallery depicts the way of life and the environment of the Hudson Bay area. The Urban Gallery has a reconstruction of a Winnipeg street in the 1920's, and has some moving displays that describe the difficulties that faced new immigrants. Probably the highlight of a visit here is the *Nonsuch*, a full-scale replica of the ketch that left London in 1668 for Hudson Bay and returned laden with furs. It was this success that brought the famous Hudson's Bay Company into existence. The museum is open daily, ((204) 956-2830.

Close by stands the **Ukrainian Cultural and Educational Centre**, 184 Alexander Avenue East, ((204) 942-0218. Housed within this old building is an art gallery and a museum that contains archival material and presents changing exhibitions on the history and rich culture of the Ukrainian people, the second largest group of immigrants to settle in the province. Exhibits include samples of embroidery, ceramics,

indoor plumbing, electric lighting, and was fitted with all kinds of household gadgetry. It is closed on Fridays and Mondays.

The magnificent **Legislative Building**, ((204) 945-3700, stands at the junction of Broadway and Osborne Street, an excellent example of neoclassical architecture, built in 1919 and designed by English architect Frank Worthington Simon. It is an H-shaped structure made of Tyndall limestone, a substance rich in fossil deposits that gives it a special texture. Atop its dome stands the gold-plated figure of the **Golden Boy**. This

carving, costumes, and the delicately painted Easter eggs called pysankys.

Moving south along Main Street and opposite the railway station there's a tiny park in which you can see **Upper Fort Garry Gate**, all that remains of the early nineteenth-century Hudson's Bay Fort. To the east along Broadway, another Winnipeg landmark carries on the name — the **Fort Garry**, a chateau-like hotel built by the Grand Trunk Railway in 1913. South of Broadway, you can take a look at what high-tech meant to the late Victorians at **Dalnavert**, 61 Carlton Street, ((204) 943-2835, a house that was built for the son of John A. Macdonáld, Canada's first Prime Minister. It is a red-brick building that was built with

figure of a boy holds the torch of progress in one hand and carries a sheaf of wheat in the other to symbolize its importance in the development of Winnipeg. It is the work of French sculptor Charles Gadet, and it has become itself a symbol of the city. The building is set in lovely grounds dotted with statuary honoring the city's various ethnic groups with depictions of some of their distinguished countrymen. One statue of particular note is that of Louis Riel. The interior of the building is also quite spectacular and

OPPOSITE: Trading on the floor of the Winnipeg Commodity Exchange. ABOVE: Part of the façade of the Legislative Building, LEFT, and the towers of the Ukrainian church at the Ukrainian Cultural and Educational Centre.

free tours are conducted between mid-June and Labor Day that allow visitors a look at the Legislative Chamber.

Winnipeg has a superb **Art Gallery** housed in an unmissable wedge-shaped building at 300 Memorial Boulevard, ((204) 786-6641. It has a varied collection of international art, but is most famous for its wonderful collection of Inuit works, which are exhibited in continually changing displays. The gallery hosts some major temporary exhibitions, and is a center for other cultural events. It is open Tuesday to Sunday, admission is free.

Across the Red River lies the **St Boniface** district, the oldest French-speaking community in Canada and the largest in the west. French traders lived in the area from 1738 when Pierre Gaultier de la Varendrye arrived here. In 1819, following the building of a church here, a French community began to develop that included French Canadians and Metis. The **St Boniface Basilica** that stands today is a modern structure built among the ruins of an earlier cathedral that burned down in 1968. In the old cemetery lies the body of Louis Riel, who was executed following the defeat of the Northwest Rebellion.

Next to the basilica stands an oak structure that was built in 1846 as a convent for the Grey Nuns who arrived here from Montreal. It now contains the **St Boniface Museum** which has a large collection of artifacts belonging to the Metis and to other early settlers in the district and includes some memorabilia of Louis Riel. The museum is open daily; for information telephone (204) 237-4500. Also in the area is the **Church of the Precious Blood**, an interesting modern structure that is shaped like a teepee.

At the southern edge of the city you can visit **Riel House**, which stands close to the river at 330 River Road, St Vital, ((204) 257-1783. It was the home of the Riel family although Louis Riel never lived there. It has been restored to the year 1885, when Riel was executed. Moving eastwards, a striking glass pyramid houses the **Canadian Royal Mint** at 520 Lagimodière Boulevard, ((204) 257-3359. The mint produces coins for various countries, and guided tours show you

all the processes and high-tech equipment involved in making money.

Assiniboine Park over in the west end of the city is a large, pleasant park with recreation areas, a miniature railway, flower beds, an English garden where a statue of Queen Victoria stands, and an attractive old pavilion where you can sometimes catch a game of cricket. It also contains a zoo with a population of around 1,200 and a conservatory where there are tropical plants, birds, and monkeys. The park is on the southern bank of the Assiniboine River about 11 km (seven miles) from downtown at 2355 Corydon Avenue, ((204) 986-3130. For zoo information telephone (204) 888-3634.

For those interested in aircraft, the **Western Canadian Aviation Museum**, ((204)

786-5503, is located at Winnipeg International Airport west of downtown, and has some historical aircraft on display. The museum is open daily.

One very pleasant way to see Winnipeg is to take a **river cruise** down the Assiniboine and Red Rivers. There are daytime and nighttime cruises on the *M.S. Lady Winnipeg* and *M.S. Lady Rouge*, or aboard the *Lord Selkirk II*, which has three dining rooms. There's also the option of a paddlewheeler cruise on the *M.S. Paddlewheel Queen* or the *M.S. Paddlewheel Princess*. Contact Paddlewheel Cruises, 2285 Main Street, ((204) 339-1696. For details of the *Lady Winnipeg* and the *Lady Rose*, contact River Tours at 312 Nairn Avenue, ((204) 669-2824, and for details of the *Lord Selkirk II* get in touch

with Riverboat Management Ltd, 69 Birchbark Bay, ((204) 582-2331.

Winnipeg celebrates its rich ethnic mix in August with the colorful **Folklorama** festival that takes place in 40 pavilions throughout the town, each representing a different culture. There are parades, traditional dancing, music, crafts, and wonderful opportunities to sample different foods. You buy a "passport" which gains you admission to the various pavilions and also allows you to travel on the special buses that shuttle you between pavilions. For details of the events contact Folklorama, Winnipeg Convention Centre, 375 York Avenue, Winnipeg R3C 3J3, ((204) 944-9793. In mid-July the four-day

Feathers for sale in the Old Market Square.

Winnipeg Folk Festival is held at Birds Hill Park approximately 32 km (20 miles) northeast of the city. Among the sounds at this internationally famous celebration are gospel, bluegrass, and many other kinds of music. For details contact the Winnipeg Folk Festival, 8-222 Osborne Street South, ((204) 284-8487.

Excursions

Lower Fort Garry, 32 km (20 miles) north of Winnipeg along Highway 9, was built by the Hudson's Bay Company in the 1830's

and is the only remaining stone fort of that era in North America. It has been carefully restored and visitors can see the various living quarters, the fur loft, and the governor's residence as they were when the fort functioned as an important trading post. Before you begin your tour of the buildings, it's a good idea to watch the film shown in the reception area which fills you in on the background. Inside the compound, costumed "workers" will demonstrate crafts in the various workshops. In the grounds you'll see a restored York boat, a vessel that was designed for transporting furs. Buses run to the fort from the downtown bus station, or you could arrive in style aboard one of the river cruises from Winnipeg (see

above for details). The fort is open daily from early May to Labor Day and on weekends during September. Telephone (204) 669-2824 for information.

The **Steinbach Mennonite Village Museum** lies 61 km (38 miles) southeast of Winnipeg, about two and a half kilometers (one and a half miles) outside the village of Steinbach, a living museum where you can see a working mill and watch the Mennonites demonstrate their crafts, just as they would have in the nineteenth century. The Mennonite sect is one that is totally committed to pacifism and has been frequently persecuted because of its beliefs. The Mennonites who settled in Manitoba came from Russia in the 1870's and '80's, and this heritage village presents a colorful picture of their way of life. There is a restaurant here which serves traditional Mennonite food. The village is open daily from May to September, ((204) 326-9661. To get there from Winnipeg, take Highway 1 then 12, and watch for signs just north of Steinbach.

A great way of seeing the prairie is to take a trip aboard the *Prairie Dog Central*, an early twentieth-century steam train that takes you on a two-hour trip to **Grosse Isle**, 58 km (36 miles) northwest of Winnipeg. It's worth the trip not only to see the countryside rolling by, but also for the delightful experience of traveling in grand old-fashioned style. The train runs two trips on Sundays between June and September and leaves from St James Street Station, 1661 Portage Avenue, ((204) 284-2690.

Sports

Football fans can see the Blue Bombers play their Canadian Football League opponents at the Winnipeg Stadium to the west of downtown, ((204) 775-9751. Winnipeg's National **Hockey** League team are the Winnipeg Jets, and their home ground is the Winnipeg Arena, near the Winnipeg Stadium at 1430 Maroons Road, ((204) 772-9491. Throughout the year there's either **harness racing** or **thoroughbred racing** at Assiniboia Downs, 14 km (nine miles) west of the city at 3975 Portage Avenue, ((204) 885-3330.

There are **hiking** trails and **cycling** paths in the city parks, details of which are available from information centers. The public **swimming** pools are mostly indoors, and one of the largest is the Pan-Am Pool at 25 Poseidon Bay, ((204) 284-4030. There are several public and private **tennis** courts throughout the city and seven public **golf** courses. There are several **skating** rinks throughout Winnipeg, and when the snow comes there's **snowmobiling** at Birds Hill Provincial Park, about 32 km (20 miles) northeast of the city.

There's excellent **fishing** in the province, as you would expect with so many lakes, but

The **Exchange District** (see under Sights) has specialty shops and boutiques, while the **Old Market Square** at Bannatyne Avenue and King Street has a variety of stalls selling food, bric-a-brac, arts and crafts. **Osborne Village** at Osborne Street by the Legislative Building is an area brimming with interesting shops that sell antiques, imported and local arts and crafts, and clothing. For unusual gifts you could also try the gift shop in the **Ukrainian Cultural and Education Centre** at 184 Alexander Avenue East, next to the Museum of Man and Nature.

you need to venture outside Winnipeg. The Tourist Information Centres can help you with information on where to go and how to get there. Likewise they can help you with details of the excellent **canoe** routes that the province is famous for.

Shopping

Winnipeg has several shopping malls, of which one of the newer ones is **Portage Place**, a large complex that links up with the two major department stores on Portage Avenue — Eaton's, which is itself part of a complex, and The Bay. **Winnipeg Square** is another large underground shopping mall underneath the corner of Portage Avenue and Main Street.

Nightlife

Winnipeg has a lively nightlife. To find out what's going on check the entertainment listings that appear in the daily *Winnipeg Free Press* and the *Winnipeg Sun*. The **Manitoba Centennial Centre**, 555 Main Street, ((204) 956-1360, is the hub of Winnipeg's very sophisticated cultural scene. It is a complex comprising the Centennial Concert Hall, the Manitoba Theatre Centre, the Warehouse Theatre, and the excellent Manitoba Museum of Man and Nature.

The theatre season in Winnipeg really gets under way between September and

OPPOSITE: Walking out the past in Lower Fort Garry. ABOVE: The landmark windmill at the Steinbach Mennonite Village Museum.

early May, and during those months the **Manitoba Theatre Centre**, 174 Market Avenue, ℂ (204) 942-6537, stages a variety of comedy and serious drama, while the smaller **Warehouse**, ℂ (204) 942-6537, also part of the Manitoba Centennial Centre, stages experimental productions. There are several other companies scattered around town, including the innovative **Gas Station Theatre**, 445 River Avenue, ℂ (204) 284-2757.

The most cherished and famous of Winnipeg's cultural institutions is the **Royal Winnipeg Ballet**, which performs a pro-

gram of classical and modern works at the Centennial Concert Hall, 555 Main Street, ℂ (204) 956-1360, and also gives a free open-air performance in Assiniboine Park in the summer. The acclaimed **Winnipeg Symphony Orchestra** and the **Manitoba Opera Association** also perform at the Centennial Concert Hall.

A mixture of jazz, folk, and classical music can often be heard at the **Art Gallery**, 300 Memorial Boulevard, ℂ (204) 786-6641, and there's jazz or blues at the **Blue Note**, 220 Main Street. You'll find rock and other live music playing at various bars and clubs in the town, often in hotel lounges. Winnipeg has quite a lively nightclub scene and one that is rapidly changing, like the city itself. The Exchange District is a night-time hot spot where a favorite hang-out is **De Soto's**, 173 McDermott Street, ℂ (204) 943-4444.

ABOVE: A Filipino wedding in Winnipeg.
OPPOSITE: A sight for sore eyes (and teeth) in downtown Winnipeg.

WHERE TO STAY

For a list of Bed & Breakfast accommodation in the area contact an Information Centre or B&B of Manitoba, 93 Healy Street, Winnipeg R2N 2S2, ℂ (204) 256-6151. If a rural retreat appeals, contact the Manitoba Farm Vacations Association, 525 Kylemore Avenue, Winnipeg R3L 1B5, ℂ (204) 475-6624, for details. The Information Centres also have information on campgrounds in the region.

Mid-range

The **Westin Hotel**, 2 Lombard Place, Winnipeg R3B 0Y3, ℂ (204) 957-1350, toll-free (800) 228-3000, is in the very center of town and is one of the top-rated hotels. There are 350 luxurious rooms, excellent service, and guests have use of a swimming pool and fitness center. There is a choice of restaurants, a cafe, in-house entertainment. The hotel is conveniently linked to a large shopping complex. The **Sheraton Winnipeg** is another top downtown hotel located close to the Convention Centre at 161 Donald Street, Winnipeg R3C 1M3, ℂ (204) 942-5300, toll-free (800) 325-3535. Rooms here are large, well-equipped, and have balconies with some excellent views from the top floors. The hotel has a pool, a sundeck, a pleasant restaurant, with nightly entertainment in the lounge. Both hotels have prices that vary between mid-range and luxury.

For some old-style grandeur, you must go to **Fort Garry**, 222 Broadway, Winnipeg R3C 0R3, ℂ (204) 942-8251, toll-free (800) 665-8088. This castle-like hotel was built by the Grand Trunk Railway in 1913 and has recently undergone extensive renovation. The refurbishment has been done with great care, so the original splendor has been preserved throughout the hotel. There are 240 elegant rooms and suites, and two beautiful dining rooms.

Also downtown, the **Holiday Inn**, 350 St. Mary Avenue, Winnipeg R3C 3J2, ℂ (204) 942-0551, is part of a complex that connects with the Convention Centre. There are 390 pleasant rooms, indoor and outdoor pools, fitness facilities, and a good range of services. There's a choice of restaurants within the hotel, and several more inside the complex. Prices here vary between luxury and mid-range. **The Delta Winnipeg**, 288 Portage Avenue, Winnipeg R3C 0B8, ((204) 956-0410, is a downtown high-rise hotel with 270 rooms above its own multi-story parking facility. The rooms are smart, the service is first-rate, and the rooms all have good views. There are two attractive restaurants, one formal and one more casual, and a comprehensive range of amenities that include a fitness center, an indoor swimming pool, a cinema, and a supervised children's activity center.

For accommodation with lots of character and excellent service, book in at the **Marlborough Inn**, 331 Smith Street, Winnipeg R3B 2G9, ((204) 942-6411, which is in the town's financial district. It is a Victorian Gothic building with a grand interior of vaulted ceilings, stained glass, and polished wood. The rooms are stylish with modern conveniences, and the hotel has a delightful restaurant as well as a coffee shop.

The **Place Louis Riel**, 190 Smith Street, Winnipeg R3C 1J8, ((204) 947-6961, is a downtown apartment hotel that offers very good value for money. Accommodations range from studios to suites, all with kitchens, and you'll find everything you need for self-catering in the shops and facilities inside the hotel, making this a good choice for families.

Inexpensive
The **Gordon Downtowner Motor Hotel** at 230 Kennedy Street, Winnipeg R2K 2M2, ((204) 943-5581, with comfortable, convenient accommodation, bars and a restaurant, is excellent value. The **Charterhouse Hotel**, 330 York Avenue, Winnipeg R3C 0N9, ((204) 942-0101, is a good downtown choice. It has 90 rooms, some of which have balconies, a dining room, and a swimming pool, while the **St Regis**, 285 Smith Street, Winnipeg R3C 1J8, ((204) 942-0171, has basic but pleasant accommodation, and a nice atmosphere.

Just outside the city, **Journey's End**, 3109 Pembina Highway, Winnipeg R3T 4R6, ((204) 269-7390, toll-free (800) 668-4200, demonstrates again the reliable quality of this hotel chain. In the St Vital district at the eastern edge of town, the **Travelodge**, 20 Alpine Street, Winnipeg R2M 0Y5, ((204) 255-6000, toll-free (800) 255-3050, has attractively furnished, well-equipped rooms, and there's a dining room and nightclub on the premises.

There's a **YWCA** at 447 Webb Street, ((204) 943-0381, centrally positioned, offering dormitory accommodation and some shared rooms. Guests have use of the swimming pool. During the summer break the **University of Manitoba** has accommodation for visitors. For details contact the Conference Co-ordinator, 26 MacLean Crescent, Pembina Hall, ((204) 474-9942.

WHERE TO EAT

Winnipeg's diverse ethnic mix makes for some exciting dining, and a surprisingly large number of restaurants for a city of its size. Many of the restaurants, like the shops, are closed on Sundays.

Moderate to Expensive
Restaurant Dubrovnik, 390 Assiniboine Avenue, ((204) 944-0594, is one of the city's best restaurants. It is in a large Victorian house on the riverbank, with a charming interior that has retained many of the original features. Some beautiful examples of Yugoslavian craftwork adorn the walls. The food is continental but with Yugoslavian specialties on the menu, and it is quite delicious. Proof of its excellence lies in its popularity, so be sure to make a reservation. Prices vary between expensive and moderate. In Osborne Village, **Victor's** at 454 River Street, ((204) 284-2339, is housed within a large old building that also contains shops. It has an

attractive interior that features stained glass windows and the continental cuisine shows flair and innovation. Another popular dining spot is the **Royal Crown Revolving Restaurant**, at Fort Garry Place, 83 Garry Street, ((204) 947-5103. The menu here is continental on the whole, and the interior is quite plush. There are two restaurants which revolve in different directions, the Tiara Dining Room being the more exclusive of the two. Although the food is quite good, people come here mainly for the panoramic views of the city. The **Velvet Glove** in the Westin Hotel, 2 Lombard Place, ((204) 957-1350, is a top-rated restaurant that specializes in continental food prepared to gourmet standards. The setting is one of formal elegance amid deep tones of wood and brass, and the dining booths add an element of intimacy. Prices vary quite a lot, but unless you choose some particularly expensive dishes your bill is likely to be moderately priced.

The Exchange District is a lively area both by day and by night, and one of its top eating spots is **Oliver's** at 185 Lombard Avenue, ((204) 943-4448, which is housed within a renovated office building. The upstairs restaurant is very grand and furnished with antiques, giving it a rather lofty air. Steaks and seafood feature heavily on the suitably traditional menu, and lighter fare is served at lunchtime. **Churchill's**, in the Marlborough Inn, 331 Smith Street, ((204) 942-6411, bears out the Gothic exterior of this lovely hotel with arches, stained glass, and Victorian furnishings creating a delightful atmosphere. The menu concentrates on steaks, seafood, and continental dishes, and there is quite a good wine list. Over in the French district of St Boniface, **Le Beaujolais**, 131 Provencher Boulevard, ((204) 237-6276, serves traditional French and nouvelle dishes, all expertly prepared, and expertly served in attractive surroundings.

For good northern Italian cooking in an elegant setting, either go to **Cibo's** at 282 Bannatyne Avenue, ((204) 943-4922, or go upstairs at **Amici**, 326 Broadway, ((204) 943-4997. There's some delicious Swiss fare at the **Old Swiss Inn**, 207 Edmonton Street, ((204) 942-7725, where you'll find more than fondue on the menu, and warm,

friendly surroundings. **Hy's Steak Loft**, 216 Kennedy Street, serves good quality steaks and seafood in old-fashioned surroundings, and **Rae and Jerry's** in the west end of the city at 1405 Portage Avenue, ((204) 783-6155, is another popular steak house that includes chicken and fish dishes on its menu. Prices here vary between inexpensive and moderate. For steaks served in a rather different way, go to the **Ichiban Japanese Steak House**, 189 Carlton Street, ((204) 942-7493, where they get the Japanese treatment, and there's also a wide choice of other traditional dishes. The decor here is very easy on the eye, and an artificial brook adds the soothing sound of running water.

Inexpensive

The **Garden Creperie**, 349 York Street, ((204) 957-0221, in the Convention Centre complex, is a smart restaurant that has pancakes with just about every kind of filling, both savory and sweet. One of Winnipeg's ever-popular restaurants is the **Bistro Dansk**, 63 Sherbrook Street, ((204) 775-5662. It is a cheerful, friendly place with good Danish food and pleasant, helpful staff. Further along the street, **Impressions Cafe**, 102 Sherbrooke Street, ((204) 772-8049, is a busy place where people come to meet, chat, and linger over a sandwich or an omelette.

D'8 Schtove at 1842 Pembina Avenue, ((204) 275-2294, serves some delicious Mennonite food which, to give you an idea, features country sausages, soups, stroganoffs, and pirogi (which are rather like large ravioli but come with a variety of interesting stuffings).

The north end of town has a plethora of delis and cafes that make for some interesting and enjoyable dining. **Alycia's**, 559 Cathedral Avenue, ((204) 582-8789, serves home-made Ukrainian food in cozy surroundings decorated with traditional arts and crafts. Both **Oscar's**, 1204 Main Street, ((204) 589-8269, and **Simon's**, 1322 Main Street, ((204) 589-8289, are well-established Jewish delicatessens which are open into the small hours. For some tastes of Indonesia, try **Betsy's Place** at 1134 Main Street North.

In Osborne Village you can go English at the **Tea Cozy**, 99 Osborne Street, ((204) 475-

1027. Here you can eat breakfast, or have a spot of lunch, or take tea with crumpets, cakes, or biscuits. For a completely different cultural experience, **Carlos and Murphy's**, 129 Osborne Street, ((204) 284-3510, has a bar and a restaurant serving good Mexican food in a congenial atmosphere.

Winnipeg's **Chinatown** lies to the north of the Exchange District, stretching between James and Logan avenues and covering an eight-block area. As is the norm, you'll find several good-value Chinese restaurants here and a variety of Chinese cuisines.

HOW TO GET THERE

Flights from the U.S.A., Canada, and elsewhere in Manitoba arrive at Winnipeg International Airport, ((204) 983-8410. The airport is approximately six kilometers (four miles) northwest of downtown, about a 20-minute drive away, but allow longer during rush hours. There's a frequent city bus service between the airport and downtown, and an airport limo runs between the airport and some of the big hotels.

The VIA Rail station is downtown at 101-123 Main Street, ((204) 949-1830 or (204) 944-8780 for recorded information. Trains run to and from Vancouver via Regina, Calgary, Banff, and via Saskatoon, Edmonton, and Jasper. From the east the line runs into Winnipeg via Montreal, Ottawa, and Sudbury. Once a week between July and September VIA Rail runs a train to Hudson Bay, stopping at Churchill and Thompson.

The bus station is downtown at 487 Portage Place. Greyhound buses, ((204) 775-8301, operate to and from this terminal. Grey Goose Lines, 301 Burnell Street, ((204) 786-8891, links Winnipeg with other towns in Manitoba.

Winnipeg is quite isolated, so if you're driving the chances are that wherever you're coming from (unless it's the airport), you'll have quite a long drive ahead. The Trans-Canada Highway (Highway 1) runs through the city, linking it with Toronto, 2,093 km (1,300 miles) east, and Calgary, 1,359 km (844 miles) to the west. Minneapolis in Minnesota is 734 km (456 miles) from Winnipeg via I-94 and I-29 in the U.S., becoming Highway 75 in Manitoba.

ELSEWHERE IN MANITOBA

WHITESHELL PROVINCIAL PARK

There are wonderful opportunities for all kinds of outdoor pursuits in this large wilderness park that lies close to the Ontario border, 144 km (89 miles) east of Winnipeg. It is Canadian Shield country, an area rich in lakes, rivers, forest, and wildlife — ideal for hiking, canoeing, fishing, and all kinds of water sports. Areas of the park have been developed for tourism, and at **Falcon Lake** a recreational development offers a golf course, tennis courts, a ski resort, shops, and accommodations. If you prefer to get away from all that, there are quieter areas in the northern reaches of the park.

LAKE WINNIPEG

This vast lake lies to the north of Winnipeg and is lined with sandy beaches, making it an excellent place for relaxation and water sports. The fishing town of **Gimli** stands at the southwestern shores of the lake, 90 km (56 miles) north of Winnipeg. Back in the 1870s Icelanders came to the area in search of a new home free of the tyranny of the volcanoes that so disrupted their lives in their native land. They found that this area could offer them a good living through fishing and farming, and for a time the region was an independent country known as New Iceland. The community of Gimli retains a strong Icelandic identity and culture, and in August it celebrates the **Icelandic Festival**, a celebration of sports, music, parades, art, and traditional food. There is a museum on the waterfront that has displays on the history of the settlement.

Hecla Provincial Park encompasses a collection of islands in Lake Winnipeg. These islands are wildlife preserves and a bird-watcher's delight, while hikers, fishermen, canoeists, and winter sports enthusiasts also find much to enjoy here. Hecla Island is accessible by car, and at its northern end the **Gull Harbour Resort** manages to offer recreation facilities, attractive accommodation, and good Icelandic hospitality without marring the natural beauty of the island. The hotel is open year-round; for details telephone (204) 475-2354, toll-free (800) 475-5992.

RIDING MOUNTAIN NATIONAL PARK

This outdoor playground lies 248 km (154 miles) northwest of Winnipeg, on the highlands of a prairie escarpment. It has been partially developed in **Wasagaming** on the shores of Clear Lake, where there's a variety of accommodation and extensive recreational facilities, but the area remains largely unspoiled, with bison, elk, deer, and beaver inhabiting the parkland. In the winter there are cross-country skiing trails through the park and downhill skiing at Mount Agassiz. Close to Wasagaming the **Elkhorn Resort** has ranch-style accommodation, chalets, campsites, and organized horse riding treks. For information on the Elkhorn Resort telephone (204) 848-2802.

CHURCHILL

The small town of Churchill lies on the southwestern shore of Hudson Bay at the estuary of the Churchill River, and is one of the few places in the north accessible from the south — though not by road. It is one of the world's largest grain-handling ports, with huge grain elevators looming overhead, but it is increasingly becoming a popular tourist destination because of its substantial natural attractions. Although weather conditions are very hard here, with snow during most of the year creating a sparse, sub-arctic vegetation, the wildlife draws the visitors. It is a great place for polar bear watching, especially during September and October when migration is at its height and the bears are regularly seen wandering around the town. Specially-built buggies take visitors out on to the tundra on bear-spotting safaris. From July to early September beluga whales swim the waters of the bay, and a boat trip out to see them is usually rewarded with a playful performance. Large flocks of Canada geese, snow geese and other birds fill the skies. This is also an ideal place to witness the delightful phenomenon of the Northern Lights that beautifully illuminate the skies.

The area has quite a long history, having been inhabited for thousands of years by the Inuit and then stumbled upon by various explorers during their search for the Northwest Passage. In 1685 the Hudson's Bay Company established a trading post here and in 1731 the company began building **Fort Prince of Wales** across the estuary to protect their fur trading interests in the area. However, in an attack in 1782 by the French it proved a dismal failure, as the almost total lack of guards forced the governor to surrender without any resistance whatsoever. The remains of the fort, now a National Historic Park, can be visited by boat from the town. Guided tours are given from July to August; telephone (204) 675-8863 for information. The **Eskimo Museum** in the town, ((204) 675-2541, has an interesting collection of Inuit carvings and some ancient artifacts.

HOW TO GET THERE

Canadian Airlines International runs flights between Winnipeg and Churchill; there's also the option of a two-night VIA Rail journey from Winnipeg. One of the best ways to get there and to see more of the province is by the excellent VIA Rail 3,394-km (2,110-mile) package trip aboard the *Hudson Explorer*, which lasts six days and seven nights, and takes travelers from Winnipeg to Churchill via Flin Flon and Thompson. The package includes food, accommodation, and sightseeing trips, but as it is extremely popular, bookings have to be made almost a year in advance. For details contact VIA Rail at 123 Main Street, Winnipeg R3C 2P8, ((204) 949-1830.

OPPOSITE: Waterfowl and moose share the unspoiled beauty of Riding Mountain National Park.

Travelers' Tips

I'VE said it before and I'll say it again: the best tip I can offer any traveler is to get yourself a good travel agent. There is no substitute — not even this sparkling chapter — for the information and helpful advice that a travel agent has at his/her command. In a world where fares, schedules, even routes are changing hourly, only someone with access to the very latest information can give you the sort of guidance necessary to ensure a hassle-free holiday. I should also point out that, with the exception of the weather summaries in the WHEN TO GO

section, the information in this chapter covers all of Canada — not just the western (or eastern) half. This is because, firstly, the laws, customs, and general characteristics of the nation don't suddenly change at the Ontario/Manitoba (or Manitoba/Ontario) border. Secondly, such is the appeal of this lovely country, the visitor may well not want to restrict his or her visit to just one side of that border.

GETTING THERE

By Air

All the major international airlines fly to Canada, but Air Canada (toll-free 800/4-CANADA) has more flights to more Canadian cities than any other airline. This is true not only of flights from other continents but also flights

All aboard! A railway station, though it may be small, is never far away.

flights from the U.S. This is worth bearing in mind whatever your place of departure, because often it is cheaper to fly from Europe or elsewhere to the U.S. first and then on to Canada. Also, as you would expect, Air Canada has an extensive connector network of domestic airlines linking cities within Canada.

Another point in Air Canada's favor, from my point of view at least, is that it is a smoke-free airline. Smoking is prohibited on all its European, North American, and transatlantic routes. Even smokers agree that it makes for a distinctly more pleasant environment in which to travel.

One further, general tip regarding air travel to Canada — or anywhere else for that matter — is to get to the airport early. This, I know, is a contentious issue among frequent flyers, some of whom like to arrive at the airport just as the pilot is starting up the engines. But for me there are three compelling arguments in favor of heading for the airport ahead of time. One is that it gives you a safety margin in case you encounter a problem — a traffic jam, a flat tire, a detour — on the way. You would be surprised how many people miss planes because they didn't leave themselves time to absorb unexpected delays. Secondly, by getting to the airport early you have a much better seat selection for your flight — and the longer the flight, the more important it is to have the seat you want. (If you are flying on a British Airways jumbo jet, for example, you can often get a seat upstairs, where it is more comfortable and the service is more attentive.) Thirdly, early arrivals at the airport avoid the long queues to check in, which means that the time that would otherwise be spent standing around shepherding one's luggage slowly forward can be spent reading, shopping, having drinks, having a meal — in a word, relaxing.

By Rail

Amtrak has two trains daily from New York City to Montreal, one going through upstate New York and the other, an overnight train which begins in Washington, D.C., going through Vermont. There is also daily service from New York to Toronto, via Niagara

Falls, and from Chicago to Toronto via Detroit. For details write to Amtrak, 400 North Capitol Street, N.W., Washington D.C. 20001 or call, toll-free, (800) 872-7245.

BY BUS

Greyhound is the only company operating a cross-border service, but it has such a huge route system that you should have no difficulty in getting to virtually any point in Canada from anywhere in the U.S. It also has a hugely complicated system of fares, discount fares, seasonal rates, unlimited-travel passes, and so on. Information is available from any Greyhound office or from Greyhound Line, Inc., Greyhound Tower, Phoenix, Arizona 85077; alternatively, you can call (212) 971-6363 for information about Greyhound's service to eastern Canada and (213) 620-1200 for details of the service in the west.

BY CAR

There are 13 principal border crossing points where the American highway system connects directly with the Canadian. The crossing is usually a quick, simple matter, although in peak season you might want to avoid the busier crossing points such as Detroit-Windsor and Niagara Falls. Once in Canada, no matter where you've crossed, you are only a short drive from the Trans-Canada Highway.

TOURIST INFORMATION

Canada — or I should say the visitor to Canada — is blessed with a whole galaxy of helpful agencies designed to provide information on every subject of potential concern to tourists. In the "General Information" sections of the preceding chapters I have already listed the local and provincial agencies, and in the following pages I will give the addresses and telephone numbers of the specific-interest agencies set up to deal with enquiries relating to the various topics discussed in this chapter. Here, then, are the people who speak for the country as a whole.

IN CANADA
Tourism Canada, 235 Queen Street, Ottawa, Ontario K1A 0H6. ℂ (613) 954-3854 or 954-3980.

IN THE U.S.A.
Canadian Consulates General:
New York 16th Floor, 1251 Avenue of the Americas, New York NY 10020. ℂ (212) 586-2400.
Chicago 12th Floor, 310 South Michigan Avenue, Chicago IL 60604. ℂ (312) 992-0637.
San Francisco Suite 2100, 50 Freemont Street, San Francisco CA 94105. ℂ (415) 495-6021.

IN EUROPE
London Canadian Government Office of Tourism, Canada House, Trafalgar Square, London SW1Y 5BJ. England. ℂ (071) 629-9492 or 930-8540.
Paris Office du Tourisme du Canada, 37 Avenue Monta, Paris 75008, France.
Frankfurt Kanadisches Fremdeverkehrsampt, Biebergasse 6–10, 6 Frankfurt am Main, Germany.

IN AUSTRALIA
Sydney Canadian Government Office of Tourism, 8th Floor, AMP Centre, 50 Bridge Street, Sydney NSW 2000. ℂ (02) 231-6522.

EMBASSIES AND CONSULATES

American Embassy: 100 Wellington Street, Ottawa K1P 5T1. ℂ (613) 238-5335
American Consulates: 360 University Avenue, Toronto M5G 1S4, ℂ (416) 595-1700; Suite 1122, South Tower, Place Desjardins, Montreal H5B 1G1, ℂ (514) 281-1886; 1 Avenue Sainte-Genevieve, Quebec City G1R 4A7, ℂ (418) 692-2095; Suite 910, Scotia Square, Halifax B3J 3K1, ℂ (902) 429-2480; Room 100, 6 Donald Street, Winnipeg R3L 0K7, ℂ (204) 475-3344; Room 1050, 615 Macleod Trail SE, Calgary T2G 4T8, ℂ (403) 266-8962; Columbia Centre IV, 1199 West Hastings Street, Vancouver V6E 2Y4, ℂ (604) 685-4311.
Australian High Commisson: Suite 710, 55 O'Connor Street, Ottawa K1P 6L2, ℂ (613) 238-0844.

Australian Consulate: 22nd Floor, Commerce Court North, King and Bay Streets, Toronto M5L 1B9, ((416) 367-0783.
British High Commission: 80 Elgin Street, Ottawa K1P 5K7, ((613) 237-1530.
British Consulates: Suite 1910, 777 Bay Street, Toronto M5G 2G2, ((416) 593-1290; Suite 901, 1155 University Street, Montreal H3B 3A7, ((514) 866-5863; Suite 501, Purdy's Wharf, Lower Water Street, Halifax B3J 2X1, ((902) 429-4330.
Irish Embassy: 170 Metcalfe Street, Ottawa, ((613) 233-6281.

TRAVEL DOCUMENTS

U.S. citizens require only proof of American citizenship to enter Canada (passport, birth certificate, voter registration card, or naturalization certifcate); U.S. residents who are not citizens must show their Alien Registration Card. British and Australian visitors, as well as citizens of most European and Commonwealth countries, need a valid passport but no visa. If in doubt, check with your travel agent or the nearest Canadian embassy, high commission, or consulate.

CUSTOMS

Customs regulations are similar to those in most countries, including the usual restrictions on bringing in meats, plants, and animals. Items intended for personal or professional use do not have to be declared, and you are allowed up to 200 cigarettes, 50 cigars, and 40 ounces of wine or spirits duty-free. You can bring in gifts up to $40 in value. There are no currency restrictions.

Hunting and fishing equipment may be brought in duty-free as well, but all firearms and ammunition must be declared and a written description of each item, including serial numbers of guns, must be provided.

Details of Customs regulations are available from Revenue Canada, Customs and Excise, Connaught Building, Sussex Drive, Ottawa, Ontario K1A 0L5.

WHEN TO GO

Generally speaking, very generally speaking, the seasons in Canada's more temperate climes divide up as follows: winter occupies most of the long stretch from November to the end of March, summer occurs in June, July, and August, while the "shoulder" seasons of spring and autumn are largely confined to April to May and September to October.

The most temperate climate in all of Canada belongs to British Columbia, where mild summers fade gently into mild winters. In Vancouver, for example, the temperature seldom rises above 21°C (70°F) in summer, and seldom dips below freezing in winter. You will, however, need to take an umbrella: in December and January alone meteorologists count on seeing 42 days of rainfall, an average that drops to about seven days in July and August.

Once you are east of the Rockies, the climate abruptly changes. The Prairie Provinces of Alberta, Saskatchewan, and Manitoba are known for their climatic extremes. In all three provinces you will find summers that are hot and sunny, though punctuated by the occasional thunderstorm, followed almost immediately by winters that are cold, very cold, and generally dry. To give you some idea of the extremes of weather to be encountered on the Canadian prairies, in Saskatchewan temperatures of

ABOVE: Autumn leaves in New Brunswick. OPPOSITE: Snow sculptures adorn Quebec City's Winter Carnival.

45°C (113°F) have been recorded in summer and temperatures of -57°C (-70°F) have been recorded in winter.

Obviously, the decision of when to go will depend on what you are going for, and by now you should have a pretty good idea of what each region has to offer at what time of the year. But just to make your planning a little more precise, here are the average daytime temperatures in degrees Celsius and Fahrenheit for each month of the year in three three principal cities of western Canada:

WHAT TO TAKE

All seasoned travelers, including this one, will urge you to travel light. That is to say we agree that you should not take more than you think you will need; where we disagree is in helping you decide exactly what you do need. For my part, I think the criterion should be not the desirability of having a particular article with you at any given time, but the undesirability of not having a particular article with you when

VANCOUVER
Jan: 4°C/39°F Feb: 5°C/41°F Mar: 6°C/43°F
Apr: 9°C/48°F May:12°C/56°F Jun: 15°C/59°F
July:17°C/63°F Aug: 17°C/63°F Sept: 15°C/59°F
Oct:10°C/50°F Nov: 7°C/44°F Dec: 4°C/39°F

CALGARY
Jan: 11°C/12°F Feb: -8°C/18°F Mar:-5°C/23°F
Apr: 6°C/43°F May:10°C/50°F Jun: 13°C/56°F
July:16°C/61°F Aug: 15°C/59°F Sept: 11°C/52°F
Oct: 7°C/44°F Nov:-5°C/23°F Dec: -8°C/18°F

EDMONTON
Jan: -15°C/6°F Feb:-11°C/12°F Mar: -6°C/22°F
Apr: 4°C/39°F May:11°C/52°F Jun: 15°C/59°F
July:18°C/64°F Aug: 16°C/61°F Sept: 11°C/52°F
Oct: 6°C/43°F Nov: -4°C/25°F Dec:-11°C/12°F

you really need it. On that principle, here is my list of things you should never leave home without.

At the top of the list, by a wide margin, is a Swiss Army knife (or, to put it another way, two knives, two screwdrivers, a bottle opener, a can opener, a corkscrew, a toothpick, tweezers, nail file, and scissors). I would also throw in a miniature flashlight and a small travel alarm clock (or clock radio). And of course you will need an adaptor and/or transformer if you plan to take any electrical appliances that don't run on 110 volts or don't have an American-type plug.

Because even the most minor physical irritations or afflictions can ruin a trip if they strike at the wrong time (which is the only time they strike), I would be sure to carry eye drops, an inhaler or nose drops, a lip balm for chapped lips, aspirin or codeine, anti-diarrhoea tablets, antiseptic ointment, a few bandages and a few packets of tissues (which can also serve as toilet paper in an emergency).

Because looking good can sometimes matter as much as feeling good, I would take along a tube of concentrated detergent, a stain remover, sachets of towelettes or "wet wipes", sachets of shoe polishers, and —

please note — a compact, telescoped umbrella. Always take an umbrella, whatever your destination.

Optional near-essentials would include things like a couple of plastic cups, a coil for heating water, coffee and tea bags, a few bouillon cubes, some salt and pepper packets, and artificial sweeteners.

By the way, everything I have mentioned so far, with the exception of the umbrella, will fit easily into a medium-sized plastic freezer bag. Ah, that's another thing! Resealable, ziplock plastic bags come in very handy when traveling — not least when you want to separate items that you want to keep apart, or segregate items that are damp or dirty or might be inclined to leak.

Speaking of separating items, if you are planning to travel by air and you want to take a Swiss Army knife, or anything else that might conceivably be considered a "weapon", be sure to pack it in the luggage you intend to check. You don't want to be mistaken for an armed passenger. On the other hand, if you are taking any battery-powered gadgets — shavers, cassette players, etc. — carry them with you on the airplane or take the batteries out before packing them, Airline security personnel get understandably jumpy when unidentified objects with batteries in them show up on their X-ray screen.

Now we come to those things that you don't need to be told to take with you — passport, tickets, driver's license, health insurance card, travelers' checks, credit cards, cash — because you would be lost without them. But suppose you do suddenly find yourself without them? Then what? Hassle, that's what. But there are ways of minimizing the hassle, and indeed of reducing the risk of incurring it at all, before you go.

First of all, be sure to take with you lists of the numbers of all travel documents, cards, and checks you will be carrying, along with any telephone numbers included on them. This will greatly facilitiate their quick replacement if lost. (I also take photocopies of my passport and any travel tickets: duplicates are issued more speedily if people can see a copy of the original — much more speedily in the case of tickets or refunds.) It is a good idea, too, to get an international driver's license, obtainable from your automobile club, so that you can keep your home driver's license tucked away in a safe place. And speaking of safe places, always leave your inessential credit cards behind when you go on a trip, and of those you take with you carry only a couple in your wallet: any others should be tucked away in the same safe place as your passport, driver's license, extra travelers' checks, etc. It's just another way of ensuring that any loss causes only a temporary inconvenience.

I realize that all this may seem like carrying prudence to somewhat extreme lengths, but I can assure you that if you have the misfortune while traveling to lose your wallet, by whatever means, you will be very grateful to have a "shadow wallet" safely in reserve.

When it comes to clothing, toiletries, jewelry, and gadgetry, it's up to you to decide what and how much you want to take. Canadians are very casual in their dress, so there is no need to take formal or semi-formal wear beyond what your taste and your expected engagements require. There is, however, a need to take some warm clothing — a sweater or two perhaps, the odd woollen or corduroy garment, a windbreaker — because even in summer, even in the hottest spots, it can turn quite cool in the evenings, especially if you happen to be on or near the water.

I will leave the last word on what to take with you to my Canadian colleague Wallace Immen, who writes on travel for *The Globe and Mail* in Toronto. He says that while you should always dress comfortably for long flights, you should also dress respectably. After all, he reasons, rather depressingly, if your luggage is lost, you could be dressed like that for quite a while.

BASICS

TIME

Canada is divided into six time zones, including Newfoundland's own, typically quirky time zone, which is only a half-hour ahead of Atlantic Standard Time in the Maritime Provinces. The other four time zones correspond to, and are continuations of, the four U.S. time zones: Eastern Standard Time, Central Standard Time, Mountain Standard Time, and Pacific Standard Time.

Atlantic Time is four hours behind Greenwich Mean Time, so when it is 8 pm in London, it is 4 pm in the Maritimes (4:30 pm in Newfoundland). Quebec and all of Ontario to the east of Thunder Bay are on Eastern Time, five hours behind GMT. Manitoba and the eastern half of Saskatchewan are on Central Time; the rest of Saskatchewan, Alberta and northeast British Columbia are on Mountain Time. All of British Columbia west of the Rockies is on Pacific Time, eight hours behind GMT.

All of Canada — with the mysterious exception of eastern Saskatchewan — observes Daylight Savings Time from the first Sunday in April, when the clocks are put forward one hour, until the last Sunday in October.

ELECTRICITY

The electric current is 110-120 volts AC, the same as in the U.S., and the sockets only take American-type plugs with two flat prongs.

WEIGHTS AND MEASURES

Canadians, like just about everybody else in the world except their American neighbors and their British cousins, rely almost exclusively on the metric system. Thus, while Canadians are spared the old question, "How much is that in dollars?", they now have to face the new question, "How far is that in miles?" or "What is that in pounds and ounces?"

To save the uninitiated the bother of having to ask such questions, and the Canadians the bother of having to answer them, I

ABOVE: Winter in Canada is a time for bundling up.
OPPOSITE: The world's first steam-powered clock keeps time in Vancouver's colorful Gastown district.

have pored over countless conversion tables (they can be found in any dictionary, almanac, or appointments diary) in an effort to decide which one, or which format, would be the most useful to readers who are, by definition, on the move. In the end I decided that none of them would be of much use — unless you want to have to pick up this book (and a calculator) every time you read a label, or see a road sign, or hear a weather forecast. (Clothing sizes are a different matter, and are dealt with in the "Shopping" section of this chapter.) Therefore, to make life easier for those not yet numerate in metrics, I have devised my own rough-and-ready (and of course approximate) system for making instant conversions on the spot. It is not only simple, but easy to memorize, so long as you remember that the colloquial term "a bit" here represents one-tenth of whatever it is next to. Thus:

One meter = a yard and a bit; One kilometer = a half-mile and a bit; One kilogram = two pounds and a bit (500g = 1 lb & a bit); One liter = a bit more than an American quart and a bit less than a British quart

For converting to degrees Fahrenheit, simply double the figure you are given in Celsius and add 30, topping it up by a couple of degrees when you get above 20°C. The temperature you come up with won't be precisely accurate, but it will be close enough.

HEALTH

You really haven't much to worry about, because health hazards are few and the health care is excellent. It can be expensive, though, so American visitors should check to make sure that their health insurance provides coverage in Canada, and overseas visitors should arrange short-term medical coverage for the period they expect to be there. An excellent medical emergency policy, which also includes personal travel insurance, is available from Europ Assistance Ltd., 252 High Street, Croydon, Surrey CR0 1NF, England. ((081) 680-1234. A similar policy, similarly priced, is offered by Wexas International, 45-49 Brompton Road, London SW3 1DE, England. ((071) 589-3315.

Another wise precaution is to carry a card in your wallet giving your blood type and listing any allergies or chronic conditions (including the wearing of contact lenses) that might affect treatment in an emergency.

Beyond that, it's always a good idea to have insect repellent with you, because in summer Canada has plenty of insects to repel, especially black flies and mosquitoes. A sunscreen lotion is also advisable, as the Canadian sun has a burning power out of all proportion to its heating power.

MONEY

Canadian currency resembles American currency in every important respect except value: the coins are in the same denominations and go by the same names (penny, nickel, dime, etc.), the paper notes are all the same size (but in different colors according to value). There is, however, a gold-colored $1 coin nicknamed the "loonie" after the bird that appears on it.

American dollars are widely accepted, at their greater value, but using them introduces an unnecessary complication into a transaction, as well as an unnecessary discourtesy.

As in all countries with hard currencies, the banks offer the best exchange rates — much better than hotels, for example. Banking hours are 10 am to 3 pm weekdays, though most banks stay open later on Fridays. All major credit cards are accepted anywhere you are likely to go; consequently you are advised to carry a minimum of cash. If you prefer using non-plastic money, take it in the form of dollar travelers' checks. They can be cashed everywhere, with proper identification (e.g. passport, driver's license), although the larger denominations will not always be welcome in places like restaurants that don't like being used as banks.

In general, however, I would recommend floating through Canada on little rafts of plastic. Provided that you pay your credit card bills promptly when they come in, you will not only benefit from the detailed accounting they supply but you will have saved the cash deposits often required by hotels, for example, while borrowing the money for your travel expenses interest-free.

CRIME

Crime? What crime? Canada may well be the most law-abiding of the world's industralized nations. Violent crime isn't exactly unheard of, but it's not heard of very often. The streets of Canada's cities are as safe at night as they are in the daytime.

All this law-and-orderliness notwithstanding, one should still take the same basic precautions here that a sensible person would take anywhere: leaving valuables in the hotel safe, locking your hotel room and car, not leaving valuable items visible in your car when unattended, not carrying all your cash and cards with you when you go out, not going for late-night strolls through slum areas. In short, exercise your common sense, secure in the knowledge that Canadians can be counted on to exercise their common decency.

GETTING AROUND

BY AIR

The country's two major carriers, Air Canada and Canadian Airlines International, handle the bulk of the middle- and long-distance air traffic, while dozens of local carriers connect the remaining dots on the map. Thus there are very few places in Canada, even including remote offshore islands, that are not accessible by air.

Air fares in Canada are predictably unpredictable, but it is worth noting that Air Canada offers Flexipass tickets which allow vistors to travel at reduced rates between any of 28 Canadian cities. Both Air Canada and Canadian Airlines International offer a variety of holiday packages, called Canadapass and Canadian Routes respectively, that cater to almost every conceivable holiday requirement at special prices. Ask your travel agent for details, or contact:

Air Canada Place Air Canada, 500 Blvd Dorchester Ouest, Montreal, Quebec H2Z 1X5. ℂ (514) 879-7000, toll-free (800) 4-CANADA.

Canadian Airlines International 2800-700 Second Street SW, Calgary, Alberta T2P 2W2. ℂ (403) 235-8100, toll-free (800) 426-7000.

BY RAIL

There are two main railways in Canada, Canadian Pacific (CP) and Canadian National (CN), both of whose passenger services are operated by the government-owned

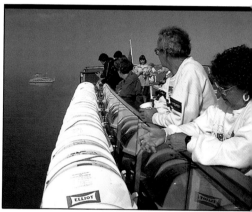

VIA Rail. Sadly, the VIA Rail network is shrinking due to cuts in government funding, but there is still regular service between the major cities, especially in eastern Canada, and it is still possible to make the spectacular transcontinental journey by train in the comfort of your own rolling bedroom or roomette.

VIA Rail also issues a Canrailpass and a Youth Canrailpass, which make possible substantial savings by allowing unlimited travel over specified areas for varying period of time in both high season and low season. Your travel agent will have all the particulars. Alternatively, you can get in touch with:

VIA Rail 935 La Gauchetikre Ouest, Montreal, Quebec H3C 3N3. ℂ (514) 871-1331, toll-free (800) 663-0667.

The ferry across the St. Lawrence to Rivière-du-Loup, at the base of the Gaspé Peninsula.

BY BUS

Where there's a way, there's a willing bus to take you wherever you want to go in Canada. Greyhound has a nationwide route system, and there are five or six large regional companies that reach into the nooks and crannies that Greyhound misses. Moreover, most of the bus lines participate in Greyhound's Ameripass coupon program, which allows unlimited travel at a discounted rate. In addition, there is the Across Canada Ticket and the International Canadian Pass, as well as the Tourpass Voyageur in Quebec and Ontario.

BY CAR

Canada, only slightly less than the U.S., is a motorist's dream. The highway system may not be as sprawling as in the U.S., but it doesn't have to be, since most of the places visited by tourists and natives alike are within easy driving distance of the Trans-Canada Hghway. And the gasoline may not be as cheap as in the U.S., but it's a lot cheaper than it is in Europe.

All the major American car-rental firms (Hertz, Avis, Budget) are represented across the country, as is the largest Canadian company, Tilden, which is affiliated with National Car Rental in the U.S. and has over 370 offices all over Canada. If you are planning to rent a car in the summer, it would be a good idea to reserve one before you leave home.

BY FERRY

There are both car and passenger ferry services available on most of Canada's major lakes and rivers, as well as between the mainland and the offshore islands. Ferries across the St. Lawrence and to Prince Edward Island and Vancouver Island don't require reservations, but other ferries should be booked in advance — well in advance if you are taking a car with you. Information is available from your travel agent or from:

Marine Atlantic P.O. Box 250, North Sydney, Nova Scotia B2A 3M3. ((902) 794-7203, toll-free (800) 341-7981.

M.S. Chi-Cheemaun Owen Sound, Ontario N4K 4K8. ((519) 596-2510.

British Columbia Ferry Corporation 818 Broughton Street, Victoria, British Columbia V8W 1E4. ((604) 669-1211.

BY LOCAL TRANSPORT

Taxis can always be found at airports, railway stations, and major hotels. They can also be hailed in the street fairly easily in the larger cities; elsewhere they can be ordered by telephone. Rates are quite reasonable by American or European standards, and a tip of 15 percent or so is normal. In some prov-

The midnight sun shines on a lonely northern road.

inces not all the taxis have meters, making it advisable to agree on the fare before beginning a journey.

In Toronto and Montreal the subway system provides a handy way of getting around. Subway tickets, which can be bought singly or in books, are on sale at newsagents as well as at the subway stations. If you choose to travel by bus, be sure to have the exact fare with you, as bus drivers do not carry change.

DRIVING

You will, of course, be required to have a valid driver's license. I would also strongly recommend — indeed, I have already recommended in the section on "What to Take"

— that you get an international driving permit as well. In addition, you will need a non-resident's Interprovincial Motor Vehicle Liability insurance card.

The driving regulations will be familiar to anyone used to driving in the U.S. or on the Continent: you drive on the right and overtake on the left, vehicles approaching from the right have the right of way at intersections, the use of seat belts is compulsory (except in Prince Edward Island and Alberta), and driving under the influence of alcohol will incur stiff penalties.

The speed limit on highways is usually 100 kph (60 mph), on smaller roads 80 kph (50 mph), and in towns 80 kph down to 50 kph (30 mph). You must stop if you come upon a school bus with its red lights flashing. You may turn right at a red light (except in Quebec) if you stop first and make sure the road is clear.

Note: It is a very bad idea to commit a traffic offense in Quebec, as the fines are much harsher there than elsewhere in Canada.

There are plenty of 24-hour service stations flanking the major highways, while those in town tend to close around 9 pm (7 pm in small towns, and all day on Sundays). Gasoline (or petrol) is sold by the liter, and is available in all grades. Most stations

take credit cards, and most are now self-service.

In the event of an accident, you should get to a telephone and dial the operator ("0") who can connect you with the police and emergency services. In case of a breakdown, members of automobile clubs affiliated with the Canadian Automobile Association can call the CAA toll-free at (800) 336-4357. Non-members can call the CAA at (613) 820-1400 and request towing services for which there will be a charge. For additional information contact:

The Canadian Automobile Association 1775 Courtwood Crescent, Ottawa, Ontario K2C 3J2. ((613) 226-7631.

ACCOMMODATION

There is little point in discussing Canadian guest accommodations in any great detail because they are pretty much what you would expect them to be, and you will usually get pretty much what you pay for. In any

case, every provincial tourism office will be more than happy to send you a comprehensive and detailed guide to the full range of accommodations available in their particular province.

If there are any surprises to be encountered on the accommodation front, they are contained in that phrase, "full range": the range is very full indeed. Apart from an unusually varied selection of hotels and motels, there are country inns, effency apartments, bed & breakfast places, youth hostels, YMCAs and YWCAs, "tourist homes", university and college residences, wilderness lodges, campgrounds, and farms and ranches.

To say that one is spoiled for choice is to put it mildly. Wherever you go in Canada, you will find that there are types of accommodation to appeal to every taste and to suit every budget. If luxury and comfort are your priorities, there are deluxe hotels to rank with any in the world. If convenient locations while motoring are important, you will be pleased to know that there are motels in every price range sprinkled along the nation's main roads and highways. If economy is the paramount consideration, you will be able to get rooms at a YMCA, YWCA, college, university hostel, or tourist home in all but the most remote spots — and sometimes even there. If conversation and "character" count alongside economy, there is bound to be a bed & breakfast house to fit the bill.

If you will be staying in one place for a longish period, particularly with children or in a group, you will get both privacy and savings (on food) in an efficiency apartment in one of Canada's many apartment hotels. If you will be staying in one place for a shortish period, you will get privacy and savings and funny stories later in one of Canada's many campgrounds. If rustic charm is what you're looking for, there are delightful country inns spread across the country. If you want to get into serious rusticity, there is no better way than to stay on one of the hundreds of working farms and ranches that offer accommodation as well as hearty meals and healthy activities. And if you just want to get away from it all and hunt or fish or think about the human condition, there are some wonderful lodges in remote wilderness areas where Nature starts at your front door.

If you are looking for a home away from home, you should consider a holiday home exchange with a Canadian family. I can recomend two companies arranging such exchanges:

Interhome Holidays Canada, Inc. 156 Randall Street, Oakville, Ontario L6J 1P4. ((416) 849-9888.

West World Holiday Exchange, 1707 Platt Crescent, North Vancouver, B.C. V7J 1X9. ((604) 987-3262.

If budgetary considerations are uppermost, you can get further information from:

The Canadian Hostelling Association, 1600 James Naismith Drive, 6th Floor, Suite 608, Gloucester, Ontario K1B 5N4. ((613) 748-5638.

The YMCA National Council 2160 Yonge Street, Toronto, Ontario M4S 2A1.

For YMCA and YWCA residence directories you should phone (416) 485-9557 for the YMCA and (416) 593-9886 for the YWCA.

The only way to appreciate fully the extent of the choices available to you in other types of accommodations is to contact the government tourism offices in the individual provinces. As I said, they will be more than happy to provide you with comprehensive guides to the range of accomodation on offer.

EATING OUT

It must be said that Michelin-star-spangled restaurants are few and far between in Canada. But that is not to say that you can't eat well, wonderfully well, in every part of the country. The secret — if you can call something so obvious a secret — is to concentrate on the special delicacies for which each part of the country is best known.

Thus, in the eastern half of the country, you will want to sample some of the many cod dishes, and the seal flipper pie, which Newfoundland has made famous. In Nova Scotia, you must try the clam chowder, Digby scallops, Lunenberg sausage, and "Solomon Gundy", a pickled-herring-and-

chopped-meat concoction that is much better than it sounds. In Prince Edward Island, the Malpeque oysters and the local cheeses are the star attractions. In New Brunswick, go for the broiled Atlantic salmon and the steamed fiddleheads, which are the new shoots of an edible fern unique to the province. In all of the Maritimes you should treat yourself to the glorious desserts made with any of the berries with which the area abounds. And in all of these provinces you will find, in my opinion, the finest lobster in the world.

Quebec, once the heart of New France, would be called New Normandy if it were named after its stomach, for its distinctive cuisine still remains based on the French peasant cooking of its early Norman (and, to a lesser extent, Breton) settlers. Not that you can't get classic — or nouvelle — French cooking in Quebec; you can, famously, in both Montreal and Quebec City. But you can get that in New York, or Los Angeles, or Mexico City, or in dozens of other cities around the world. What makes Quebec special is the way provincial Canadian

---

OPPOSITE: Ottawa's renowned Château Laurier.
ABOVE: A leisurely lunch in Montreal.

foodstuffs have been used to create provincial French food. A few examples: soupe aux pois, a thick pea soup; tourtires, delicious meat pies (the meat is usually pork, but can be hare or even venison); cretons, pork pâte usually served with rye bread; cipaille, a pastry-layered game-and-potato pie; andouillette aux fines herbes, a spicy pork tripe sausage; trempette, fresh baked bread saturated with maple syrup and covered in whipped cream. Maple syrup, in fact, is a theme running through (or over) almost all of Quebecois cooking — in sauces, in desserts, in curing ham — which is hardly surprising, given that the province literally oozes with maple syrup. What is perhaps surprising is that Montreal rivals new York as a Mecca for worshippers of the great deli sandwich.

Happily, the French influence — and the maple syrup — doesn't stop running when you get to Ontario, although here the culinary emphasis shifts to the province's game birds — you must have the Haliburton pheasant—and its dazzling variety of freshwater fish from Ontario's countless lakes and rivers. There is also, in Toronto, a rapidly growing array of first-rate ethnic restaurants: Greek, Italian, Chinese, Indian, Polish, Hungarian, and even Japanese. One of my favorite sushi bars, in fact, is in the middle of Toronto.

In the western half of the country, you will want to go for the Pacific salmon, shrimp, black cod, and king crab in British Columbia. And for a change from all the wonderful seafood, you should try the lamb from Saltspring Island or the moose steaks from the Yukon. Afterwards, or any other time for that matter, you can enjoy the fresh fruit from the Okanagan Valley.

In Alberta, The Steak is the thing. Even if you are not normally a beefeater, you will be won over by Alberta's beef. Only in Argentina have I ever tasted steaks to compare with the ones you can get here. In fact, across all the Prairie Provinces the beef is exceptional — as is the freshwater fish from the thousands of lakes and rivers carved into the prairies. In Saskatchewan and Manitoba, I

would urge you to order wildfowl — especially the partridge and wild duck — and even the prosaic farm birds, which are tastier here than almost anywhere else because they eat better here. In these provinces, too, you will come across a sort of Borscht Belt, where the large Ukrainian population has left its mark on the menus in the form of spicy sausages, dumplings, and a variety of cabbage dishes.

On the other hand, if you are just looking for a pit stop where you can refuel quickly, you will find coffee shops, diners, and fast-

food places everywhere you go — many of them open 24 hours a day.

As in the U.S., Canadian restaurants generally tend to be informal and welcoming. They also tend to serve meals at earlier hours than Europeans are used to, so if you are counting on having a late lunch or dinner you would be wise to check on kitchen closing times first.

DRINKING

Canadians are funny about drinking (alcohol, I mean). I remember the first time I was ever in Canada I asked a shopkeeper where I might find the nearest liquor store. This

A quick lunch.

simple question caused utter consternation, followed by endless consultations, followed by… blank. The reason, it turned out, was that liquor stores — or just ordinary grocery stores or supermarkets selling liquor — do not exist outside Quebec. To buy liquor by the bottle, except in parts of Quebec, you have to go to an official government outlet — of which there are maddeningly few, maddeningly out of the way, maddeningly closed at night and on Sundays and holidays — and there, but only there, are you allowed to conduct your thirsty transaction. Why this should be the case I cannot say. What I can say is that it interferes with one's budgeting more than with one's drinking, because even the happiest of Happy Hours is not as economical as a couple of self-catered cocktails, and a Rémy in your room is better value than any post-prandial drink in a restaurant.

Even the most convivial imbibing is complicated by local laws, which come in various shades of blue. In some places you can get a drink if you're 18, in other places you have to be 19. In some places the bars close at midnight, in other places they stay open as late as 4 am. In most places you can only buy a drnk on Sundays at a restaurant or a hotel dining room, and then only if you buy a meal. In a few places you can't buy a drink — period — whatever day it is. All very strange.

Equally stange, Canadians are not great whisky drinkers, although they make some excellent whiskies. But they are great beer drinkers, although the beer they make is at best mediocre, at worst comparable to what passes for beer south of the border. The only logical, or easily understandable, element that I have been able to detect in Canadian drinking habits is their reluctance to drink much of the wine they produce.

TIPPING

When buying something you can never be absolutely certain of getting exactly what you pay for, but when tipping you can always make certain that you pay for what you got. That said, I would never tip less than 10 percent except in extreme circum-stances. Once upon a time I was given to the retributive tactic of rewarding insultingly bad service with an insultingly low tip, but I soon came to realize that all I accomplished thereby was to add an unpleasant sequel to an unsatisfactory experience. As a rule, then, I would tip more or less 15 percent — more if the service is outstanding, less if it is not so good. I would tip porters $1 a bag, chambermaids $1 a day — rounding off the total upwards in deserving cases, downwards in undeserving ones.

SHOPPING

The same rule applies with shopping as with dining: look for the local specialties. This means that in the Maritime Provinces you may want to check out the hand-knit sweaters, hunting jackets, and fishermen's gear such as oilskins. In Quebec you will be amazed to learn how many things can be made from maple syrup. In Ontario you will want to inspect the Indian basketwork. In the Prairie Provinces, especially Alberta, you will find every item of cowboy attire you could possibly want. And in British Columbia, you should look over the elaborately carved handcrafts of the West Coast Indians.

There is one caveat that should be borne in mind when shopping for Native Canadian arts and crafts. Although these items, when genuine, are among the loveliest things to buy in Canada, they are often swamped by cheap imitations. Be suspicious of any handcrafted article that strikes you as a bargain. To be certain that you are getting the real thing, either buy from a crafts guild or cooperative or from a museum shop.

Shops in Canada are generally open from 9:30 am to 6 pm, Monday to Saturday, except in the big shopping malls and the "underground cities" of Toronto and Montreal, where shops are frequently open late and sometimes even on Sundays.

If you are shopping for clothes, the following table will enable you to convert Canadian sizes to their British and European equivalents. (Canadian and American sizes are the same.)

Men's suits

Canadian	British	European
34	34	44
35	35	46
36	36	48
37	37	49½
38	38	51
39	39	52½
40	40	54
41	41	55½
42	42	57

Women's dresses and blouses

Canadian	British	European
6	8	36
8	10	38
10	12	40
12	14	42
14	16	44
16	18	46
18	20	48

Men's shoes

Canadian	British	European
7	6	39½
8	7	41
9	8	42
10	9	43
11	10	44½
12	11	46
13	12	47

Women's shoes

Canadian	British	European
4½	3	35½
5	3½	36
5½	4	36½
6	4½	37
6½	5	37½
7	5½	38
7½	6	38½
8	6½	39
8½	7	39½
9	7½	40

The following sizes are the same in Canada and Britain:

Men's shirt collars

Canadian	European
14	36
14½	37
15	38
15½	39
16	41
16½	42
17	43

Men's sweaters:

Canadian	European
SMALL	
34	87
MEDIUM	
36	91
38	97
LARGE	
40	102
42	107
EXTRA LARGE	
44	112
46	117

Men's trouser waists

Canadian	European
24	61
26	66
28	71
30	76
32	80
34	87
36	91
38	97

CAMPING

Canada is a camper's paradise. There are thousands upon thousands of campgrounds throughout the country, campgrounds of every size and description. Many are in the national and provincial parks, some are municipally owned, others are privately run. Most are open from May until late September, with campsites costing from $10 to $15. Facilities usually include toilets, showers, a laundry, picnic tables, campfire sites, and power hook-ups for caravans. The fancier ones will also have a shop and a restaurant. Generally speaking, the privately run campgrounds will have more amenities and will be more expensive, while the public ones in the national and provincial parks will be more beautifully situated.

From lush river valleys to vast open prairies, Canada has a landscape to suit every taste.

As most campgrounds are run on a first-come, first-served basis, during the high season—July and August—it's a good idea to start looking for a site no later than mid-afternoon.

There are however, three nocturnal nuisances that can thoroughly spoil a camping holiday if you come unprepared. The first is that familiar bane, the mosquito. So bring plenty of insect repellent, as well as a tent fitted with a mosquito net. The second nuisance is the scavenging animal — often, in Canada, a bear. These creatures can be discouraged by never keeping food in or near the tent (unless it's in the car), and by always disposing of uneaten food and washing up immediately after meals. No leftovers, no problems. Thirdly, the temperature at night can suddenly drop, leaving you shivering unless you have brought enough warm clothing. For lists of campgrounds write to the national tourism office or the provincial offices in the provinces you plan to visit. There is also a very informative publication, *National Parks,* available free from the Canadian Parks Service, Ottawa, Ontario K1A 0H3. ((819) 997-2800.

HUNTING

It's small wonder that great herds of hunters migrate to Canada every year, usually in the autumn: one of Canada's richest natural resources is its superabundance of game. There is big game on the ground — moose, elk caribou, deer, bear — and there is small game in the air — partridge, ducks, and geese.

Each province has its own rules and regulations concerning hunting, in addition to which there are a few federal laws. For example, all guns and ammunition must be declared at Customs, while an export license is required if you want to take skins or hunting trophies out of the country. Hunting is strictly forbidden in the national parks, and foreigners are only permitted to hunt in the forests if accompanied by an official guide. No buffalo, polar bear, mink, or beaver may be hunted, and there are restrictions on the hunting of certain migratory birds. For the specific regulations of each province, as well as license applications, write to the provincial tourist information office or to the Ministry of Natural Resources, Wildlife Branch, Queen's Park, Toronto, Ontario M7A 1W3.

FISHING

The situation regarding fishing in Canada almost exactly mirrors that regarding hunting: there is a superabundance of fish to be caught, and the laws regulating the catching of them vary from province to province. In the Maritimes there is the Atlantic salmon and, offshore, bluefin tuna, cod, mackerel, and halibut. In British Columbia there is the Pacific salmon and, offshore, sea bass. In between there is pike, perch, grayling, whitefish, goldeye, muskie, bass, and every kind of trout known to man.

All non-resident anglers must have a fishing permit, which is available from any tourist office in the province where you intend to fish, as well as from local sporting goods stores and marinas. A separate license is required for fishing in national parks, which is valid for all parks and is available from any park office or from Parks Canada, Ottawa, Ontario K1A 1G2.

SKIING

Not for nothing is Canada referred to colloquially as the "Great White North." It has snow the way Brazil has coffee. Where the snow lies flat, you get wonderful cross-country skiing. Where it lies at an angle, you get wonderful downhill skiing. And where it doesn't lie at all, or not enough of it, there is snowmaking equipment to compensate for Nature's oversight. Wonderful skiing is not hard to find in Canada.

What is perhaps surprising, given the country's size and topography, is that you rarely have to go very far to find good skiing. Even in Newfoundland and the Maritimes, even in Manitoba and Saskatchewan, there are some decent ski runs. And in Ontario there are excellent ski areas near both Toronto and Ottawa. But it is in Quebec and the Rockies that you find ski slopes of a variety and grandeur unsurpassed anywhere in the world. It is no accident that there are over 130 ski areas in Quebec's Laurentian Mountains alone, nor was it a fluke that the 1988 Winter Olympics were held in the mountains outside of Calgary.

If you like skiing, and you plan to go to Canada between November and March, prepare to be made very happy.

PUBLIC HOLIDAYS AND FESTIVALS

NATIONAL HOLIDAYS

NEW YEAR'S DAY: January 1
GOOD FRIDAY
EASTER MONDAY
VICTORIA DAY: Monday nearest May 24
CANADA DAY: July 1
LABOR DAY: First Monday in September
THANKSGIVING DAY: Second Monday in October
REMEMBRANCE DAY: November 11
CHRISTMAS DAY: December 25
BOXING DAY: December 26

PROVINCIAL HOLIDAYS

Epiphany (Quebec): January 6
Ash Wednesday (Quebec): First Wednesday in Lent
St. Patrick's Day (Newfoundland): Monday nearest March 17
St. George's Day (Newfoundland): Monday nearest April 23
Ascension Day (Quebec): Fortieth day after Easter
St. Jean Baptiste Day (Quebec): June 24
Discovery Day (Newfoundland): Monday nearest June 24
Memorial Day (Newfoundland): Monday nearest July 1
Orangeman's Day (Newfoundland): Monday nearest July 12
Civic Holiday (almost everywhere except Quebec): First Monday in August
All Saints Day (Quebec): November 1

FESTIVALS

JANUARY
New Year's Day Polar Bear Swim in Vancouver
Montreal Winter Festival
Toronto International Boat Show
Ice Canoe Race in Toronto

FEBRUARY
Quebec City Winter Carnival
North York (Ontario) Winter Carnival
Vernon (British Columbia) Winter Carnival
Winterlude in Ottawa
Chinese New Year in Vancouver
Toronto International Auto Show

MARCH
Outdoors Show in Montreal
Springtime Craft Show and Sale in Toronto
"Sugaring Off" parties in Eastern Townships (Quebec)

APRIL
National Home Show in Toronto
International Book Fair in Quebec City
Stratford Shakespeare Festival season opens

MAY
Blossom Festival in Niagara Falls
International Mime Festival in Montreal
Festival of Spring in Ottawa
Scotia Festival of Music in Halifax
International Theatre Fortnight in Quebec City
Banff Arts Festival season opens
Shaw Festival season opens in Niagara-on-the-Lake

JUNE
Charlottetown Summer Festival season opens
Molson Grand Prix in Montreal
Midnight Sun Golf Tournament in Yellowknife (Northwest Territories)
All That Jazz Festival in Toronto
Nova Scotia Tattoo in Halifax
Montreal International Jazz Festival

JULY
Quebec International Summer Festival in Quebec City
Just For Laughs Festival in Montreal
Loyalist Days in Saint John (New Brunswick)
Molson Indy auto race in Toronto
The Calgary Stampede
Klondike Days in Edmonton

Nova Scotia International Tattoo in Halifax
Shediac (New Brunswick) Lobster Festival
Antigonish (Nova Scotia) Highland Games
Caribana, Caribbean music festival in Toronto
National Ukrainian Festival in Dauphin (Manitoba)

AUGUST
Montreal International Film Festival
Gaelic Mod — Scottish Highlands Festival in St. Ann's (Nova Scotia)
Festival By the Sea in Saint John (New Brunswick)
Canadian National Exhibition in Toronto
The Americas Cycling Grand Prix in Montreal
Old Home Week in Charlottetown (Prince Edward Island)
Folklorama in Winnipeg
Buffalo Days in Regina
Tyne Valley (Prince Edward Island) Oyster Festival
Player's International Tennis Championships in Montreal and Toronto
Expo-Quebec in Quebec City
Acadian Festival in Caraquet (New Brunswick)
Quidi Vidi Lake Regatta in St. John's (Newfoundland)
Canadian Open golf championship in Toronto

SEPTEMBER
Festival of Festivals in Toronto
Niagara Grape and Wine Festival in St. Catharines (Ontario)
The Montreal Marathon
The Molson Export Challenge horse race in Toronto
Montreal International Music Festival

OCTOBER
Oktoberfest in Kitchener (Ontario)

NOVEMBER
Royal Agriculture Winter Fair in Toronto

DECEMBER
Quebec Crafts Show in Quebec City
Christmas Ice Bridge at Niagara Falls

MAIL

Although main post offices in Canada may open as early as 8 am and close as late as 6 pm on weekdays, and some are open on Saturday mornings, you can avoid disappointment by going between 9 am and 5 pm, Monday to Friday. In fact, you can

avoid post offices altogether for most purposes, as stamps can be bought at hotels and vending machines in airports, railway stations, shopping centers, drugstores and many small shops.

Letters and postcards can be mailed at most hotels' front desks or at any red mailbox.

If sending mail to a Canadian address, it will speed things up considerably if you use the (admittedly complicated) zip code. Also, I am told by the postal authorities that every year there are some Americans who think it is just as good to use American stamps as Canadian ones. It's not.

If you want to receive mail in Canada but are unsure of your exact whereabouts

From the Atlantic to the Pacific: a house on Cape Breton Island and a telephone booth in Vancouver's Chinatown.

at a given time, you can have mail sent to you c/o "General Delivery" at the mail post office in the town or city where you wish to pick it up. But remember that it must be picked up within 15 days or it will be returned to sender. Alternatively, if you have an American Express card, or traveler's checks from American Express or Thomas Cook, you can have mail sent to you at any office of either company. It should be marked "Client Mail," and it will be held for you for as long as a month.

Telegrams are handled by CNCP Tele-communications, while most good hotels now have telex and/or fax facilities available for guests' use.

TELEPHONES

The Canadian telephone system is completely integrated with that of the United States, which means that it is splendidly efficient and economical, and that no international codes are necessary for calls between the U.S. and Canada. As in the U.S., for information on local telephone numbers dial 411; for information on long-distance numbers dial 1-555-1212. For calls re-

quiring operator assistance — such as long-distance personal or collect calls, or for emergency calls — dial 0.

To place a long-distance call within the same area code, dial 1 + the number you are calling. To place a call outside your area code, dial 1 + area code + telephone number. For direct dialing of overseas calls, dial 011 + country code + city code + telephone number.

Calls placed in the evening or on the weekend are less expensive, although any call from a hotel will incur a (usually steep) surcharge. There are public telephones just about everywhere, but they only accept Canadian quarters.

RADIO AND TELEVISION

I am tempted to say that if you are in Canada you shouldn't be indoors, and leave it at that. I am further tempted to say that if you do find yourself indoors in North America, you definitely shouldn't be watching television. You know the reasons; you've probably seen a number of them already, wherever you live. Even so, it's difficult to convey the feeling of dull despair that comes over you when you contemplate a galaxy of up to 40 television channels — not one of which is shining brightly enough to engage your attention for more than a few minutes.

If it's any consolation, though, you are better off watching television in Canada then in the U.S., simply because you have a choice of programs in addition to the American ones (which nonetheless predominate even in areas beyond the reach of American stations). And its precarious finances notwithstanding, the CBC (Canadian Broadcasting Corporation) manages to produce some worthy programming of its own, while the French-language channels serve up the occasional treat. But don't be surprised when you switch channels to escape Teenage Mutant Ninja Turtles only to be confronted with Popeye et son fils.

For rabid sports fans — and that includes the author of these lines — there is one exceedingly bright spot in Canadian TV programming. What's more, it appears at a time in the week when you might reasonably be expected to be otherwise unoccupied. At 9:30 am Eastern Standard Time on Saturday mornings from September until May the cable Sports Network televises live an English First Division soccer match. A good way to start the weekend.

The Canadian radio dial, like the American, features end-to-end music — classical, pop, rock, country, jazz — interspersed with talk-shows, phone-ins, and news.

NEWSPAPERS AND MAGAZINES

Canadian journalism, too, closely resembles its American counterpart. With the exception of the Globe and Mail, which is published in Toronto, the newspapers are all local papers. Certainly, some big-city papers such as the Toronto Star are national, even international, in stature, but their main emphasis remains on coverage of their own communities. This enlightened parochialism benefits the visitor not only by providing a useful introduction to topics of local interest, but also by providing through its listings and advertisements a comprehensive guide to local events and entertainments. As a matter of fact, many of the places to go and things to do that I have recommended in this book were originally suggested to me by articles or reviews I came upon in the local press. So don't neglect this valuable resource whenever you arrive in a new place.

All of the larger news agents in Canada have shelves that are identical to the ones you would expect to find in comparable shops in the United States — except that in addition to all the American newspapers and magazines you get the Canadian ones as well. I wish I could say that in my frequent browsings among these shelves I discovered a Canadian periodical of compelling interest. But I didn't. You can't have everything.

Recommended Reading

BROOK, STEPHEN. Maple Leaf Rag. Pan Books, London 1989.

HARDY, ANNE. Where To Eat In Canada. Oberon Press, Ottawa 1990.

MACKAY, CLAIRE. The Toronto Story. Annick Press, Toronto 1990.

MacKAY, DONALD. Flight from Famine: The Coming of the Irish to Canada. McClelland & Stewart, Toronto 1990.

MACLENNAN, HUGH. Papers. University of Calgary Press, Calgary 1986.

MALCOLM, ANDREW H. The Canadians. Times Books, New York 1985.

MCNAUGHT, KENNETH. The Penguin History of Canada. Penguin Books, London 1988.

MORTON, DESMOND. A Peculiar Kind of Politics. University of Toronto Press, Toronto 1982.

MORTON, WILLIAM L. The Canadian Identity. University of Wisconsin Press, Madison 1973.

PATTERSON, FREEMAN. The Last Wilderness: Images of the Canadian Wild. Canadian Geographic Society, Vanier, Ontario 1991.

MUISE, D.A., ed. Reader's Guide to Canadian History, Vol. I. University of Toronto Press, Toronto 1982. Vol. II ed. GRANATSTEIN, À.L. & STEVENS, P. University of Toronto Press, Toronto 1982.

RICHLER, MODECAI. The Apprenticeship of Duddy Kravitz. Penguin Books, London 1991. Broadsides. Vintage Books, London 1991. Papers. University of Calgary Press, Calgary 1987.

WALLACE, DONALD C. & FLETCHER, FREDERICK À. Canadian Politics through Press Reports. Oxford University Press, Toronto 1985.

Quick Reference A–Z Guide
to Places and Topics of Interest with Listed Accommodation, Restaurants and Useful Telephone Numbers

* Star ratings for accommodation and restaurants indicate price relationships only. Refer to the text for rates, facilities and recommendations

A

accommodation, general 182
Alberta 25, 89–129
 historical background 25
alcohol 184
Alert Bay 79
 attractions 79
 U'Mista Cultural Centre 79
Angel Glacier 125
Appalachian region 32
Athabasca Falls 123
Athabasca Glacier 123

B

Bamfield 78
 attractions 78
 West Coast Trail 78
Banff 91, 116, 119–122, 128–129
Banff National Park 116–129
 access 128–129
 Brewster Transportation, ((403) 762-6767 129
 Greyhound bus station, ((403) 762-2286 129
 VIA Rail Station, ((403) 762-3722 or 852-3168 129
 accommodation 126–127
 ***Banff Park Lodge, ((403) 762-4433, toll-free (800) 661-9266 126
 ***Banff Springs Hotel, ((403) 762-2211, toll-free (800) 268-9411 126
 **Inns of Banff Park, ((403) 762-4581, toll-free (800) 661-1272 126
 **Mount Royal Hotel, ((403) 762-3331 126
 **Rundle Manor Apartment Hotel, ((403) 762-5544 126
 **Swiss Village Lodge, ((403) 762-4581, toll-free (800) 661-1272 127
 *Banff International Hostel, ((403) 762-4122 127
 *Red Carpet Inn, ((403)762-4184 127
 *YWCA, ((403) 762-3560 127
 Bed & Breakfast, Bed & Breakfast Bureau, ((403) 762-5070 126
 attractions
 Banff Centre, ((403) 762-6300 120
 Banff Park Museum, ((403) 762-3324 120
 Banff Springs Hotel 121
 Cave and Basin Centennial Centre, ((403) 762-4900 120
 Cave and Basin Hot Springs 120
 cultural activities 126
 hoodoos rock formations 121
 Luxton Museum, (403) 762-2388 120
 Mount Norquay 121
 Natural History Museum, ((403) 762-4747 120
 sport, active 125
 golf, Banff Springs Hotel, ((403) 762-6801 125
 Sulphur Mountain Gondola Lift 121
 Tunnel Mountain 121
 Upper Hot Springs Pool, ((403) 762-2056 121
 Whyte Museum of the Canadian Rockies, ((403) 762-2291 120
 background 118
 environs 121–122
 Icefields Parkway 122
 Johnston Canyon 121
 Lake Louise 122
 Lake Minnewanka 121
 Sunshine Village 121
 Two-Jack Lake 121
 festivals 120, 126
 Banff Festival of Arts ((403) 762-6300 (June to August) 126
 Banff Festival of the Arts (June to August) 120
 general information 119
 Banff Park Information Centre, ((403) 762-4256 119
 Banff/Lake Louise Chamber of Commerce, ((403) 762-3777 119
 Superintendent, Banff National Park, ((403) 762-3324 119
 nightlife 126
 outdoor recreation 125
 restaurants 128
 Aardvark's, ((403) 262-5500 128
 Drifter's Inn, ((403) 762-4525 128
 Giorgio's, ((403) 762-5114 128
 Grizzly House, ((403) 762-4055 128
 Melissa's, ((403) 762-5114 128
 Paris Restaurant, ((403) 762-3554 128
 Rose and Crown, ((403) 762-2121 128
Barkley Sound 78
Batoche National Historic Park 145
Battleford 146
 attractions 146
 Battleford National Historic Park 146
Bow Lake 122
British Columbia 25, 35, 37–87
 historical background 24–25
Broken Group Islands 78
Buffalo Pound Provincial Park 139

C

Calgary 91, 101–117
 access 113–117
 Airporter Bus, ((403) 291-3848 116
 Calgary International Airport, ((403) 292-8477 113
 Greyhound bus station, ((403) 265-9111 116
 VIA Rail station, (toll-free (800) 665-8630 116

accommodation 110–113
  ***Delta Bow, ((403) 266-1980,
    toll-free (800) 268-1133 110
  ***International Hotel, ((403) 265-9600,
    toll-free (800) 661-8627 110
  ***Skyline Plaza Hotel, ((403) 266-7331,
    toll-free (800) 648-7200 110
  ***Westin Hotel, ((403) 266-1611,
    toll-free (800) 228-3000 110
  **Best Western Hospitality Inn,
    ((403) 278-5050, toll-free (800) 528-1234 111
  **Marlborough Inn & Convention Center,
    ((403) 248-8888, toll-free (800) 661-1464 111
  **Prince Royal Inn All Suite Hotel, ((403)
    263-0520, toll-free (800) 661-1592 110
  **Sandman Hotel, ((403) 237-8626,
    toll-free (800) 663-6900 110
  **The Hotel Calgary Plaza, ((403) 263-7600,
    toll-free (800) 661-8684 111
  *Elbow River Inn & Casino,
    ((403) 269-6771 111
  *Flamingo Motor Hotel, ((403) 252-4401 111
  *Homeplace Guest Ranch & Trail Trips,
    ((403) 931-3245 113
  *Lord Nelson Inn, ((403) 269-8262 111
  *Stampeder Inn, ((403) 243-5531 111
  *Stanley Park Inn, ((403) 287-2700,
    toll-free (800) 661-1889 111
  *Sun Bow Inn, ((403) 289-1973 111
  *The Palliser Hotel, ((403) 262-1234,
    toll-free (800) 268-9411 110
  *University of Calgary, ((403) 220-3210 113
  *York Hotel, ((403) 262-5581 111
  *YWCA, ((403) 263-1550 113
attractions
  Alberta Science Centre and Centennial
    Planetarium, ((403) 221-3700 104
  Calaway Park 106
  Calgary Tower, ((403) 266-7171 103
  Calgary Zoo, ((403) 232-9300 104
  cultural activities:
    Centre for the Performing Arts,
      ((403) 294-7444 (information) 109
    Jubilee Auditorium and Pumphouse
      Theatre, ((403) 263-0079 109
    Energeum, ((403) 297-4293 104
    Fish Creek Park, ((403) 297-5293 106
    Fort Calgary Park 104
    Glenbow Museum, ((403) 264-8300 or
      237-8988 103
    Grain Academy museum, ((403) 263-4594 105
    Heritage Park, ((403) 255-1858 105
    indoor garden 103
    Inglewood Bird Sanctuary, ((403) 269-6688 104
    Lunchbox Theatre 103
    Museum of the Regiments,
      ((403) 240-7002 105
    Olympic Hall of Fame 106
    Olympic Saddledome 104
    Prehistoric Park 104
    Prince's Island Park 104
  sport, active 108
    golf, Inglewood course, ((403) 272-3949 109
    golf, McCall Lake, ((403) 250-5677 109

    horse-riding, Fish Creek Riding Stables,
      ((403) 251-6955 109
    ice scating, Olympic Speed Skating Oval,
      ((403) 220-7890 109
    kart racing: Kart Gardens International,
      ((403) 250-9555 109
    . Lindsay Park Sports Centre 109
  sport, spectator
    equestrian events, Spruce Meadows,
      ((403) 254-3200 108
    football, McMahon Stadium,
      ((403) 284-1111 108
    harness and horse-racing: Grandstand in
      Stampede Park, ((403) 261-0214 108
    hockey, basketball, Olympic Saddledome,
      ((403) 261-0455 108
    stock car and motorcycle racing, Race City
      Speedway, ((403) 251-6955 108
  Stampede Park 104
  The Olympic Park, ((403) 247-5404 106
background 102
environs 107
  Drumheller Dinosaur and Fossil Museum,
    ((403) 823-2593 107
  Fort Macleod 107
  Fort Macleod Museum 107
  Head-Smashed-In Buffalo Jump,
    ((403) 553-2731 107
  Red Deer River Valley Badlands 107
  Royal Tyrrell Museum of Palaeontology,
    ((403) 823-7707 107
festivals
  Calgary Stampede (July),
    toll-free (800) 661-1260 106
general information 102
  Calgary Visitor & Convention Bureau,
    ((403) 262-2766 or toll-free
    (800) 661-1778 103
  Information Office, ((403) 261-8616 103
nightlife 110
restaurants 113
  *Franzi's Gasthaus, ((403) 228-6882 113
  *Take Ten Cafe, ((403) 270-7010 113
  *Unicorn Pub, ((403) 233-2666 113
  **La Chaumiere, ((403) 228-5690 113
  **Owl's Nest, ((403) 267-2823 113
  **Sky's Rotisserie and Wine Bar,
    ((403) 266-7177 113
  **The Green Street Cafe, ((403) 266-1551 113
  **The Three Greenhorns, ((403) 264-6903 113
  **Traders, ((403) 266-7331 113
  *4th Street Rose, ((403) 228-5377 113
  *Greek Village, ((403) 244-1144 113
  *The Cafe 1886, ((403) 292-8477 113
shopping 109
Campbell River 79–81
accommodation 80
  ***Painter's Lodge and Fishing Resort,
    ((604) 286-1102, toll-free (800) 663-7090 80
  *Strathcona Park Lodge, ((604) 286-2008 80
attractions 79
  Cape Mudge Indian Village Museum 79
  Discovery Pier 79
  Quadra Island 79
  recreation center 79

restaurants 80
camping, general 186–187
Canada , general information on travelling
  arrival
    customs 174
    getting around 179–181
      by air 179
      by bus 180
      by car 180
      by train 179
      ferry services 180
      local transportation 180
    getting to 172
      by air 172
      by bus 173
      by car 173
      by rail 172
    travel documents 174
Canadian Pacific Railway 25
  historical background 25
Canadian Shield region 32
Cape Breton Island 22
  historical background 22
Cape Scott 79
Cape Spear (Newfoundland) 31
Cavell Lake 125
Chemainus 73
Churchill 168
  access 168
    VIA Rail (Winnipeg) ((204) 949-1830 168
  attractions 168
    Eskimo Museum, ((204) 675-2541 168
    Fort Prince of Wales 168
    National Historic Park, ((204) 675-8863 168
Clear Lake 168
climate 31–33
Columbia Icefield 123
Comex 79–80
Comox Valley 79
  attractions 79
    recreational center 79
  accommodation 80
Courtenay 79–80
  accommodation 80
currency 178
Cypress Mills Provincial Park 150–151
D **Denman** 79
Dinsoaur Provincial Park 108
driving 181
Drumheller 107
  attractions 107
    Dinosaur Trail 107
    Drumheller Dinosaur and Fossil Museum,
      ((403) 823-2593 107
    Royal Tyrrell Museum of Palaeontology,
      ((403) 823-7707 107
  environs 108
    Dinsoaur Provincial Park 108
Duncan 73, 80
  accommodation 80
    **Best Western Cowichan Valley Inn,
      ((604) 748-2722 80
  attractions
    British Columbia Forest Museum,
      ((604) 748-9389 73

Cowichan Valley 73
Lake Cowichan 73
E eating out, general 183
Echo Valley Provincial Park 139
Edmonton 91–101
  access 101
    Greyhound bus terminal,
      ((403) 421-4211 101
    VIA Rail Station, ((403) 429-5431,
      toll-free (800) 665-8630 101
  accommodation 98–99
    ***Chateau Lacombe, ((403) 428-6611,
      toll-free (800) 268-9411 98
    ***Fantasyland Hotel & Resort, ((403)
      444-3000, toll-free (800) 661-6454 99
    ***Hilton International Edmonton,
      ((403) 428-7111, toll-free (800) 268-9275 98
    ***Ramada Renaissance Inn, ((403) 423-4811,
      toll-free (800) 268-8998 99
    ***Sheraton Plaza Edmonton, ((403) 423-2450,
      toll-free (800) 228-3000 99
    ***Westin Hotel, ((403) 426-3636,
      toll-free: (800) 228-3000 98
    **Alberta Place Suite Hotel, ((403) 423-1565,
      toll-free (800) 661-3982 99
    **Edmonton House All Suite Hotel,
      ((403) 424-5555, toll-free (800) 661-6562 99
    **Edmonton Inn, ((403) 454-9521, toll-free
      (800) 661-7264 99
    **Renford Inn at Fifth, ((403) 423-5611,
      toll-free (800) 661-6498 99
    *Chateau Louis Motor Inn, ((403) 452-7770,
      toll-free (800) 661-9843 99
    *Continental Inn, ((403) 484-7751 99
    *Edmonton Centre Travelodge,
      ((403) 428-6442, toll-free (800) 255-3050 99
    *La Bohème, ((403) 474-5693 99
    *Mayfair Hotel, ((403) 423-1650 99
    *YMCA, ((403) 421-9622 100
    *YWCA, ((403) 429-8707 100
    Bed & Breakfast 100
  attractions
    Aviation Hall of Fame, ((403) 424-2458 93
    cinema: Princess Theatre, ((403) 433-0979 98
    Civic Centre 93
    Convention Centre, ((403) 424-2458 93
    cultural activities: Citadel Theatre 98
    cultural activities: Jubilee Auditorium,
      ((403) 427-9266 98
    Edmonton Art Gallery, ((403) 422-6223 93
    Fort Edmonton Park, ((403) 428-2992 94
    Habitat gallery 94
    Indian gallery 94
    Legislature Building, ((403) 427-7362 93
    Museum of Telecommunications
      Equipment 93
    Muttart Conservatory, ((403) 428-2939 or
      (403) 428-5226 94
    Natural History gallery 94
    Old Strathcona Historic Area 95
    Provincial Museum, ((403) 427-1730 94
    Space and Sciences Centre,
      ((403) 452-9100 95
    sport, active 97
      City Recreation Park 97

golf, Riverside Golf Course,
  ((403) 428-5330   97
golf, Victoria Golf Course and Driving
  Range (River Road), ((403) 428-5349   97
golf, Victoria Golf Course and Driving
  Range (Rundle Park), ((403) 428-5342   97
Kinsmen Sports & Aquatic Centre,
  ((403) 428-7970   97
Mill Wood's Recreation Centre,
  ((403) 428-2888   97
sport, spectator   97
baseball, John Ducey Park,
  ((403) 429-2934   97
Canadian football, Commonwealth
  Stadium, ((403) 429-2881   97
harness racing, ((403) 471-7210   97
hockey, Edmonton Northlands Coliseum   96
Strathcona Archaeological Centre,
  ((403) 427-2022   96
West Edmonton Mall   95
background   92–93
environs   96
Elk Island National Park   96
Ukrainian Cultural Heritage Village,
  ((403) 662-3640   96
festivals   96, 98
Folk Music Festival (August)   98
Fringe Theatre Festival (August)   98
Jazz City, (late June/early July)   98
Klondike Days festival (July)   96
general information   93
Alberta Tourism Information Centre,
  ((403) 297-6574   102
Edmonton Tourism Visitor Centre,
  ((403) 422-5505 or 988-5455   93
Travel Alberta, ((403) 427-4321,
  toll-free (800) 661-8888   93
nightlife   98
Blues on Whyte, ((403) 439-3981   98
Sidetrack Cafe, ((403) 421-1326   98
Yardbird Suite, ((403) 432-0428   98
Yuk-Yuk's, ((403) 466-2131   98
restaurants   100–101
**Carvery, ((403) 426-3636   100
**Hy's Steak Loft, ((403) 424-4444   100
**La Bohème, ((403) 474-5693   100
**La Ronde, ((403) 428-6611   100
**Shogun, ((403) 482-5494   100
**Sushi Tomi, ((403) 422-6083   100
**Un-Heard-Of, ((403) 432-0480   100
*Bistro Praha, ((403) 424-4218   100
*Mongolian Food Experience,
  ((403) 426-6806   100
*Russian Tea Room, ((403) 426-0000   101
*Smokey Joe's Hickory Smokehouse,
  ((403) 489-3940   100
*The Silk Hat, ((403) 428-1551   100
*Uncle Albert's Pancake House,
  ((403) 439-6609   100
shopping   97
Edmonton Centre   97
West Edmonton Mall   97
Elk Island National Park   96
attractions
Ukrainian Pioneer Home   96

general information   96
Astotin Interpretive Centre ((403) 922-5790   96
embassies and consulates   173–174
Englishman Falls Provincial Park   74
explorers   20
Alexander Mackenzie   23
David Thompson   23
Henry Hudson   21
Jacques Cartier   20
John Cabot   20
Sanuel de Champlain   21
Simon Fraser   23
Vikings   20
F   **Falcon Lake**   167
attractions   167
recreational development   167
flora and fauna   32–33
food, general   183
Fort Macleod   107
Fort Qu'Appelle   139
Fort Walsh   150
attractions   150
Farewell's Trading Post   150
Fort Walsh National Historic Park,
  ((306) 662-3590   150
G   **Gabriola Islands**   74
Galcier National Park   87
Roger's Pass   87
Gaspé Peninsula   32
geography and climate   31–33
getting around   182
Gimli   167
attractions   167
Lake Winnipeg   167
festival   167
Icelandic Festival (August)   167
Gold River   79
Gold rush   24
Grosse Isle   162
H   health   178
Hecla Provincial Park   167
Hector Lake   122
historical background   20–22, 24, 27
British Canada   22–24
Canada today   27–29, 31
Dominion of Canada   24–27
French Canada   21
New France   21–22
Seven Years War   22
the first europeans   20
War of Spanish Succession   21
holidays and festivals   189–190
Hornby Islands   79
Hudson Bay   21
historical background   21
I   **Icefields Parkway**   122
attractions
Athabasca Glacier   123
Bow Lake   122
Columbia Icefield   123
Mistaya Canyon   122
Peyto Lake   122
Sunwapta Pass   122
Weeping Wall   122

general information 123
Interpretive Centre, ((403) 762-6736 123

J **Jasper** 91, 116, 123
Jasper National Park 116–129
access 128–129
Greyhound bus station, ((403) 852-3926 129
VIA Rail station, ((403) 852-4102,
toll-free (800) 561-8630 129
accommodation 126–127
***Chateau Jasper, ((403) 852-5644,
toll-free (800) 661-9323 127
***Jasper Park Lodge, ((403) 852-3301,
toll-free (800) 642-38174 127
**Jasper Inn, ((403) 852-4461,
toll-free (800) 661-1933 127
**Lobstick Lodge, ((403) 852-4431,
toll-free (800) 661-9317 127
**Tekkara Lodge, ((403) 852-3386 127
**Whistler's Motor Hotel, ((403) 852-3361,
toll-free (800) 282-9919 127
*Athabasca Hotel, ((403) 852-3386 128
Bed & Breakfast, Bed & Breakfast Bureau,
((403) 762-5070 126
room reservation service: Jasper Experience,
((403) 852-5656 126
attractions
Jasper Tramway 123
Lake Annette 123
Lake Beauvert 123
Lake Edith 123
Patricia Lake 123
Pyramid Lake 123
sport, active: golf 126
sport, active: golf, Jasper Park Lodge,
((403) 852-3301 or 852-6090 126
background 118
environs 123–125
Angel Glacier 125
Cavell Lake 125
Maligne Canyon 123
Maligne Lake 124
Maligne Valley 123
Medicine Lake 124
Miette Hot Springs 124
Mount Edith Cavell 125
Spirit Island 124
general information 119
Jasper National Park Centre,
((403) 852-6161 119
Jasper National Park Chamber of Commerce,
((403) 852-3858 119
Visitor Information Centre,
((403) 852-4401 119
outdoor recreation 125
restaurants 128
L & W, ((403) 4114 128
Something Else Greek Taverna,
((403) 852-3850 128
The Beauvallon, ((403) 852-5644 128
Tokyo Tom's, ((403) 852-3780 128
Villa Caruso, ((403) 852-3920 128

K **Katepwa Point Provincial Park** 139
Kelowna 81–82, 84, 86
access 87
Greyhound station, ((604) 860-3835 87

accommodation 86
***Capri Hotel, ((604) 860-6060 86
***Lake Okanagan Resort, ((604) 769-3511 86
***Lodge Motor Inn, ((604) 860-9711 86
*Ponderosa Motel, ((604) 860-2218 86
*Willow Inn Hotel, ((604) 762-2122 86
attractions
Big White Ski Area 85
Calona Wines (winery) 85
Centennial Museum, ((604) 763-2417 84
Hiram Walker Distillery 85
lake cruising 84
Lake Okanagan 84
Last Mountain skiing area 85
general information 82
Okanagan Similkameen Tourist Association,
((604) 769-5959 82
Travel Infocentre, ((604) 545-0771 82
restaurants 84, 87
aboard *M.V. Fintry Queen*, ((604) 763-2780 84
Carmelle's Creperie, ((604) 762-6350 87
Hollywood on Top, ((604) 763-2777 87
Jonathan L. Segals, ((604) 860-8449 87
Kuper Island 73

L **L'Anse aux Meadows** 20
historical background 20
La Ronge 150
attractions
Lac la Ronge Provincial Park,
((306) 425-4234 150
Lac la Ronge Provincial Park 150
general information 150
Ladysmith 74, 80
accommodation 80
Yellowpoint Lodge, ((604) 245-7422 80
Lake Annette 123
Lake Beauvert 123
Lake Cowichan 73
Lake Edith 123
Lake Louise 116, 122–123, 127–129
access 128–129
accommodation 126–127
***Chateau Lake Louise, ((403) 522-3991 127
***Post Hotel, ((403) 522-3989,
toll-free (800) 661-1586 127
**Lake Louise Inn, ((403) 522-3791,
toll-free (800) 661-9237 127
Bed & Breakfast, Bed & Breakfast Bureau,
((403) 762-5070 126
attractions
Chateau Lake Louise 122
Lake Louise Gondola 122
Moraine Lake 122
Lake Okanagan 81
Lake Winnipeg 167
attractions
Gull Harbour Resort, ((204) 475-2354,
toll-free (800) 475-5992 167
Hecla Provincial Park 167
Louisberg 22
historical background 22
Lower Fort Garry 162

M **MacMillan Provincial Park** 74
mail services 190
Maligne Lake 124

Manitoba 25, 153–169
  historical background 25
Maple Creek 150
Meadow Lake Provincial Park 150
  general information, ((306) 236-3382 150
Meares Island 78
media 191–192
Miette Hot Springs 124
Mistaya Canyon 122
money 178
Moose Jaw 138
  attractions
    Saskatchewan Air Show (July) 138
    Western Development Museum,
    ((306) 693-6556/693-5989 138
    Wild Animal Park, ((306) 691-0111 138
  environs 139
    Buffalo Pound Provincial Park 139
Mount Agassiz 168
Mount Edith Cavell 125
Mount Robson 123
Mount Washington 79
Mt. Logan (Canada's highest mountain) 31

N **Nanaimo** 60, 74, 80
  accommodation 80
    **Coast Bastion Inn, ((604) 753-6601 80
    **Dorchester Hotel, ((604) 754-6835 80
    *Colonial Motel, ((604) 754-4415 80
  attractions 74
    Nanaimo Bathtub Race 74
    Nanaimo Centennial Museum,
    ((604) 753-1821 74
    recreational parks and lakes 74
    Shakespeare Plus Festival 74
  general information 60
    Tourism Association of Vancouver Island,
    ((604) 754-8474 60
  restaurants 80
national parks 32
New Brunswick 23, 25
  early settlers 23
  historical background 25
Newcastle Island Provincial Park 74
Newfoundland 25, 32
  historical background 25
North Battleford 146
  attractions
    Western Development Museum 146
Northwest Passage 21
Nova Scotia 23, 25
  early settlers 23
  historical background 25

O **Okanagan River** 81
Okanagan Valley 81–87
  See also Osoyoos; Penticton and Vernon
Ontario 25
  historical background 25
Osoyoos 81–82, 85
  attractions
    Osoyoos Lake 82
    watersports 82

P **Pacific Rim National Park** 76, 78–80
  accommodation 80
  attractions
    Bamfield 78

Barkley Sound 78
Broken Group Islands: canoeing and
  kayaking 78
rain forest trails 78
West Coast Trail 78
whale-spotting 78
Parksville 74, 76, 79–80
  accommodation 80
Patricia Lake 123
Pelee Island (Lake Erie) 31
Penticton 81, 83–84, 86, 87
  access 86–87
    Greyhound station, ((604) 493-4101 87
  accommodation 86
    ***Coast Lakeside Resort, ((604) 493-8221 86
    **Best Western Telstar Inn, ((604) 493-0311 86
    *Kozy Guest House, ((604) 493-8400 86
    *Three Gables Hotel, ((604) 492-3933 86
    *Ti-Ki Shore, ((604) 492-8769 86
  attractions
    Apex Recreation Area 84
    Art Gallery of the South Okanagan,
    ((604) 492-6025 83
    Casabella Wines, ((604) 492-0621 83
    lake cruises 83
    Okanagan Game Farm, ((604) 497-5405 83
    Okanagan Lake 83
  general information 82
    Penticton Chamber of Commerce and
    Visitor's Information Centre,
    ((604) 492-4103 82
Peyto Lake 122
Port Alberni 74, 76
  accommodation 80
  attractions
    canoeing, kayaking, diving 76
Port Hardy 79, 80
  restaurants 80
Port McNeill 79
Port Renfrew 76
Port Royal 21
  historical background 21
postal services 190
Prairies 32
Prince Albert 149
Prince Albert National Park 133, 149
Prince Edward Island 24–25
  historical background 20, 24–25
Pyramid Lake 123

Q **Qu'Appelle Valley** 139
Qualicum Beach 79–81
  accommodation 80
    **Qualicum College Inn, ((604) 752-9262,
    toll-free (800) 663-7306 80
    *George Inn, ((604) 752-9236 80
Quebec 21, 25
  historical background 21, 25

R **Radar Hill** 78
recommended reading 192
Regina 133–142
  access 142
    Greyhound bus station,
    ((306) 787-3340 142
    VIA Rail station, ((306) 359-1822,
    toll-free (800) 665-8630 142

accommodation 140–141
***Hotel Saskatchewan, ((306) 522-7691,
   toll-free (800) 667-5828 *140*
***Regina Inn, ((306) 525-6767,
   toll-free (800) 667-8162 *140*
***Sheraton Inn Regina, ((306) 569-1666,
   toll-free (800) 325-3535 *140*
**Chelton Inn, ((306) 569-4600,
   toll-free (800) 667-9922 *140*
**Imperial 400 Motel, ((306) 584-8800 *141*
**Landmark Inn, ((306) 586-5363 *141*
**Regina Travelodge, ((306) 586-3443,
   toll-free (800) 255-3050 *141*
**Sandman Inn, ((306) 586-2663,
   toll-free (800) 663-6900 *141*
**Seven Oaks Motor Inn, ((306) 757-0121,
   toll-free (800) 667-8063 *141*
*Inntowner Motor Inn, ((306) 525-3737,
   toll-free (800) 667-7785 *141*
*Journey's End, ((306) 789-5522,
   toll-free (800) 668-4200 *141*
*North Star Motel, ((306) 352-0723 *141*
*Plains Motor Hotel, ((306) 757-8661 *141*
*Turgeon International Hostel,
   ((306) 522-4200 *141*
*YMCA, ((306) 757-9622 *141*
*YWCA, ((306) 525-2141 *141*
attractions
   cultural activities: Globe Theatre,
     ((306) 525-9553 *140*
   cultural activities: Saskatchewan Centre of the
     Arts, ((306) 565-0404 *140*
   Diefenbaker Homestead,
     ((306) 522-3661/565-2742 *137*
   Government House,
     ((306) 787-5717/5726 *137*
   Legislative Building, ((306) 787-5358 *136*
   Museum of Natural History,
     ((306) 787-2815/2818 *136*
   Norman Mackenzie Art Gallery,
     ((306) 522-4242 *136*
   RCMP Centennial Museum,
     ((306) 780-5838 *137*
   Regina Plains Museum,
     ((306) 352-0844/352-0861 *138*
   Saskatchewan Centre of the Arts,
     ((306) 565-0404 *137*
   Saskatchewan Science Centre,
     ((306) 791-7900 *136*
   Sergeant Major's Parade *138*
   sport, active *139*
     golf, Saskatchewan Golf Association,
     ((306) 975-0834 *139*
     horse riding, ((306) 757-5462 *140*
   sport, spectator *139*
   Sunset Retreat Ceremony *138*
   Wascana Centre *135*
   Waterfowl Park, ((306) 522-3661 *137*
background 135
environs 138–139
   Moose Jaw *138*
festivals 138
   Buffalo Days *138*
general information 135
   Chamber of Commerce, ((306) 527-4685 *135*

Tourism Regina, ((306) 789-5099 or
   (306) 527-4685 *135*
Tourism Saskatchewan, ((306) 787-2300,
   toll-free (800) 667-7538 *135*
U.S. Saskatchewan Parks and Renewable
   Resources, ((306) 787-2700, or toll-free
   (800) 66-PARKS *135*
nightlife 140
   Celebrations, ((306) 525-8989 *140*
   Stage West, ((306) 800-8162 *140*
restaurants 141–142
   Bartleby's, ((306) 565-0040 *142*
   C.C. Lloyd's Dining Room,
     ((306) 569-4650 *142*
   Elephant & Castle, ((306) 757-4405 *142*
   Mieka's, ((306) 522-6700 *141*
   Roxy's Bistro, ((306) 352-4737 *141*
   The Diplomat, ((306) 359-3366 *141*
   Upstairs Downstairs, ((306) 525-1496 *141*
Riding Mountain National Park *168*
Rocky Mountains *31*
Roger's Pass *87*
   accommodation 87
   Best Western Glacier Park Lodge,
     ((604) 837-2126 *87*
   general information 87
   Roger's Pass Information Centre
     ((604) 837-6274 *87*

⊡ safety *179*
San Josef Provincial Parks *79*
Saskatchewan *25, 131–150*
   historical background 25
Saskatchewan River *26*
Saskatoon *142–149*
   access 149
   Greyhound bus station, ((306) 933-8000 *149*
   Saskatoon International Airport,
     ((306) 975-4754 *149*
   VIA Rail terminal, ((306) 384-5665 *149*
   accommodation 147–148
   ***Holiday Inn, ((306) 244-2311,
     toll-free (800) 465-4329 *148*
   ***Ramada Renaissance, ((306) 665-3322,
     toll-free (800) 268-9889 *148*
   ***Sheraton Cavalier, ((306) 652-6770,
     toll-free (800) 325-3535 *147*
   **Delta Bessborough, ((306) 244-5521,
     toll-free (800) 268-1133 *148*
   **Saskatoon Inn, ((306) 242-1440,
     toll-free (800) 667-8789 *147*
   *Journey's End Motel, ((306) 934-1122,
     toll-free (800) 668-4200 *148*
   *King George Hotel, ((306) 652-4672,
     toll-free (800) 667-1234 *148*
   *Parktown Motor Hotel, ((306) 244-5564,
     toll-free (800) 667-3999 *148*
   *Senator Hotel, ((306) 244-6141 *148*
   Travelodge Hotel, ((306) 242-8881,
     toll-free (800) 255-3050 *148*
   YWCA, ((306) 244-0944 *148*
   attractions
   Bessborough Hotel *144*
   cultural activities: Saskatoon Centennial
     Auditorium, ((306) 975-7777 *147*
   Forestry Farm Park and Zoo *145*

Kiwanis Park 144
Mendel Art Gallery and Civic Conservatory,
    ((306) 975-7610 144
sport, active: horse riding, Sandhills Stable,
    ((306) 955-4311 147
sport, spectator: horse racing, Marquis
    Downs Racetrack, ((306) 242-6100 147
Ukrainian Museum of Canada,
    ((306) 244-3800 144
University of Saskatchewan Biology
    Museum 144
University of Saskatchewan Gordon
    Snelgrove Gallery 144
University of Saskatchewan John Diefenbaker
    Centre 144
University of Saskatchewan Museum of
    Antiquities 144
University of Saskatchewan Observatory 144
University of Saskatchewan,
    ((306) 966-5788 144
W.W. Northcote River Cruises 144
Western Development Museum,
    ((306) 931-1910 144
background 143
environs 145
Batoche National Historic Park,
    ((306) 423-6227 145
Battleford 146
North Battleford 146
festivals 145, 147
Folkfest, (August) 145
Shakespeare on the Saskatchewan Festival,
    ((306) 653-2300 (July and August) 147
Vesna Festival, (June) 145
nightlife 147
Texas, ((306) 373-8080 147
restaurants 148–149
**Aerial's Cove, ((306) 665-3322 148
**Bessborough Hotel, ((306) 244-5521 148
**Cousin Nik's, ((306) 374-2020 148
**John's Prime Rib, ((306) 244-6384 148
**Lucci's (Italian food) 148
**R.J. Wiloughby, ((306) 244-2311 148
**Whiteside's, ((306) 665-3322 148
*Adonis, ((306) 652-9598 149
*Ambassador, ((306) 373-4888 149
*Artful Dodger, ((306) 653-2577 149
*Fuddruckers, ((306) 955-7777 149
*St Tropez Bistro, ((306) 652-1250 148
shopping 147
general information 144
Saskatoon Visitor's Bureau,
    ((306) 242-1206 144
Visitor and Convention Bureau,
    ((306) 242-1206 144
shopping, general 185
Sooke 66–67, 71
accommodation 71
**Sooke Harbour House, ((604) 642-3421 71
restaurants 71
Sooke Harbour House, (604) 642-3421 71
Southern Gulf Islands 74
sport, general
    fishing 188
    hunting 188
    skiing 188

Sproat Lake 76
St. Lawrence Lowlands region 32
St. Lawrence River 22, 32
    historical background 22
St. Lawrence Seaway 27
Steinbach 162
    attractions 162
Strathcona Park 79
    attractions
        Della Falls 79
        Golden Hinde 79
Sunshine Village 121
Sunwapta Falls 123
Sunwapta Pass 122

T telephones 191
Thetis Island 73
time zones 177
tipping 185
Tofino 76
    accommodation 80
    restaurants 80
tourist information offices 173
Trans-Canada Highway 27

U Ucluelet 76, 80
    accommodation 80

V Vancouver 38–59
    access 58
        BC Ferries, information, ((604) 669-1211 58
        BC Rail station, ((604) 984-5246,
            toll-free (800) 665-8630 58
        Greyhound buses, ((604) 662-3222 58
        Maverick Lines, ((604) 662-8051,
            toll-free (800) 972-6301 58
        Pacific Coach Lines, ((604) 662-8074 59
        Trans-Canada Railway station,
            ((604) 669-3050, toll-free (800) 665-8630 58
    accommodation 53–56
        ***Four Seasons, ((604) 689-9333,
            toll-free (800) 268-6282 53
        ***Hotel Vancouver, ((604) 684-3131,
            toll-free (800) 268-9411 53
        ***Hyatt Regency Vancouver, ((604) 687-6543,
            toll-free (800) 233-1234 54
        ***Le Meridien, ((604) 682-5511,
            toll-free (800) 543-4300 54
        ***Pan Pacific Vancouver Hotel,
            ((604) 662-8111, toll-free (800) 663-1515 54
        ***The Delta Place, ((604) 687-1122,
            toll-free (800) 268-1133 53
        ***The Georgian Court Hotel,
            ((604) 682-5555, toll-free (800) 663-1155 54
        ***The Westin Bayshore, ((604) 682-3377,
            toll-free (800) 228-3000 54
        ***Wedgewood Hotel, ((604) 689-7777,
            toll-free (800) 663-0666 54
        **Granville Island Hotel and Marina,
            ((604) 683-7373, toll-free (800) 663-1840 55
        **Hotel Georgia, ((604) 682-5566,
            toll-free (800) 663-1111 54
        **Lonsdale Quay Hotel, ((604) 986-6111 55
        **Park Royal Hotel, ((604) 926-5511 55
        **Sylvia Hotel, ((604) 681-9321 55
        **The Barclay Hotel, ((604) 688-8850 54
        *Dominion Hotel, ((604) 681-6666 55
        *Kingston Hotel, ((604) 684-9024 55

*Nelson Place Hotel, ((604) 681-6341 55
*St Regis Hotel, ((604) 681-1135 55
*The Patricia, ((604) 255-4301 55
*YMCA, ((604) 681-0221 55
*YWCA, ((604) 662-8188 55
A B & C Bed and Breakfast of Vancouver,
    ((604) 986-5069 56
Bed & Breakfast 56
Canada-West Accommodations,
    ((604) 929-1429 56
Old English Bed and Breakfast Registry,
    ((604) 986-5069 56
SFU Housing and Conference Services,
    ((604) 291-4201 55
Town and Country Bed and Breakfasts in
    B.C., ((604) 731-5942 56
University of British Columbia at Point Grey,
    ((604) 228-2963 55
Vancouver International Hostel,
    ((604) 224-3208 55
attractions
Asian Garden 46
Bloedel Conservatory 46
Brockton Point 43
Canada Place 40
Canadian Pacific Railway Station 41
Capilano Suspension Bridge 46
Chinatown 42
Chinese Cultural Centre 42
cinema 53
    CN IMAX Theatre, ((604) 682-4629 40, 53
    OMNIMAX Theater, ((604) 687-OMNI 46
    Pacific Cinematheque, ((604) 688-3456 53
    The Ridge Theatre, ((604) 738-6311 53
    Vancouver East Cinema,
       ((604) 253-5455 53
cultural activities 51–52
    Anna Wyman Dance Theatre,
       ((604) 662-8846 52
    Arts Club Revue 52
    Ballet British Columbia, ((604) 669-5954 52
    Comedy Punchlines Theatre,
       ((604) 684-3015 52
    Firehall Arts Centre, ((604) 689-0926 52
    Orpheum Theatre, ((604) 684-2787 51
    Queen Elizabeth Theatre, ((604) 665-3050 51
    Robson Square Media Centre,
       ((604) 660-2830 52
    Robson Square Plaza 52
    The Arts Club Theatre, ((604) 687-1644 52
    The Vancouver East Cultural Centre,
       ((604) 254-9578 52
    Theatresports, ((604) 688-7013 52
    Vancouver Chamber Choir,
       ((604) 738-6822 52
    Vancouver Opera 52
    Vancouver Playhouse, ((604) 665-3050 51
    Vancouver Playhouse, ((604) 665-3050,
       ((604) 665-3050 52
    Vancouver Symphony Orchestra,
       ((604) 684-9100 52
    Vancouver Ticket Centre, ((604) 280-3311
       (information), (604) 280-4444 (credit card
       booking) 51
Dr Sun Yat-Sen Classical Chinese Garden 42

Ferguson Point 43
Fort Langley National Historic Park,
    ((604) 888-4424 48
Fraser Valley 48
Gastown 41
Gordon Southam Observatory,
    ((604) 738-2855 44
Granville Island 43
Great Hall 44
Grouse Mountain 46
H.R.Macmillan Planetarium,
    ((604) 736-4431 44
Harbour Centre, ((604) 689-0421 41
Heritage Harbour 44
Lions Gate Bridge 46
Lonsdale Quay Market 46
Lost Lagoon 42
Lynn Canyon Park, ((604) 987-5922 46
Maritime Market 44
Maritime Museum, ((604) 736-4431 44
Mount Seymour Provincial Park 47
Museum of Anthropology, ((604) 228-3825 44
MV Britannia, ((604) 987-5211. 47
Nitobe Memorial Garden 44
OMNIMAX Theater, ((604) 687-OMNI 46
Physick Garden 46
Public Market 44
Queen Elizabeth Park, ((604) 872-5513. 46
recreation: cycling 49
recreation: hiking 49
Robson Square 41
Robsonstrasse 41
rock concerts: BC Place Stadium 52
rock concerts: Metro, ((604) 687-5566 52
Royal Hudson 2860 47
Sam Kee Building 42
Scenic Drive 42
Science World, ((604) 687-7832 46
Shannon Falls 47
shopping 50
Skyride 46
sport, active 49–50
    canoeing 49
    fishing, B.C. Department of Fisheries,
       ((604) 666-2268 or toll-free
       (800) 663-9333 50
    fishing, Greater Vancouver Regional District
       Parks Department, ((604) 432-6350 50
    golf, Whistler course, ((604) 932-4222. 49
    golf, University Golf Course,
       ((604) 224-7513 49
    heli-skiing and glacier skiing, Whistler
       Resort Association, ((604) 932-4222 or
       toll-free (800) 685-3650 49
    sailing 49
    scuba diving, The Diving Locker,
       ((604) 736-2681 49
    skiing, Mount Seymour, ((604) 986-2261 49
    skiing, Vancouver area information,
       ((604) 669-SNOW 49
    swimming, Aquatic Centre,
       ((604) 689-7156 50
    swimming, UBC Aquatic Center,
       ((604) 228-4521 50
    tennis 49

whitewater rafting 49
windsurfing 49
sport, spectator 48–49
Baseball 48
Football 48
hang gliding 48
harness racing 48
horse racing 48
ice hockey 48
ski racing 48
skiing, Cypress Bowl, ((604) 926-5612 49
St Roch 44
Stanley Park 42
steam-powered clock 42
UBC Botanical Garden, ((604) 228-4208 46
University of British Columbia 44
Van Dusen Botanical Gardens,
((604) 266-7194. 46
Vancouver Aquarium, ((604) 682-1118 43
Vancouver Art Gallery, ((604) 682-5621 41
Vancouver Museum, ((604) 736-4431 44
Vanier Park 44
Whistler Resort, ((604) 932-4222,
toll-free 685-3650 47
Wreck Beach 44
background 38–40
general information 40
The Travel Infocentre, ((604) 683-2000 or
toll-free (800) 663-6000 40
Tourism British Columbia, ((604) 387-1642
or toll-free (800) 663-6000 40
nightlife 51–52
Alma Street Cafe, ((604) 222-2244 52
Amnesia, ((604) 682-2211 52
Basin Street Cabaret, ((604) 688-5351 52
Club Soda, ((604) 733-4141 52
Commodore Ballroom, ((604) 681-7838 52
Gastown district 51
Glass Slipper, ((604) 682-0706 52
Graceland, ((604) 688-2648 52
Granville Island 51
JR Country Club, ((604) 681-2211 52
Landmark Jazz Bar, ((604) 687-9312 52
Pelican Bay, ((604) 683-7373 52
Richard's on Richards, ((604) 687-6794 52
Shampers, ((604) 684-6262 52
Sneaky Pete's, ((604) 681-9561 52
The Classical Joint Coffee House,
((604) 689-0667 52
The Hot Jazz Society, ((604) 873-4131 52
The Railway Club, ((604) 681-1625 52
Town Pump, ((604) 683-6695 52
restaurants 56–58
A Kettle of Fish, ((604) 254-9606 57
Bishop's, ((604) 738-2025 57
Bridges, ((604) 687-4400 57
Chartwell, ((604) 689-9333 56
Gerard's, ((604) 682-5511 56
Heaven and Earth India Curry House,
((604) 732-5313 58
Heidelberg House, ((604) 682-1661 58
Hy's Mansion, ((604) 689-1111 57
Il Giardino, ((604) 669-2422 57
Kamei Sushi, ((604) 684-5767 57
Kiri Mandarin Restaurant, ((604) 682-8833 57

Le Crocodile, ((604) 669-4298 57
Le Gavroche, ((604) 685-3924 56
Old Spaghetti Factory, ((604) 684-1288 58
Piccolo Mondo, ((604) 688-1633 57
Quilicum, ((604) 681-7044 58
Raintree, ((604) 688-5570 56
Saigon, ((604) 682-8020 58
Salmon House on the Hill, ((604) 926-3212 57
Teahouse Restaurant, ((604) 738-2025 57
The Cannery, ((604) 254-9606 57
The Only Fish and Oyster Cafe,
((604) 681-6546 58
The Pink Pearl, ((604) 253-4316 58
Tojo's, ((604) 872-8050 56
Topanaga, ((604) 733-3713 58
William Tell, ((604) 688-3504 56
Yang's, ((604) 873-2116 58
Vancouver Island 59–74, 76, 78–81
attractions
Alert Bay 79
Botanical Beach 67
British Columbia Forest Museum,
((604) 748-9389 73
Cameron Lake 74
Campbell River 79
Cape Scott 79
Chemainus 73
Comex 79
Courtenay 79
Denman 79
Duncan 73, 80
Englishman Falls Provincial Park 74
Friendly Cove 79
Gabriola Islands 74
Gold River 79
Hornby Islands 79
Ladysmith 74, 80
Lake Cowichan 73
Little Qualicum Falls Provincial Park 74
Long Beach 76
MacMillan Provincial Park 74
Malahat Drive 66
Meares Island 78
Mount Washington 79
Nanaimo 60, 74, 80
Pacific Rim National Park 76
Parksville 74, 79
Port Alberni 74, 76
Port Hardy 79
Port McNeill 79
Port Renfrew 67, 76
Qualicum Beach 79
Radar Hill 78
San Josef Provincial Parks 79
skiing: Forbidden Plateau 79
Sooke 66
Southern Gulf Islands 67
Sproat Lake 76
Strathcona Park 79
Thetis and Kuper Islands 73
Tofino 76
Ucluelet 76
See also Victoria
access 80
background 60

General information 60
  Tourism Association of Vancouver Island,
    ((604) 876-3088 60
Vernon *81, 85–87*
access 87
  Greyhound station, ((604) 545-0527 87
accommodation 85–86
  *The Windmill House, ((604) 549-2804 86
  Okanagan High Country Bed and Breakfast,
    ((604) 542-4593 85
attractions
  Cedar Hot Springs 85
  O'Keefe Historic Ranch 85
  Polson Park oriental gardens 85
  Silver Star Ski Resort 85
  Vernon Museum and Archives 85
general information 82
  Travel Infocentre, ((604) 545-0771 82
restaurants 86–87
  The Keg and Cleaver, ((604) 542-0202 87
  The Vernon Station Restaurant,
    ((604) 549-3112 87
Victoria *60–73*
access 72–73
  Black Ball Transport, ((604) 386-2202 73
  British Columbia Ferry Corporation,
    ((604) 386-3431 73
  British Columbia Steamship Company,
    ((604) 386-1124 73
  by catamaran from Seattle, Victoria Clipper,
    ((604) 382-8100 73
  E&N (VIA Rail) Station,
    toll-free (800) 561-8630 73, 81
  Island Coach Lines, ((604) 385-4411 81
  Orient Stage Lines Ltd, (604) 723-6924 81
  Pacific Coach Line terminal,
    ((604) 385-5731 73
accommodation 69–71
  ***Beaconsfield Inn, ((604) 384-4044 69
  ***Empress Hotel, ((604) 384-8111 or
    toll-free (800) 828-7447 69
  ***Executive House Hotel, ((604) 388-5111,
    toll-free: (800) 663-7001 in the U.S 70
  ***Hastings House, ((604) 537-2362 or
    toll-free (800) 661-9255 70
  ***Hotel Grand Pacific, ((604) 386-0450 70
  ***Laurel Point Inn, ((604) 386-8721,
    toll-free (800) 663-7667 70
  **Best Western Carlton Plaza,
    ((604) 388-5513 70
  **Château Victoria Hotel, ((604) 382-4221,
    toll-free (800) 663-5891 70
  **Holland House Inn, ((604) 384-6644 70
  **Oak Bay Beach Hotel, ((604) 598-4556 70
  **Olde England Inn, ((604) 388-4353 70
  **The Captain's Palace, ((604) 388-9191 70
  **The Victoria Regent Hotel,
    ((604) 386-2211 70
  *Cherry Bank Hotel, ((604) 385-5380 71
  *Hotel Douglas, ((604) 383-4157 71
  *James Bay Inn,Z (604) 384-7151 71
  *Strathcona Hotel, ((604) 383-7137 71
  Abigail's Hotel, ((604) 388-5363 69
  campus accommodation,
    ((604) 721-8396 71

Fort Victoria Campground,
  ((604) 479-8112 71
Victoria YM-YWCA, ((604) 386-7511 71
Victoria Youth Hostel, ((604) 385-4511 71
attractions
  Art Gallery of Greater Victoria,
    ((604) 384-4104 64
  Beacon Hill Park 64
  British Columbia Provincial Museum,
    ((604) 387-3701 63
  Butchart Gardens, ((604) 652-4422 66
  Carillon Tower (museum), ((604) 387-3041
    (recorded information) or ((604) 387-3701
    (office hours) 63
  Chinatown 64
  Craigdarroch Castle, ((604) 592-4233 64
  Craigflower Manor 65
  cultural activities 68
    Belfry Theatre, ((604) 385-6815 68
    Royal Theatre, ((604) 386-6121 68
    University Centre Auditorium,
      ((604) 386-6121 68
    Victoria Symphony Orchestra,
      ((604) 385-6515 68
    Victorian Jazz Society, ((604) 388-4423 68
  Emily Carr Museum, ((604) 387-3080 64
  Empress Hotel 61
  English Village, ((604) 388-4353 65
  Fable Cottage Estate, ((604) 658-5741 65
  Fisherman's Wharf 63
  Helmcken House heritage building 63
  Maritime Museum, ((604) 385-4222 64
  Old Town district 63
  Parliament Buildings 61
  Royal London Wax Museum
    ((604) 388-4461 63
  Sealand oceanarium, ((604) 598-3373 65
  sport, active 67–68
    golf, Cedar Hill Golf Course,
      ((604) 477-8314 68
    golf, Victoria Golf Club,
      ((604) 598-4321 68
    swimming, Crystal Pool Recreation Centre,
      ((604) 383-2522 67
    yachting, Horizon Yacht Centre,
      ((604) 595-6677 67
  The Crystal Garden 61
  Thunderbird Park 63
  Undersea Gardens, ((604) 382-5717 63
general information 60
  Infocentre, ((604) 382-2127 60
nightlife 68–69
  Harpo's, ((604) 385-5333 69
  Hermann's Dixieland Inn, ((604) 388-9166 69
  Merlin's Nightclub, ((604) 388-6201 69
  Pagliacci's, ((604) 386-1662 69
  pubs 69
    The Forge, ((604) 383-7137 69
    The Rail, ((604) 385-2441 69
restaurants 72
  ***Empress Dining Room, ((604) 384-8111 72
  **Causeway Restaurant, ((604) 381-2244 72
  **Chauney's, ((604) 385-4512 72
  **Chez Pierre, ((604) 388-7711 72
  **La Petite Colombe, ((604) 383-3234 72

**Larousse, ((604) 386-3454 72
*Herald Street Caffe, ((604) 381-1441 72
*James Bay Tearoom, ((604) 382-8282 72
*Japanese Village, ((604) 382-5165 72
*Millos, ((604) 382-4422 72
*Pagliacci's, ((604) 386-1662 72
*Taj Mahal, ((604) 383-4662 72
Empress Hotel (for afternoon teas),
  ((604) 384-8111 61

W Wasagaming 168
  attractions
  Elkhorn Resort, ((204) 848-2802 168
Waskesiu 149
  attractions
  Nature Centre 149
  Prince Albert National Park 149
  Waskesiu Lake 149
  general information 149
  Prince Albert National Park,
    ((306) 663-5322 149
  Waskesiu Chamber of Commerce,
    ((306) 922-3232 149
Waterton National Parks 91
weather 174
weights and measures 177
Western Cordillera region 32
what to take 177
Whistlers Mountain 123
Whiteshell Provincial Park 167
Winnipeg 156–167
  access 167
  Grey Goose Lines, ((204) 786-8891 167
  Greyhound bus station, ((204) 775-8301 167
  VIA Rail station, ((204) 949-1830 or
    (204) 944-8780 167
  Winnipeg International Airport,
    ((204) 983-8410 167
  accommodation 164–166
  **Fort Garry, ((204) 942-8251,
    toll-free (800) 665-8088 164
  **Holiday Inn, ((204) 942-0551 164
  **Marlborough Inn, ((204) 942-6411 165
  **Place Louis Riel, ((204) 947-6961 165
  **Sheraton Winnipeg, ((204) 942-5300,
    toll-free (800) 325-3535 164
  **The Delta Winnipeg, ((204) 956-0410 165
  **Velvet Glove, ((204) 957-1350 166
  **Westin Hotel, ((204) 957-1350,
    toll-free (800) 228-3000 164
  *Charterhouse Hotel, ((204) 942-0101 165
  *Gordon Downtowner Motor Hotel,
    ((204) 943-5581 165
  *Journey's End, ((204) 269-7390,
    toll-free (800) 668-4200 165
  *St Regis, ((204) 942-0171 165
  *Travelodge, ((204) 255-6000,
    toll-free (800) 255-3050 165
  Bed & Breakfast: B&B of Manitoba,
    ((204) 256-6151 164
  farmstays: Manitoba Farm Vacations,
    ((204) 475-6624 164
  University of Manitoba, ((204) 474-9942 165
  YWCA, ((204) 943-0381 165
  attractions
  Art Gallery 160

Assiniboine Park and zoo, ((204) 986-3130 160
Canadian Royal Mint, ((204) 257-3359 160
Centennial Centre, ((204) 956-2830 158
Centennial Concert Hall 158
Church of the Precious Blood 160
cultural activities 163–164
Dalnavert House, ((204) 943-2835 159
Electric Railways Chambers Building 158
Exchange District 158
Fort Garry 159
Legislative Building, ((204) 945-3700 159
Manitoba Museum of Man and Nature 158
Market Square 158
Planetarium 158
Prairie Dog Central steam train to the
  prairies, ((204) 284-2690 162
Riel House, ((204) 257-1783 160
river cruises 161
  Paddlewheel Cruises, ((204) 339-1696 161
  River Tours, ((204) 669-2824 161
  Riverboat Management Ltd,
    ((204) 582-2331 161
sport, active 162
sport, spectator 162
  Football, ((204) 775-9751 162
  hockey, Winnipeg Arena,
    ((204) 772-9491 162
  horse racing, ((204) 885-3330 162
St Boniface 160
St Boniface Basilica 160
St Boniface Museum 160
Ukrainian Cultural and Educational Centre,
  ((204) 942-0218 159
Upper Fort Garry Gate 159
Urban Gallery 158
Western Canadian Aviation Museum,
  ((204) 786-5503 160
Winnipeg Commodity Exchange,
  ((204) 949-0495 158
background 157
environs 162
  Grosse Isle 162
  Lower Fort Garry, ((204) 669-2824 162
  Steinbach Mennonite Village Museum,
    ((204) 326-9661 162
festivals 161
  Folklorama, ((204) 944-9793 (August) 161
  Winnipeg Folk Festival, ((204) 284-8487 162
general information 158
  Travel Information Centre, ((204) 945-3777,
    toll-free (800) 665-0040 158
  Travel Manitoba, ((204) 945-3777,
    toll-free (800) 665-0040 158
  Winnipeg Convention and Visitors Bureau,
    ((204) 943-1970 158
nightlife 164–166
  Art Gallery, ((204) 786-6641 164
  De Soto's, ((204) 943-4444 164
restaurants 165–166
  ***Le Beaujolais, ((204) 237-6276 166
  ***Oliver's, ((204) 943-4448 166
  ***Royal Crown Revolving Restaurant,
    ((204) 947-5103 166
  ***Victor's, ((204) 284-2339 165
  **Amici, ((204) 943-4997 166

**Churchill's, ☏ (204) 942-6411 *166*

**Cibo's, ☏ (204) 943-4922 *166*

**Hy's Steak Loft, ☏ 9204) 942-7725 *166*

**Ichiban Japanese Steak House,
☏ (204) 942-7493 *166*

**Old Swiss Inn, ☏ (204) 942-7725 *166*

**Restaurant Dubrovnik, ☏ (204) 944-0594 *165*

*Alycia's, ☏ (204) 582-8789 *166*

*Bistro Dansk, ☏ 9204) 775-5662 *166*

*D'8 Schtove, ☏ (204) 275-2294 *166*

*Garden Creperie, ☏ (204) 957-0221 *166*

*Impressions Cafe, ☏ (204) 772-8049 *166*

*Oscar's, ☏ (204) 589-8269 *166*

Betsy's Place, ☏ (204) 475-1027 *166*

Carlos and Murphy's, ☏ (204) 284-3510 *167*

Chinese restaurants *167*

Rae and Jerry's, ☏ (204) 783-6155 *166*

Simon's, ☏ (204) 589-8289 *166*

Tea Cozy, ☏ (204) 475-1027 *166*

shopping 163

Y **Yorkton** *150*

attractions 150

Western Development Museum,
☏ (306) 783-8361 *150*